T0301824

A Research Agenda for Social Entrepreneurship

Elgar Research Agendas outline the future of research in a given area. Leading scholars are given the space to explore their subject in provocative ways and map out the potential directions of travel. They are relevant but also visionary.

Forward-looking and innovative, Elgar Research Agendas are an essential resource for PhD students, scholars and anybody who wants to be at the forefront of research.

Titles in the series include:

A Research Agenda for Global
Environmental Politics
Edited by Peter Dauvergne and Justin Alger

A Research Agenda for New Institutional
Economics
*Edited by Claude Ménard and Mary M.
Shirley*

A Research Agenda for Regeneration
Economies
Reading City-Regions
*Edited by John R. Bryson, Lauren Andres and
Rachel Mulhall*

A Research Agenda for Cultural Economics
Edited by Samuel Cameron

A Research Agenda for Environmental
Management
*Edited by Kathleen E. Halvorsen, Chelsea
Schelly, Robert M. Handler, Erin C. Pischke
and Jessie L. Knowlton*

A Research Agenda for Creative Tourism
Edited by Nancy Duxbury and Greg Richards

A Research Agenda for Public
Administration
Edited by Andrew Massey

A Research Agenda for Tourism
Geographies
Edited by Dieter K. Müller

A Research Agenda for Economic
Psychology
*Edited by Katharina Gangl and Erich
Kirchler*

A Research Agenda for Entrepreneurship
and Innovation
*Edited by David B. Audretsch, Erik E.
Lehmann and Albert N. Link*

A Research Agenda for Financial Inclusion
and Microfinance
*Edited by Marek Hudon, Marc Labie and
Ariane Szafarz*

A Research Agenda for Global Crime
Edited by Tim Hall and Vincenzo Scalia

A Research Agenda for Transport Policy
Edited by John Stanley and David A. Hensher

A Research Agenda for Tourism and
Development
*Edited by Richard Sharpley and David
Harrison*

A Research Agenda for Housing
Edited by Markus Moos

A Research Agenda for Economic
Anthropology
Edited by James G. Carrier

A Research Agenda for Social
Entrepreneurship
*Edited by Anne de Bruin and Simon
Teasdale*

A Research Agenda for Social Entrepreneurship

Edited by

ANNE DE BRUIN

Professor of Economics, School of Economics and Finance, and Director, New Zealand Social Innovation and Entrepreneurship Research Centre, Massey University, New Zealand

SIMON TEASDALE

Professor of Public Policy and Organisations, and Assistant Vice Principal of Global Challenges Research, Glasgow Caledonian University, UK

Elgar Research Agendas

Edward Elgar
PUBLISHING

Cheltenham, UK • Northampton, MA, USA

Published by
Edward Elgar Publishing Limited
The Lypiatts
15 Lansdown Road
Cheltenham
Glos GL50 2JA
UK

Edward Elgar Publishing, Inc.
William Pratt House
9 Dewey Court
Northampton
Massachusetts 01060
USA

A catalogue record for this book
is available from the British Library

Library of Congress Control Number: 2019938889

This book is available electronically in the **Elgar**online
Business subject collection
DOI 10.4337/9781788972321

MIX
Paper from
responsible sources
FSC® C013056

ISBN 978 1 78897 231 4 (cased)
ISBN 978 1 78897 232 1 (eBook)

Typeset by Servis Filmsetting Ltd, Stockport, Cheshire
Printed and bound in Great Britain by TJ International Ltd, Padstow, Cornwall

Contents

Contributors

Ghadah Alarifi is an Assistant Professor at Princess Nourah bint Abdulrahman University in Saudi Arabia. She holds a PhD in Management from Royal Holloway University of London and her research focus is in the area of social entrepreneurship. Ghadah is also a social entrepreneur who co-founded and spearheaded Cell Network (a women's professional network) in 2011 to support professional women to enhance their careers through networking, mentorship and training, and she is currently the chairperson of CellA. She gives consultations to third sector organisations in Saudi Arabia.

Andy Brady is Senior Lecturer at Anglia Ruskin University and his research interests focus on social entrepreneurship, networks and sustainability. Andy is the founder and director of 3rd Sector Futures, the specialist unit working with charities, social enterprises and voluntary organisations, and course leader for the Higher Education Certificate in Charity & Social Enterprise Management. He has more than 20 years of social sector experience including lead business coach for the Ariane de Rothschild Fellowship, a transnational social entrepreneurship programme (2013–2017). Andy currently chairs Social Enterprise East of England, the regional membership organisation for social enterprises across six English counties.

Deborah Burand is an Associate Professor of Clinical Law at NYU School of Law where she directs the International Transactions Clinic and co-directs the Grunin Center for Law and Social Entrepreneurship. Prof. Burand has served as general counsel to the Overseas Private Investment Corporation. She also has worked in the microfinance sector, most recently as the Executive Vice President for Strategic Services of the Grameen Foundation. Earlier in her career, she was a senior attorney in the Federal Reserve Board's Legal Division and at the US Department of the Treasury, and practised corporate law in a global law firm.

Erin Castellas, PhD, is Chief Impact Officer at Impact Investment Group and an adjunct fellow with the Centre for Social Impact, Swinburne University, Australia. Erin has over 15 years' experience working at the interface between social, environmental and economic outcomes. She has a deep interest in how values intersect with value.

Léo-Paul Dana, a graduate of McGill University and of HEC-Montreal, is Professor at Montpellier Business School and a member of the Entrepreneurship & Innovation chair, which is part of LabEx Entrepreneurship (University of Montpellier, France). This 'laboratory of excellence' is funded by the French government in recognition of high-level research initiatives in the human and natural sciences (LabEx Entreprendre, ANR-10-LabEx-11-01). He has published extensively in a variety of leading journals including *Entrepreneurship & Regional Development, Entrepreneurship: Theory & Practice, International Small Business Journal, Journal of Small Business Management, Journal of World Business* and *Small Business Economics.*

Anne de Bruin is founder and director of the New Zealand Social Innovation and Entrepreneurship Research Centre and Professor of Economics, Massey University. Her research is published in leading journals including *Entrepreneurship Theory and Practice, Entrepreneurship & Regional Development (ERD)* and *International Small Business Journal.* She is Associate Editor of the *Social Enterprise Journal,* is on other editorial boards including *Journal of Management and Organization* and *International Journal of Gender and Entrepreneurship* and has co-edited several journal special issues including recently 'The collaborative dynamic in social entrepreneurship' for *ERD.* Anne is a Fulbright New Zealand Scholar.

Pascal Dey is Associate Professor at Grenoble Ecole de Management, France, and a Senior Research Fellow at the University of St. Gallen, Switzerland. Much of Pascal's work unfolds at the intersection of entrepreneurship, politics and society and has been chiefly informed by critical sociological and philosophical theories. Pascal's most recent interest lies in issues pertaining to social imagination, willful ignorance and illegality. Pascal is the co-director of the PhD programme at Grenoble Ecole de Management and senior editor of *Organization Studies.*

Bob Doherty is Professor of Marketing and Chair of Agrifood at the University of York and leads a four-year interdisciplinary research programme on food resilience titled 'IKnowFood' (GFS funded). Bob is also the research theme leader for food in the York Environmental Sustainability Research Institute (YESI). Bob specialises in research on the management aspects of social enterprise hybrid organisations competing in the food industry. He is currently a trustee on the board of the Fairtrade Foundation. Prior to moving into academia Bob spent five years as the Head of Sales and Marketing at the Fairtrade pioneer Divine Chocolate Ltd.

Mary Duniam, PhD, is situated in the University College of University of Tasmania and lectures in Applied Business and Agribusiness. Dr Duniam is an active board member on several community organisations (including social enterprises) and is Deputy Mayor within local government in Tasmania. Dr Duniam's research has primarily focused on social entrepreneurship and the relationship between social enterprises and local government on the island state of Tasmania.

Angela M. Eikenberry is the David C. Scott Diamond Alumni Professor of Public Affairs in the School of Public Administration at the University of Nebraska at Omaha (UNO). Her research focuses on the social, economic and political roles of philanthropy, voluntary associations, nonprofit organisations and social enterprises in democratic governance. In 2016 she received the UNO campus-wide Award for Distinguished Research or Creative Activity. She recently co-edited a textbook on nonprofit management – *Reframing Nonprofit Management: Democracy,*

Inclusion, and Social Change (Melvin & Leigh, 2018) – and is currently President of the Association for Research on Nonprofit Organizations and Voluntary Action (ARNOVA).

Robyn Eversole is Professor and Deputy Director at the Centre for Social Impact, Swinburne University. An anthropologist who studies regional development in Australia, Latin America, and the Asia-Pacific, her work focuses on practical development challenges and how communities and organisations can catalyse social change. Her books include *Knowledge Partnering for Community Development* (Routledge, 2015), *Regional Development in Australia: Being Regional* (Routledge, 2016), and *Anthropology for Development: From Theory to Practice* (Routledge, 2018).

Helen Haugh, PhD, is a Senior Lecturer and Research Director for the Centre for Social Innovation, Cambridge Judge Business School. Helen's research interests focus on social and community entrepreneurship and social innovation, especially community-led regeneration in rural communities, cross-sector collaboration and innovations in governance. Helen's social economy research has been supported by the Monument Trust and The Esmée Fairbairn Foundation, and the research for this chapter was funded by the Edmond de Rothschild Foundations and the Isaac Newton Trust.

Richard Hazenberg (BA, MA, PhD) is Director and Research Leader of the Institute for Social Innovation and Impact at the University of Northampton. Richard has research interests in the areas of social innovation, impact investment and public service innovation. He has contributed to international/national government policy through papers, conferences and roundtable meetings (including for the European Commission; OECD; Cabinet Office; and HM Treasury). Prof. Hazenberg is on the editorial board of the *Social Enterprise Journal* and is a reviewer for a number of international peer-review journals including *Policy and Politics*, the *Journal of Social Policy* and *Small Business Economics.*

Malin Henriksson holds a PhD from Linköping University within the area of technology and social change. Her thesis from 2014 develops an intersectional framework on planners' images of sustainable mobility and combines qualitative methods with feminist theory. Today, Malin works as a researcher at the Swedish National Road and Transport Research Institute. Her research largely concerns transport, mobility, justice and power.

Colette Henry is Professor and Head of Department of Business Studies at Dundalk Institute of Technology (DkIT), Ireland, and Adjunct Professor of Entrepreneurship at UiT-The Arctic University of Norway. She is founder and Editor of the CABS-listed *International Journal of Gender & Entrepreneurship* (IJGE), and has published widely on women's enterprise, entrepreneurship education and training, social enterprise, creative industries and veterinary business. She holds the Diana International Research Trailblazer Award and the Sten K Johnson European Entrepreneurship Education Award for her work on gender and entrepreneurship education, respectively. She is also a fellow of the Academy of Social Sciences.

Ella Henry is a Māori woman, and Senior Lecturer in Māori Indigenous Development, at Auckland University of Technology, New Zealand. Ella holds a PhD in Māori Development, which focused on Māori entrepreneurship in screen production, and a Master of Philosophy, focusing on Māori women and leadership. Ella has published her research in leading journals, for example *Entrepreneurship & Regional Development*, the *Journal of Management & Organization* and *Organization* (Sage), co-edited a book on Indigenous aspirations and rights with Indigenous scholars Ana Maria Peredo and Amy Klemm Verbos, and co-written another on the Māori screen industry.

Diane Holt (BSc, MSc, PhD) is Professor of Management at Essex Business School, University of Essex, UK. She is the Principal Investigator on the Trickle Out Africa Project (2011 to present) which considers the impact of social and environmental enterprises on poverty alleviation and sustainable development across the 19 countries of Southern and Eastern Africa. She has published over 100 peer-reviewed journal articles, book chapters and conference papers in areas such as social entrepreneurship, hybrid businesses, green supply chain management, the role of business in development, and ecopreneuring.

Martin Hultman, Associate Professor at Chalmers University, is widely published in energy, climate and environmental issues in journals such as *Environmental Humanities, History & Technology*, and *Hydrogen Energy*. Especially notable are *The Making of an Environmental Hero: A History of Ecomodern Masculinity, Fuel Cells and Arnold Schwarzenegger* in Routledge handbook *Gender and the Environment* and the books *Discourses of Global Climate Change* and *Ecological Masculinities*. Hultman has organised field-defining conferences on ecopreneurship and climate denialism, edited special issues about gender/environment as well as on ecopreneurship, currently being a research leader of masculinities and energy, circular economies and scrutinising climate change denial.

Nils Johansson, PhD, is a researcher in the meeting point between materiality, technology and humans. His work takes an interest in how waste relates to institutions by problematising the circular economy, diving into issues such as why policies fail to reduce waste amounts. Nils has also written extensively on the becoming of resources, by uncovering the role of political support in the construction of mining and recycling practices. His work has been published in a broad range of journals within the fields of waste, organisation and policy and he is currently the research leader for several waste-related projects.

Anna Kaijser has a background in gender studies and anthropology, and a PhD in sustainability science. In her research she explores power dynamics involved in the meaning-making around environmental matters. Her most widely acknowledged piece of work, *Climate Change through the Lens of Intersectionality*, advances feminist intersectional analysis of climate change. In other past projects she has explored environmental struggles in contemporary Bolivia and conflicts around infrastructure development and natural resources in Sweden. Her current work is focused on imaginaries of the circular economy, and the potential for rethinking this notion in more inclusive ways.

Pichawadee Kittipanya-ngam is an Assistant Professor of Operations Management at Thammasat Business School, Thailand. She is also a research affiliate at the Institute for Manufacturing, University of Cambridge. Pichawadee specialises in research and practices in supply chain and management aspects of social enterprises. She is also a founder of *Cambridge Babies*, a social project that encourages early years development. The project, in collaboration with Cambridge Thai Foundation, annually donates part of its profits as scholarships to Thai students at the University of Cambridge. She is also an academic associate at iAcademy pte., a social enterprise in the education sector operating in Nepal.

Endrit Kromidha is a Senior Lecturer in Entrepreneurship and Innovation at the University of Birmingham. His research looks at entrepreneurship financing, collaborative innovation, social entrepreneurship and public sector digital innovation systems. Endrit has published in a number of business, management, entrepreneurship and e-government journals. He is particularly interested in the use of digital platforms for entrepreneurship, access to finance and development.

Kate V. Lewis, PhD, is Reader in the Department of People and Performance in the Faculty of Business and Law at Manchester Metropolitan University. She is also a member of the University Centre for Research and Knowledge Exchange in Decent Work and Productivity. Kate is also a Visiting Professor at Plymouth Marjon University, an External Affiliate of the New Zealand Social Innovation and Entrepreneurship Research Centre at Massey University, and a Consulting Editor for the *International Journal of Gender and Entrepreneurship*.

Laurent Marti is a PhD student at the Yunus Centre for Social Business and Health, Glasgow Caledonian University, UK. Mainly building on relational process ontologies, his current research focuses on entrepreneurial processes in the digital creative industries and the third sector as well as on mental health literacy and stigma. Amongst others, he has published on visual methods in management studies and the contingent effects of emerging technologies in entrepreneurial finance.

Chris Mason is Associate Professor of Social Impact and Principal Research Fellow at the Centre for Social Impact Swinburne, at Swinburne University of Technology, Melbourne. His work centres on the discursive processes cutting across policy-making and organisational change. His studies of social enterprise explore many different facets of these processes, from the shaping effects of social enterprise policy discourses to the narratives explaining organisational responses to paradoxes. His multidisciplinary approach has been applied to a variety of critical social issues, such as exploring the role of social enterprise in addressing youth health inequity, and understanding how social enterprise tackles homelessness and affordable housing issues in Australia.

Bev Meldrum (BSc, MA) is a PhD student at the Graduate School of Business, University of Cape Town, South Africa. Her research focuses on social entrepreneurship and innovation, in particular within the informal economy in Sub Saharan Africa. She is also a social entrepreneur, having worked in both the UK and more recently South Africa for the past 20 years.

Jarrod Ormiston, PhD, is Assistant Professor in Social Entrepreneurship at the School of Business and Economics, Maastricht University, Netherlands. Jarrod's action research focuses on supporting refugee and migrant entrepreneurs and working with social enterprises to enhance their impact. Jarrod's PhD explored the role of impact assessment in social entrepreneurship and impact investment. His research interests include social entrepreneurship, impact investment, refugee entrepreneurship, and innovative pedagogies in entrepreneurship education. Jarrod has worked as a consultant to the Australian Government, the OECD and United Nations on entrepreneurship and education.

Paul Robson was appointed to a Professorship of Entrepreneurship and Strategy at Royal Holloway, University of London in January 2011, after a short spell as Professor of Entrepreneurship at Kingston University. Prior to that he worked for four years as a Reader in Entrepreneurship at Durham University Business School. He spent the period 2001–2005 in Aberdeen, Scotland. He started his career working as a Research Fellow at the Centre for Business Research, Cambridge University, over the period 1996–2000.

Michael J. Roy, PhD, is Professor of Economic Sociology and Social Policy at the Yunus Centre for Social Business and Health, Glasgow Caledonian University, UK. Michael has published extensively on social enterprise, particularly on their health and well-being impacts. His research has been funded by a variety of national governments, transnational bodies and international agencies. He is Deputy Editor in Chief of *Social Enterprise Journal*, and serves on the board of *Voluntas: the International Journal of Voluntary and Nonprofit Organizations*. Michael received the Helen Potter Award of Special Recognition for 2017 from the US-based Association for Social Economics.

Roger Spear is Emeritus Professor of Social Entrepreneurship at Open University, Member of Ciriec Scientific Committee, and founder member of EMES research network on social enterprise. He is guest professor in the Centre for Social Entrepreneurship, Roskilde University, contributing to an International Masters in Social Entrepreneurship. Recent research projects are: *A Map of Social Enterprises and Their Eco-systems in Europe*; *Developing an Ecosystem of Support for Social Enterprise*; *Social Enterprise in the UK: Models and Trajectories*; a Policy and Practice study of *Cities, the Social Economy and Inclusive Growth* (JRF project); and four EC Peer Reviews: Belgium, France, Croatia, and Norway.

Simon Teasdale is Professor of Public Policy and Organisations, and Assistant Vice Principal Global Challenges Research at Caledonian University. He is also Editor of *Social Enterprise Journal*. Simon's research focuses on the interface between public policies and organisational behaviour, with a particular emphasis on how social entrepreneurs shape, and are shaped by, policy discourses. This work has been funded by the OECD, European Union, the UK's Economic and Social Research Council and Medical Research Council, and has been published in journals such as *Economy and Society, Journal of Social Policy, Organization, Policy and Politics*, and *Public Management Review*.

Björn Wallsten is currently working as a Senior Research Officer at Formas – a Swedish Research Council for Sustainable Development. In his research, Björn has been concerned with questions regarding how natural resources become and are transformed in social processes. Primarily, he has scrutinised minerals and metals, their political framing and how they flow and/or become stocks in the built environment. He is an appointed member of The Swedish National Committee for History of Technology and Science.

Rafael Ziegler co-founded, in 2009, the social-ecological research group GETIDOS at the University of Greifswald and the IÖW Berlin, after studies in philosophy and economics at the London School of Economics and McGill University. His work is inspired by social innovations not only as a source of empirical materials but also as a spring of new ideas and concepts. His focus is on social innovation in relation to water, justice and sustainability. Dr Ziegler has worked as a deputy professor for environmental ethics in Greifswald. He is currently a guest professor at the Institute for the Environment, Sustainable Development and Circular Economy (IEEDEC) in Montreal.

1 Exploring the terrain of social entrepreneurship: new directions, paths less travelled

Anne de Bruin and Simon Teasdale

The field of social entrepreneurship (SE) is reaching maturity (Sassmannshausen and Volkmann 2018). However, there remain numerous new directions and paths less travelled for exploring the varied and complex SE terrain. This book draws together sixteen chapter contributions from developing paths of the SE field, to signpost directions ahead. In this chapter we integrate and build on these rich insights, paving the way for a future research agenda to advance the maturing SE field.

While some scholars suggest that mainstream entrepreneurship theories are sufficient to explain SE (Dacin et al. 2010), the field has been enriched by the application of different disciplinary approaches including management, public administration, economics, sociology, public health, and development studies. Up to this point methods have been predominately qualitative, arguably reflecting what a decade ago was characterised as a 'pre-paradigmatic' stage of field development (Nicholls 2010a), ranging from macro-studies of policy ecosystems to ethnographies. Economic theories have sought to explain the emergence of SE (Santos 2012) while realist evaluations (Roy et al. 2017) and systematic reviews (Calò et al. 2018; Roy et al. 2014) have been used to understand the impact of SE. Signs are emerging that scholars (and governments) are beginning to amass the datasets necessary for large-scale quantitative analysis (Estrin et al. 2013). While many authors use the terms social innovation, entrepreneurship and enterprise almost interchangeably, other scholars have focused on differentiating between them (de Bruin et al. 2014). Social innovation and SE are closely aligned. Despite this, the primary focus of this book is on SE, since a dual focus would have resulted in only thin coverage of both fields. However, the intricate and integral weaving together of the two fields is neatly captured in the final chapter of the book, Chapter 17 by Ziegler. The temporal perspective, future-orientation in capitalism and social imaginary ideas which are the crux of a chapter nominally focused on social innovation, are equally applicable to SE. As Ziegler aptly highlights, albeit in an endnote (note 1), his focus is on a strand of SE that relates to innovation and for brevity he refers to social innovations and social innovators, although this is not to assert that all social entrepreneurs are innovative. In similar vein, Luke and Chu (2013) show that not all social enterprises are entrepreneurial; although many chapters in this volume do not make such sharp distinctions between social enterprises and SE.

We can trace the emergence of SE as a concept to early academic papers such as that by Waddock and Post (1991) who defined social entrepreneurs as "private sector citizens who play critical roles in bringing about catalytic changes in the public sector agenda and the perception of certain social issues" (p. 393). This definition reflects the attention paid to Schumpeter's hero entrepreneur extending out of economics and business management literature, and into domains of public administration and social policy. It also reflects the relabelling of the activities of US nonprofits within a frame that might appeal to donors at a time when capitalism had become the only game in town. Early work by pioneers of the academic field such as Dees (1998) maintained a focus on change agents in the social sector, and, similar to early work in the more mainstream field of entrepreneurship, began to trace out the traits of successful social entrepreneurs. A focus on exemplars of SE helped to establish people like Nobel laureate Muhammad Yunus as emblematic of SE (Choi and Majumdar 2014). But limiting SE to a 'rare breed' of heroic individuals (Dees 1998; Martin and Osberg 2007) effectively places boundaries around the concept which exclude potential beneficiaries from involvement in the solutions for the social problems they face (Eikenberry and Kluver 2004; see also Chapter 4 by Eikenberry). Yet, as researchers began focusing on SE as a *process*, the field of SE widened from a limiting focus on systemic change. Zahra et al. (2009) developed a typology of social entrepreneurs rooted in different theoretical traditions and distinguishable by the ways they act, the scale at which they operate, and their effects on the social equilibrium. This opened up the idea that the tools and concepts of SE research might be applied to a much wider variety of approaches, and from a variety of (macro- meso- and micro-) perspectives.

Therefore, our goal for this book was not only to showcase the range and depth of advances that currently characterise the SE field but also to move the field forward with re-thinking and blue-sky thinking on directions for covering new ground in exploring SE. Toward this end, we invited a range of scholars to contribute. They ranged from those who were already distinguished by their expertise on SE topics, some of whom also sought the opinions of their early career colleagues, to mid-career scholars with scholarly expertise on particular aspects and applications of SE. We also sought contributions from other established research areas that could draw out implications for SE – legal scholarship (Chapter 6), gender (Chapter 12), Indigenous research (Chapter 13) – as well as cover less traversed regional contexts (Chapters 14 and 15). Additionally, we attempted to bring in research contributions from emerging societal trends, for example the circular economy–ecological entrepreneurship–SE nexus (Chapter 11). Together this sets the scene for chapters that stretch imaginaries of both the futuristic and the everyday (see Chapters 16 and 17).

We abstain from providing an overview and summary of each of the chapters in the book. We leave it to the readers to glean first-hand the valuable insights these chapters offer. However, we do allude to the other chapters where relevant and generally we underscore and build on them in our discussion in this chapter of the less developed contours of the SE field and the scope they present for research.

Contours of the SE terrain

In this section we take up some unresolved issues and gaps in the literature and point to directions for further exploration.

Contestation

It is notable that most usages of the concept of SE are positively imbued. To some extent, the enthusiastic portrayal of social entrepreneurs is a consequence of field-building exercises (Nicholls 2010a). In its early days the concept was treated more neutrally. For example, Breton and Breton (1969) conceptualise the social entrepreneur as the initiator of a social movement. Social movements grow around a shared conception of what possesses social value, and understandings of the causes of the problems they seek to tackle. However, whereas social movement scholars accept this contestation, within SE research there has been a tendency to avoid the 'dark side' (Williams and K'nife 2012). At heart, social value is a contested concept – what has value to one group may not necessarily be seen as having value by another. To illustrate, recent work (Chandra 2017) highlights the potential of SE to overcome terrorism through "disengag[ing] individuals enthralled to ideology and trapped by their own past behaviour" (p. 657). But from our privileged vantage point we should be mindful that the activities of Nelson Mandela and the African National Congress were once classified as terrorism by governments not only in South Africa, but also the United Kingdom. This of course is an extreme example, but we need to be alert to SE as modern form of colonialism which imposes a dominant set of values (Dey and Steyaert 2010). One route towards avoiding the contested nature of what has social value might be focusing on positively intended social change (Stephan et al. 2016). This reveals interesting paths less travelled for future research. Exploring SE as a site where contested ethics and values are played out between opposing factions offers much potential (Dey and Teasdale 2016). This in turn raises questions around the contested ethics and values of SE. Research from other fields may provide insights into methodological tools, such as Q methodology, designed to explore subjectivity and beliefs (Baker et al. 2006).

Hybridity, competing logics

Some authors switch interchangeably between SE and social enterprise, with the implication being that social entrepreneurs create and lead social enterprises. Others suggest SE extends well beyond social enterprises, perhaps because of the commercial constraints implied by social enterprise (e.g. Zahra et al. 2009). From this perspective, SE is not constrained to a single sector or subsector of the economy. The concept of hybridity perhaps offers a more useful lens through which to understand SE, since, as Chapter 15 by Holt and Meldrum illustrates, it is more adaptable to different cultural contexts.

The basic premise of hybridity is that social ventures bridge institutional fields (Tracey et al. 2011) by virtue of existing at the intersection between private, public and civil society, and so must accommodate the diverse logics, practices and values of these fields (Evers and Svetlik 1993). As such their bridging of institutional fields (Tracey et al. 2011) leads them to negotiate conflicting logics within the organisation, particularly around commercial and collective objectives (Doherty et al. 2014; Pache and Santos 2013). In the context of this book, SE involves conscious or unconscious strategies aimed at negotiating conflicting logics within the organisation (Doherty et al. 2014). These strategies more usually are aimed at alleviating tensions, selective coupling (or decoupling) (Pache and Santos 2013) or optimising conditions whereby social mission and commercial goals are in broad alignment (Battilana and Lee 2014).

While hybridity poses challenges to social entrepreneurs, it also offers opportunities to draw upon different organisational identities for different purposes. Drawing upon identity theory, Wry and York (2015) show how social entrepreneurs might be single minded (aligned either to a social or commercial logic), mixed (whereby role-based identity conflicts with personal identity), or balanced, whereby multiple role identities align with different logics. This begins to help explain how social ventures might normalise organisational complexity and hybridity. Nevertheless, it may also now be questioned whether social enterprises should continue to be classified as hybrid organisations (McMullen 2018). However, addressing questions of identity and reconciliation of tensions of multiple identities remain especially relevant, especially in the face of collaborative arrangements and partnerships including cross-sector interactions of social enterprises, nowadays an enduring ethic of SE (de Bruin et al. 2017).

Rurality

Extant studies have shown that SE can play an important role in rural development and catalysing solutions to socio-economic challenges in sparsely populated remote areas (Farmer et al. 2008; Steiner and Teasdale 2017; see also Chapter 10 by Eversole and Duniam). (Some) rural areas may have particular attributes (dense networks of trust and social capital) which lend themselves to SE (Lang and Fink 2018). Environmental sustainability, food insecurity in rural areas and vulnerability of smallholder farmers, agriurban and alternative food initiatives and food supply chain are all related issues that are being increasing tackled in the social economy and by social enterprises and offer fruitful areas for investigation (see Chapter 9 by Doherty and Kittipanya-ngam).

Measuring social value

While a constructivist perspective certainly poses challenges towards measuring social impact, academic literature on social impact measurement is wide and varied. Nicholls (2009) developed the construct of blended value accounting, showing how social entrepreneurs creatively use reporting practices as strategic tools to access resources. In many ways this is not dissimilar to the ways in which mainstream businesses present their annual accounts. But one notable difference is that in most countries, legislation determines which financial data should be reported, and to what standards. The quest to legitimise a single approach to social impact reporting brings to mind the battles fought between Betamax and VHS in the 1980s as academics, practitioners, and accountancy firms seek to establish their own/chosen models as dominant practice (see also Chapter 5 by Ormiston and Castellas on the potential for practice insights for social impact measurement). Perhaps the most widely written-about method of social impact reporting is Social Return On Investment (SROI) (Arvidson et al. 2013), but it is widely accepted that SROI offers no realistic basis for comparing social performance of different types of social purpose organisation. Indeed, it is questionable whether such a basis for comparison is ever achievable, or even desirable, since it may push organisations to focus on what is measurable at the expense of experimentation and innovation (McMullen and Warnick 2016). While it may be feasible to ask organisations to collect data on immediate outputs, understanding longer-term impacts is expensive as well as subjective. Accordingly, there are good arguments that this should be left to funders (Ebrahim and Rangan 2014).

Critical perspectives and governmentality

Attempts by funders to measure social performance have been portrayed as embodying the high watermark of a new public management culture (Hall et al. 2012). The 'rational' thinking here was that if it were possible to place financial proxies on the activities and outputs of organisation, allocating resources would become a simple task easily aligned to political objectives. Perhaps recognising the futility of such command and control approaches, governments across the world, but particularly in market-liberal societies such as the UK, Australia and the US, have attempted to increase the supply of social ventures and manipulate their activity towards particular political objectives through more subtle 'governmentality' approaches such as discourse and the manipulation of material incentives. Discursive analysis of SE texts has sought to reveal how language functions in maintaining/changing power relations. Scholars (Dart 2004; Dey and Steyaert 2012; Dey and Teasdale 2016; Eikenberry and Kluver 2004; Ruebottom 2013) note that many of these texts (both academic and policy) highlight the role of the hero social entrepreneur as moving behind the constraints imposed by bureaucratic governments and well-meaning but ultimately patronising and ineffective charities through the adoption of business-like approaches (see Dees 1998; Yunus 2011). Researchers adopting a discursive perspective have focused on resistance to dominant SE discourse from civil society practitioners (Parkinson and Howorth 2008), the implication being that since many practitioners 'reject' the dominant discourse, such attempts to manipulate behaviour have failed. However, the language of SE has become more prevalent than such resistance would predict (Dey and Teasdale 2013), and that resistance/compliance is not a simple dichotomy (Dey and Teasdale 2016). Other studies move the focus beyond discourse to focus on how policymakers manipulate behavioural levers through a blend of financial incentives (grants and contracts) and associated performance measurement techniques (Carmel and Harlock 2008). Hall et al. (2012) analysed the role of the UK's National Health Service in seeking to increase the supply of social enterprises operating in the health sector and encourage them into particular types of behaviour through the use of market-based incentives. Their conclusions lend further support to the notion that governments have not yet developed the tools to successfully manipulate the behaviour of social entrepreneurs. In Chapter 3, Mason picks up this line of questioning using a quasi-market illustration. Nonetheless, there remains a considerable gap in our knowledge concerning how governments and social entrepreneurs collaborate and/or come into conflict, and how this changes over time and context (see Chapters 2 and 4 by Roy and Hazenberg, and Eikenberry respectively).

Field building and institutional environment/ecosystems

The importance of contextual factors supporting, and constraining, SE is increasingly highlighted in the academic literature. There is a particular focus on the roles that government can play, through legislative instruments, in reshaping markets to financially reward the creation of social value (Ebrahim et al. 2014; Teasdale et al. 2012). Here studies have focused on legal forms for social ventures (Galera and Borzaga 2009; Nicholls 2010b; Reiser 2011), and tools such as social impact bonds aimed at bringing the financial efficiency of markets (Nicholls and Teasdale 2017) to the social sphere (Edmiston and Nicholls 2018; McHugh et al. 2013).

At the macro level this has been related to the development of SE as a field (Nicholls 2010a), and some studies have begun to focus on such field building through different institutional lenses: historical (Kerlin 2013; Roy et al. 2015; Sepulveda 2015; see also Chapter 2 by Roy and Hazenberg), and discursive (Nicholls and Teasdale 2017). Interestingly, as with much of the SE literature, when viewed from the macro level, scholars tend to derive a less positive analysis, particularly towards policy attempts to create a conducive environment for SE. In many countries, it would seem that the actions of policymakers are guided towards the replacement of (albeit) imperfect systems of social protection. Future research might usefully begin to unpack resistance to such social change activities (Dacin et al. 2011).

Beyond the individual hero

Early work tended to downplay or take for granted the social aspect of SE. Effectively 'social' was used in a residual sense to reflect social purpose organisations. Mair and Martí (2006) moved the focus away from the entrepreneur and began to focus on the ways in which social entrepreneurs are embedded in communities and draw upon resources within these communities. This helped switch attention towards the collective dimension of SE. Viewed through a collective lens, this demonstrates that all SE should be seen as a form of collective action, but also highlights particular approaches to SE that explicitly emphasise this collective dimension: social movements, community cooperatives, and cross-sectoral collaborations (Montgomery et al. 2012; see also Chapter 8 by Spear). Other authors focus on community enterprises as a particular form of social venture which bring to the fore the collective dimension within SE (see Chapter 7 by Haugh and Brady).

Towards intersectionality

Interestingly, despite the attention paid within much of the discourse around SE as a means for tackling gender inequality, few studies explicitly explore SE as a gendered practice. Dempsey and Sanders (2010) show how SE can be conceived as the marketisation of reproductive labour and highlight the tensions this engenders. On the one hand, it makes such work 'meaningful', but on the other hand, through marketisation and professionalisation, SE might also serve to make meaningful work less accessible to women. To some extent this offers new insights into a quantitative literature which highlights that women may be overrepresented in the third sector and social enterprises, but the highest occupational levels are dominated by men (Teasdale et al. 2011). As such, work becomes professionalised and characterised by long hours and a 'macho' culture, and women are pushed (or pulled) away from positions of leadership.

A small number of studies have focused on efforts by social ventures to promote gender and development objectives. A study of a women's cooperative by Datta and Gailey (2012) suggests that collective entrepreneurship can empower women economically. However, work by Hayhurst (2014) indicates that when practised by international nongovernmental organisations, such SE efforts may actually further gender inequalities through focusing on short-term solutions (enabling women to cope in a 'man's world) while overlooking the broader structural inequalities and gender relations that marginalise women in the first place. In essence this is central to the critique of SE put forward by many scholars: that it can never achieve structural change through tackling the effects of inequality rather than the causes (Garrow and Hasenfeld 2014). This is a critique that has been levelled more widely at development practices in the Global South, so it is perhaps surprising that, as noted in Chapter 15 by Holt and Meldrum, there are relatively few studies of SE in the South; most existing studies focus on the efforts of Western-based NGOs and foundations (such as Ashoka) rather than on indigenous SE.

Thus, we draw attention to the need to extend the study of SE beyond the tried and tested Global North (see Chapters 14 and 15 by Alarifi, Robson and Kromidha, and Holt and Meldrum, respectively). Questions to be investigated include: What does SE mean for development, and developing and emerging economies? What does SE look like when interrogated through a postcolonial lens? How do we incorporate gender (see Chapter 12 by Lewis and Henry), and ethnicity and Indigenous perspectives (see Chapter 13 by Henry and Dana)? What is the role for SE in sustainable development? Perhaps most important, we would call for researchers to avoid focusing on particular inequalities in isolation; and begin to incorporate the concept of intersectionality in order to understand how different disadvantages combine and interact, and to explore whether hybrid organisations might possess particular advantages in overcoming multi-faceted social problems. Furthermore, intersectional research relies on bridging disciplinary boundaries and drawing on theories across disciplines. Given that diversity is a strength of the SE field, as discussed in the next section, this makes our call for intersectional analysis all the more apt.

Pluralism and multi-disciplinary advantage

A strength of the SE field is its diversity in theoretical, disciplinary and methodological approaches, and as the field has matured, we have seen signs of considerable advancement in the interdisciplinary approach to studying SE. Arguably, this stems in part from the interdisciplinary conversations and cross-pollination of ideas stimulated through events such as the International Social Innovation Research Conference which will be in its eleventh year in 2019. The combination of different perspectives can help build exciting new theory. Disciplines where SE is perhaps still underrepresented include Development Studies, Sociology and Economics. Geography is another discipline that would seemingly lend itself to further study of SE as contextually and spatially determined.

It is not new to suggest that SE as a field is characterised by a lack of large-scale quantitative studies. Some would suggest this is partly a consequence of us not (yet) possessing a general theory of SE setting out its defining characteristics and general principles. Others from a more institutionalist slant would argue that such a general theory is impossible given the contextual interdependence between micro-social entrepreneurial initiatives and their politically, culturally, socially, economically, geographically, and historically variable contexts within which they operate. In essence, social ventures emerge to fit their context, making comparison impossible. Here the work led by Defourny and Nyssens as part of the ICSEM (International Comparative Models of Social Enterprise)[1] offers an exciting way forward. The ICSEM project seeks to identify and map broad families of social enterprise and relate their prevalence to institutional factors.

Much of the existing work on SE has relied on relatively light touch case studies to help build the field. As noted above, much of this work is relatively uncritical and can lead to an overly optimistic view of the field. Where researchers have undertaken more in-depth qualitative work challenges to this perspective emerge, such as around failure (Tracey and Jarvis 2006), and SE as performance (Mauksch 2016) involving deviance and mimicry (Dey and Teasdale 2016). A common thread running through these studies is the search by social entrepreneurs to carve out a path for agency within structuralist systems. Studying the creativity of social entrepreneurs and the ways in which they negotiate the spaces of power is one way in which the concept could permeate the sociological literature more deeply.

In measuring social impact, we can learn more from disciplines such as economics and development studies, more used to studying the effects of complex social interventions. Can we adopt 'gold standard' methodological approaches such as Randomised Control Trials to the study of SE? How can we ascertain the counterfactual? We need to be mindful here of the possibility for natural experiments. Realist evaluation offers one route forward in negotiating the problems of contextual interdependence, while, philosophically at least, offering potential to bridge the structure/agency divide.

Concluding comment

Our overarching goal for the book was not to be prescriptive, but rather to stimulate the imagination in new ways. As an expedition to pave new ways to build cumulative knowledge in the maturing SE field, the book highlights future research directions that the complex dynamics and phenomena of SE offer. SE in its many and varied forms holds much promise for stimulating positive social change. This potentially includes systemic change through tackling deep-rooted global-level societal challenges such as poverty and environmental degradation; institutional change through tackling structural constraints such as improving women's empowerment in meaningful ways; and community change by tackling local-level social vulnerabilities such as inadequate housing for socio-economically disadvantaged groups. Now let the fascinating and rewarding exploration of the SE terrain pick up the pace, traversing not only gently undulating ground, but also land less trodden, rocky and steep.

NOTE

1   https://www.iap-socent.be/icsem-project.

References

Arvidson, M., F. Lyon, S. McKay and D. Moro (2013), 'Valuing the social? The nature and controversies of measuring Social Return on Investment (SROI)', *Voluntary Sector Review*, **4** (1), 3–18.

Baker, R., C. Thompson and R. Mannion (2006), 'Q methodology in health economics', *Journal of Health Services Research & Policy*, **11** (1), 38–45.

Battilana, J. and M. Lee (2014), 'Advancing research on hybrid organizing – insights from the study of social enterprises', *The Academy of Management Annals*, **8** (1), 397–441.

Breton, A. and R. Breton (1969), 'An economic theory of social movements', *The American Economic Review*, **59** (2), 198–205.

Calò, F., S. Teasdale, C. Donaldson, M. J. Roy and S. Baglioni (2018), 'Collaborator or competitor: assessing the evidence supporting the role of social enterprise in health and social care', *Public Management Review*, **20** (12), 1790–814.

Carmel, E. and J. Harlock (2008), 'Instituting the "Third Sector" as a governable terrain: partnership, procurement and performance in the UK', *Policy & Politics*, **36** (2), 155–71.

Chandra, Y. (2017), 'Social entrepreneurship as emancipatory work', *Journal of Business Venturing*, **32** (6), 657–73.

Choi, N. and S. Majumdar (2014), 'Social entrepreneurship as an essentially contested concept: opening a new avenue for systematic future research', *Journal of Business Venturing*, **29** (3), 363–76.

Dacin, P. A., M. T. Dacin and M. Matear (2010), 'Social entrepreneurship: why we don't need a new theory and how we move forward from here', *The Academy of Management Perspectives*, **24** (3), 37–57.

Dacin, M. T., P. A. Dacin and P. Tracey (2011), 'Social entrepreneurship: a critique and future directions', *Organization Science*, **22** (5), 1203–13.

Dart, R. (2004), 'The legitimacy of social enterprise', *Nonprofit Management and Leadership*, **14** (4), 411–24.

Datta, P. B. and R. Gailey (2012), 'Empowering women through social entrepreneurship: case study of a women's cooperative in India', *Entrepreneurship Theory and Practice*, **36** (3), 569–87.

de Bruin, A., E. Shaw and D. Chalmers (2014), 'Social entrepreneurship: looking back, moving ahead', in E. Chell and M. Karatas-Ozkan (eds), *Handbook of Research in Entrepreneurship and Small Business*, Cheltenham: Edward Elgar Publishing, pp. 392–416.

de Bruin, A., E. Shaw and K. V. Lewis (2017), 'The collaborative dynamic in social entrepreneurship', *Entrepreneurship & Regional Development*, **29** (7–8), 575–85.

Dees, J. G. (1998), *The Meaning of Social Entrepreneurship*, Duke University, Fuqua School of Business.

Dempsey, S. E. and M. L. Sanders (2010), 'Meaningful work? Nonprofit marketization and work/life imbalance in popular autobiographies of social entrepreneurship', *Organization*, **17** (4), 437–59.

Dey, P. and C. Steyaert (2010), 'The politics of narrating social entrepreneurship', *Journal of Enterprising Communities*, **4** (1), 85–108.

Dey, P. and C. Steyaert (2012), 'Social entrepreneurship: critique and the radical enactment of the social', *Social Enterprise Journal*, **8** (2), 90–107.

Dey, P. and S. Teasdale (2013), 'Social enterprise and dis/identification', *Administrative Theory & Praxis*, **35** (2), 248–70.

Dey, P. and S. Teasdale (2016), 'The tactical mimicry of social enterprise strategies: acting "As If" in the everyday life of Third Sector organizations', *Organization*, **23** (4), 485–504.

Doherty, B., H. Haugh and F. Lyon (2014), 'Social enterprises as hybrid organizations: a review and research agenda', *International Journal of Management Reviews*, **16** (4), 417–36.

Ebrahim, A., J. Battilana and J. Mair (2014), 'The governance of social enterprises: mission drift and accountability challenges in hybrid organizations', *Research in Organizational Behavior*, **34**, 81–100.

Ebrahim, A. and Rangan, V. K. (2014), 'What impact? A framework for measuring the scale and scope of social performance', *California Management Review*, **56** (3), 118–41.

Edmiston, D. and A. Nicholls (2018), 'Social impact bonds: the role of private capital in outcome-based commissioning', *Journal of Social Policy*, **47** (1), 57–76.

Eikenberry, A. M. and J. D. Kluver (2004), 'The marketization of the nonprofit sector: civil society at risk?', *Public Administration Review*, **64** (2), 132–40.

Estrin, S., T. Mickiewicz and U. Stephan (2013), 'Entrepreneurship, social capital, and institutions: social and commercial entrepreneurship across nations', *Entrepreneurship Theory and Practice*, **37** (3), 479–504.

Evers, A. and I. Svetlik (eds) (1993), *Balancing Pluralism: New Welfare Mixes in Care for the Elderly*, Aldershot: Avebury.

Farmer, J., A. Steinerowski and S. Jack (2008), 'Starting social enterprises in remote and rural Scotland: best or worst of circumstances?', *International Journal of Entrepreneurship and Small Business*, **6** (3), 450–64.

Galera, G. and C. Borzaga (2009), 'Social enterprise: an international overview of its conceptual evolution and legal implementation', *Social Enterprise Journal*, **5** (3), 210–28.

Garrow, E. E. and Y. Hasenfeld (2014), 'Social enterprises as an embodiment of a Neoliberal welfare logic', *American Behavioral Scientist*, **58** (11), 1475–93.

Hall, K., P. Alcock and R. Millar (2012), 'Start up and sustainability: marketisation and the Social Enterprise Investment Fund in England', *Journal of Social Policy*, **41** (4), 733–49.

Hayhurst, L. M. C. (2014), 'The "Girl Effect" and martial arts: social entrepreneurship and sport, gender and development in Uganda', *Gender, Place & Culture*, **21** (3), 297–315.

Kerlin, J. A. (2013), 'Defining social enterprise across different contexts: a conceptual framework based on institutional factors', *Nonprofit and Voluntary Sector Quarterly*, **42** (1), 84–108.

Lang, R. and M. Fink (2018), 'Rural social entrepreneurship: the role of social capital within and across institutional levels', *Journal of Rural Studies*, accessed 18 December 2018 at https://doi.org/10.1016/j.jrurstud.2018.03.012.

Luke, B. and V. Chu (2013), 'Social enterprise versus social entrepreneurship: an examination of the "why" and "how" in pursuing social change', *International Small Business Journal*, **31** (7), 764–84.

Mair, J. and I. Martí (2006), 'Social entrepreneurship research: a source of explanation, prediction, and delight', *Journal of World Business*, **41** (1), 36–44.

Martin, R. L. and S. Osberg (2007), 'Social entrepreneurship: the case for definition', *Stanford Social Innovation Review*, **Spring**, 28–39.

Mauksch, S. (2016), 'Managing the dance of enchantment: an ethnography of social entrepreneurship events', *Organization*, **24** (2), 133–53.

McHugh, N., S. Sinclair, M. J. Roy, L. Huckfield and C. Donaldson (2013), 'Social impact bonds: a wolf in sheep's clothing?', *Journal of Poverty and Social Justice*, **21** (3), 247–57.

McMullen, J. S. (2018), 'Organizational hybrids as biological hybrids: insights for research on the relationship between social enterprise and the entrepreneurial ecosystem', *Journal of Business Venturing*, **33** (5), 575–90.

McMullen, J. S. and B. J. Warnick (2016), 'Should we require every new venture to be a hybrid organization?', *Journal of Management Studies*, **53** (4), 630–62.

Montgomery, A. W., P. A. Dacin and M. T. Dacin (2012), 'Collective social entrepreneurship: collaboratively shaping social good', *Journal of Business Ethics*, **111** (3), 375–88.

Nicholls, A. (2009), '"We do good things, don't we?" "Blended Value Accounting" in social entrepreneurship', *Accounting, Organizations and Society*, **34** (6–7), 755–69.

Nicholls, A. (2010a), 'The legitimacy of social entrepreneurship: reflexive isomorphism in a pre-paradigmatic field', *Entrepreneurship Theory and Practice*, **34** (4), 611–33.

Nicholls, A. (2010b), 'Institutionalizing social entrepreneurship in regulatory space: reporting and disclosure by community interest companies', *Accounting, Organizations and Society*, **35** (4), 394–415.

Nicholls, A. and S. Teasdale (2017), 'Neoliberalism by stealth? Exploring continuity and change within the UK social enterprise policy paradigm', *Policy & Politics*, **45** (3), 323–41.

Pache, A.-C. and F. Santos (2013), 'Inside the hybrid organization: selective coupling as a response to competing institutional logics', *Academy of Management Journal*, **56** (4), 972–1001.

Parkinson, C. and C. Howorth (2008), 'The language of social entrepreneurs', *Entrepreneurship and Regional Development*, **20** (3), 285–309.

Reiser, D. B. (2011), 'Benefit corporations – a sustainable form of organization?', *Wake Forest Law Review*, **46**, 591–625.

Roy, M. J., R. Baker and S. Kerr (2017), 'Conceptualising the public health role of actors operating outside of formal health systems: the case of social enterprise', *Social Science & Medicine*, **172**, 144–52.

Roy, M. J., C. Donaldson, R. Baker and S. Kerr (2014), 'The potential of social enterprise to enhance health and well-being: a model and systematic review', *Social Science & Medicine*, **123**, 182–93.

Roy, M. J., N. McHugh, L. Huckfield, A. Kay and C. Donaldson (2015), '"The most supportive environment in the world"? Tracing the development of an institutional "ecosystem" for social enterprise', *Voluntas: International Journal of Voluntary and Nonprofit Organizations*, **26** (3), 777–800.

Ruebottom, T. (2013), 'The microstructures of rhetorical strategy in social entrepreneurship: building legitimacy through heroes and villains', *Journal of Business Venturing*, **28** (1), 98–116.

Santos, F. M. (2012), 'A positive theory of social entrepreneurship', *Journal of Business Ethics*, **111** (3), 335–51.

Sassmannshausen, S. P. and C. Volkmann (2018), 'The scientometrics of social entrepreneurship and its establishment as an academic field', *Journal of Small Business Management*, **56** (2), 251–73.

Sepulveda, L. (2015), 'Social enterprise – a new phenomenon in the field of economic and social welfare?', *Social Policy & Administration*, **49** (7), 842–61.

Steiner, A. and S. Teasdale (2017), 'Unlocking the potential of rural social enterprise', *Journal of Rural Studies*, accessed 18 December 2018 at https://doi.org/10.1016/j.jrurstud.2017.12.021.

Stephan, U., M. Patterson, C. Kelly and J. Mair (2016), 'Organizations driving positive social change: a review and an integrative framework of change processes', *Journal of Management*, **42** (5), 1250–81.

Teasdale, S., P. Alcock and G. Smith (2012), 'Legislating for the Big Society? The case of the Public Services (Social Value) Bill', *Public Money & Management*, **32** (3), 201–8.

Teasdale, S., S. McKay, J. Phillimore and N. Teasdale (2011), 'Exploring gender and social entrepreneurship: women's leadership, employment and participation in the Third Sector and social enterprises', *Voluntary Sector Review*, **2** (1), 57–76.

Tracey, P. and O. Jarvis (2006), 'An enterprising failure: why a promising social franchise collapsed', *Stanford Social Innovation Review*, **5** (Spring), 55–70.

Tracey, P., N. Phillips and O. Jarvis (2011), 'Bridging institutional entrepreneurship and the creation of new organizational forms: a multilevel model', *Organization Science*, **22** (1), 60–80.

Waddock, S. A. and J. E. Post (1991), 'Social entrepreneurs and catalytic change', *Public Administration Review*, **51** (5), 393–401.

Williams, D. A. and K. A. K. K'nife (2012), 'The dark side of social entrepreneurship', *International Journal of Entrepreneurship*, **16**, 63–75.

Wry, T. and J. G. York (2015), 'An identity-based approach to social enterprise', *Academy of Management Review*, **42** (3), 437–60.

Yunus, M. (2011), 'Social business – towards a better capitalism', in P. U. Petit (ed.), *Creating a New Civilization through Social Entrepreneurship*, Piscataway, NJ: First Transaction Publishers/Goi Peace Foundation, pp. ix–xvi.

Zahra, S. A., E. Gedajlovic, D. O. Neubaum and J. M. Shulman (2009), 'A typology of social entrepreneurs: motives, search processes and ethical challenges', *Journal of Business Venturing*, **24** (5), 519–32.

2 An evolutionary perspective on social entrepreneurship 'ecosystems'

Michael J. Roy and Richard Hazenberg

Introduction

In this chapter we focus upon the idea that the process of social entrepreneurship (SE) needs a supportive environment in order to flourish. Drawing upon biological metaphors and evolutionary theory, we show how different environmental conditions – such as historical, political, legal and economic factors – all combine to influence various types of social enterprise that can emerge in different contexts. Reflecting on extant research on social enterprise 'ecosystems', we draw upon results of a large-scale European project to present a typology of different ecosystems identified thus far and suggest ways in which research on this topic could be developed further in the future.

The first part of the chapter is concerned with our evolutionary perspective. We employ evolutionary theory to explain how even relatively small differences in environmental factors, such as occurs between nations or regions *within* a state – drawing on the example of Scotland and England – can lead to divergence in the types of social enterprise that can come to dominate. We then discuss the role of institutional and stakeholder networks in shaping different types of ecosystem, such as we see across Europe. First of all, however, we turn attention to what we mean by the term 'ecosystem'.

About ecosystems

While interest in social entrepreneurship and social enterprise in academic circles has flourished in recent decades (Doherty 2018), we are increasingly seeing the terms being employed to describe phenomena which can vary significantly depending on the place, space, culture or political or legal frameworks in which they are undertaken. It is considered that variations in social enterprise around the world are due, in large part, to the highly idiosyncratic nature of the context in which they operate (Bacq and Janssen 2011; Di Domenico et al. 2010; Kerlin 2013).

One of the principal aims of the EFESEIIS (Enabling the Flourishing and Evolution of Social Entrepreneurship for Innovative and Inclusive Societies) project, which ran from 2014 to 2016 (see Biggeri et al. 2019), was to explore such variations, and extend theory on some of the reasons for these. Supported by the European Commission's Seventh Framework Programme for Research, EFESEIIS involved 11 European partners and three non-European comparators. While employing evolutionary theory to the social sciences is an idea that has become increasingly popular in recent decades (Gough et al. 2008), this project allowed us to apply, test and adapt evolutionary theory to the idea of social entrepreneurship ecosystems for the first time (see During et al. 2016, 2019). Since the term 'ecosystem' was first used in studies of mainstream business a quarter of a century ago (Moore 1993) a stream of literature has emerged on 'entrepreneurial ecosystems' (Alvedalen and Boschma 2017; Spigel 2017; Stam 2015) to mean "the union of localized cultural outlooks, social networks, investment capital, universities, and active economic policies that create environments supportive of innovation-based ventures" (Spigel 2017, p. 49). Despite the explosion in academic and policy interest in social entrepreneurship, however, the literature on social entrepreneurship ecosystems, to which we next turn, is still in its infancy.

Social entrepreneurship ecosystems and the relevance of evolutionary theory

The term social entrepreneurship (or social enterprise) ecosystem has crept into the lexicon of policymakers over the past 10 years or so. Governments across the world, and transnational actors such as the World Bank (see Deloitte LLP 2016), have all shown an intense interest in creating a supportive environment for social entrepreneurship to flourish. Leaving aside, for the time being, the reasons why policymakers seem to have become intensely interested in the role of social enterprise to address acute social problems, particularly since the Global Financial Crisis of 2007–2008, social entrepreneurship ecosystems are usually conceived as being place based and organised at a national or regional level. That is not to say that they could not be larger (e.g. transnational) or smaller (city, or municipality level, or even neighbourhood level) but since policy is usually enacted at a regional, state or national level this is usually the size of ecosystem that policymakers are concerned with. It should not be forgotten, however, that the systems are not closed, but open: there are interconnections beyond the boundaries of the ecosystem. Moreover, just like any natural system, we cannot expect one component, such as a particular policy instrument, law, or even organisation, to be removed from its environment and expect it to thrive elsewhere without adaptation.

Academic literature on social entrepreneurship ecosystems has, however, largely failed to keep pace with policy and practice. Drawing on literature on civil society and social movements, Arthur et al. (2006) speak of the importance of an 'associative ecosystem' to address social inclusion, working alongside and supported by, the state. Grassl (2012, p. 44), meanwhile, explains that a social enterprise must be built as "a robust, integrated network of nodes and connections with the knowledge of who the constituents of the business are and where they can find value individually and together as a whole". Roy et al. (2015), drawing upon the particular example of Scotland, attempt to explain how history, geography, politics, and the country's sometimes fractious relationship with their far larger neighbour England all combine to influence the dominant type of social enterprise that we see. Building upon that work via the EFESEIIS project, we attempted to contribute to an exploration of some of the 'uneven geographies' of social enterprise (Buckingham et al. 2012; Mazzei 2017; Muñoz 2010) by taking the opportunity to compare Scotland to England (Hazenberg, Bajwa-Patel, Roy et al. 2016). We found that not only was there divergence between the social enterprise ecosystems of Scotland and England, but divergence was increasing over time. Explanations for this were found through an analysis of the political and socio-economic differences that have emerged between the two countries in the past 50 years or so, but which have accelerated through political devolution of key powers to Scotland from Westminster, and the (re-) establishment of the Scottish Parliament in 1999. Not only are there now quite different approaches to social enterprise policy when comparing the two countries, but markedly different tones and even ideologies at play in a wide range of key social policies. There is clear evidence of an emergence of a distinct 'Scottish approach' to policymaking (Cairney et al. 2016), for example, that is recognised as being especially consultative and co-operative, particularly in comparison with England.

Applying evolutionary theory (During et al. 2019), we then attempted to not only *describe* the differences, but also start to unpack the *reasons for* differences in ecosystems. We employed ecological metaphors such as:

1. *Genetic variation*: random variation, where new forms of social enterprise appear, and their survival is then dependent on how well their random changes are suited to their current environment;
2. *Phenotypes*: where environmental factors lead to variations in traits/behaviours leading to different 'species' of social enterprise emerging; and
3. *Epigenetics*: where experience and/or interaction with environmental factors alter the shape (or 'genetic coding') of the social enterprise, leading to mutation.

While both the ecosystems of Scotland and England share a similar historical (genetic) base, particularly since the two countries were joined to form the United Kingdom over 300 years ago, both countries have been subjected to very similar environmental factors (epigenetics), unsurprisingly resulting in relatively similar types of social enterprises (phenotypes) emerging. The birth of the co-operative movement of the eighteenth and nineteenth centuries, for example, emerged as a response to many of the upheavals of the industrial revolution happening in northern Britain. However, over the past 50 years or so, epigenetic influences on both ecosystems have diverged: both countries have adopted different approaches to politics (right-wing parties dominating in England, compared to Scotland becoming increasingly left-wing over the course of the twentieth century), socio-economic policy (monetarist in England, versus a favourable outlook towards Keynesian models in Scotland) and institutional structures (political devolution, in the case of Scotland). Drawing upon Teasdale's (2012) typology of social enterprise discourses, we found the Scottish ecosystem to be dominated by the 'community enterprise' (collective/social) form of social enterprise, while England was characterised by the 'social business' form (economic/individualistic). It could also be argued that northern England, with its history of cooperatives and traditionally left-wing politics, is closer to the Scottish model than the 'English' model. However, until (very) recently the north has not had the political power to shape policy in the same way that Scotland has (albeit this is now changing through the devolution of powers from London to northern cities). This again demonstrates the uneven geography of social enterprise and shows that we may see a divergence in the English ecosystem between 'community enterprise' and 'social business'. These differences are presented in Figure 2.1.

Constructing a typology of social enterprise ecosystems

We then began the process of constructing a typology of the different social enterprise ecosystems across Europe. This rather ambitious stage of the project focused on examining the presence of certain types of stakeholders, and the relationships or social networks that exist between them (Hazenberg, Bajwa-Patel, Mazzei et al. 2016). We undertook in-depth semi-structured interviews and focus groups with stakeholders in Austria, England, France, Germany, Italy, the Netherlands, Poland, Scotland, Serbia and Sweden. In total we gathered qualitative data from 258 different actors in various key areas of the social enterprise ecosystem of each country. These data were then used to produce 10 stakeholder maps – one for each country – which were then compared with each other to identify the differences and commonalities between each ecosystem. Seven key areas of interest emerged: procurement policies and regulation; financial activities for ecosystem growth; inclusive labour market practices; collaborative stakeholder systems; training and education in support of ecosystem growth; impact and dissemination; and a general 'system drivers' category. After an exhaustive (and exhausting) iterative process involving discussion with and between the various researchers involved in interpreting and analysing the data, we used our findings to identify four distinct social enterprise ecosystem types. We called these Statist-macro, Statist-micro, Private-macro and Private-micro. Figure 2.2 shows each in a quadrant relevant to their relative positions against two axes: local/international and state/private. In addition, our research identified a growing network of collaborative stakeholders and the emergence of strategic partnerships within each social enterprise ecosystem. Normatively speaking, we considered that such pluralism (labelled the Pluralist Zone) should be considered the 'ideal scenario' for the development of flourishing, sustainable and robust social enterprise ecosystems.

Employing our metaphors again drawn from evolutionary theory, we found different dominant stakeholder groups in each ecosystem, which we considered to be the result of historical (genetic) factors and environmental (epigenetic) factors, and the nature of the relations between institutions, organisations and individuals within the ecosystem. The *Statist-macro* type, under which we grouped Poland,

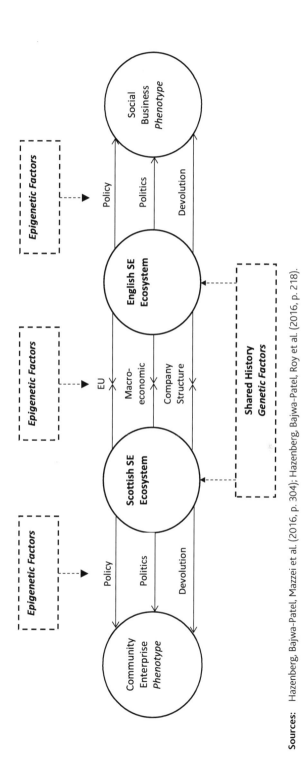

Sources: Hazenberg, Bajwa-Patel, Mazzei et al. (2016, p. 304); Hazenberg, Bajwa-Patel, Roy et al. (2016, p. 218).

Figure 2.1 Comparative development of the Scottish and English ecosystems

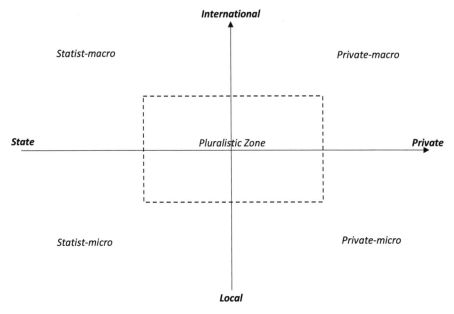

Source: Hazenberg, Bajwa-Patel, Mazzei et al. (2016, p. 317).

Figure 2.2   Social enterprise ecosystem typology

France, Serbia and Austria, was found to be characterised by a reliance on centralised state institutions directing policy and funding mechanisms to support the development of social enterprises (including heavy reliance in some ecosystems on 'international' EU funding). As such, social enterprises within this type of ecosystem, we found, tended to be fairly reliant upon grant and/or directed funding. We found too that the types of social enterprises in this ecosystem type tended to be fairly homogenous, with a particular dominance of the Work Integration Social Enterprise (WISE) form.

The *Statist-micro* type, by comparison – into which we grouped Scotland and Sweden – was also found to be reliant upon state institutions for funding, but policy support was found to be well embedded at a local level, particularly through effective use of procurement and community-based instruments of support funded by the state and European funding enacted at a fairly local level. We also found evidence of subsidised loans rather than grant support in places. The focus on local support seemed to encourage heterogeneity in social enterprise forms, albeit WISEs were also common to this ecosystem type. We found the public sector in each case seemed to frame social enterprise as an important and robust tool for labour market integration, particularly for vulnerable groups.

The *Private-macro* type (Germany and England), meanwhile, was broadly characterised by a relative lack of direct state financial subsidy, at least in comparison to the other types. That said, the state was found to have an interest in assisting social enterprises to become more market-oriented, directing policy towards supporting social enterprises to become financially sustainable through such means. Open competitive tendering of contracts was found to be a key mechanism for funding social enterprises, although there was also evidence of an emerging social investment market in both countries. While this ecosystem type was also characterised as having a focus on generating social value through the use of procurement, particularly encouraged at the level of state government, the success of such instruments varied, particularly when sub-national policy actors were tasked with local delivery. Inclusive labour market policies were found to be less common within this typology.

Finally, the *Private-micro* type (Netherlands and Italy), like the Private-macro, was characterised by state encouragement of marketisation of the social sector, with a view to widening income diversification. However, in contrast to the Private-macro type, this was not necessarily driven by state policy, but often by regional associations and local government. Capitalisation problems were found to be common in this ecosystem type, although there was significant diversity in the range of policies being used, particularly to support social enterprise as a form of labour market integration for vulnerable groups.

Future priorities for research

We are merely at the start of attempting to make sense of not only the types of social enterprise ecosystem that exist, but the reasons why we have such variation: they do not map neatly onto classical models of welfare states (viz Esping-Andersen 1990), for example. What we came up with over the course of the EFESEIIS project was merely a first attempt in understanding what are incredibly complex networks of individuals and organisations which, despite analysing them by country, can often transcend national borders. While we have focused on the level of the country, the ecosystems in which social enterprises operate on a day-to-day basis often tend to be highly localised, with important work undertaken by small, local actors. But institutions and individuals are also often intimately connected to other systems operating at different levels simultaneously: if we were to look hard enough we would undoubtedly find evidence of global structures influencing local practices and *vice versa* (viz Ban 2016). Moreover, influence upon the day-to-day practice of social entrepreneurship can come from several different directions at once: social enterprises may depend upon regional policy support for funding, while national legal frameworks often encourage a particular type of organisation to flourish; policy frameworks can be influenced by, or even rest upon, ideas such as transnational solidarity, while a broad neoliberal capitalist framework clearly shapes policies and transcends national or international borders.

In certain contexts, it could be argued, social entrepreneurship has emerged as a form of counter-hegemonic resistance to global economic priorities that have proven to be destructive to social ties and societal well-being, in much the same way as the co-operative movement emerged as a form of resistance to the dehumanising effects of industrialisation. These sites of resistance, particularly 'everyday' acts and sites of micro-resistance via social enterprise (e.g. see Dey 2014; Dey and Teasdale 2016), deserve far closer attention. Conversely, it could also be argued that the emergence of social enterprise in some regions of the world, particularly developing countries in receipt of international development support, is driven precisely by these forces of globalisation, as social enterprise 'phenotypes' are plucked from one ecosystem and deposited into another. Whilst these can still be 'owned' locally and be very successful, they have not emerged locally. To borrow a biological analogy, of relevance to the UK at least, such organisations are the Grey Squirrel of the social enterprise world (for an interesting overview of social enterprise use in international development see Hoyos and Angel-Urdinola 2018).

Moreover, as stated at the outset, scholarship on social entrepreneurship ecosystems has only just emerged, in contrast to the prominence of the term in policy literature, and in how the ecosystem idea has come to be employed in general entrepreneurship studies. The under-theorisation of the ecosystem concept makes it difficult to explain processes of social action, specifically how actions might be shaped by the structures of the social system, and indeed, how social action might influence, and bring about change in, the system itself. Ecosystems are not static but are living and breathing, always in flux. And yet they are often presented as static systems. We are still relatively unaware of how ecosystems change over time (indeed that is also a weakness of the general ecosystem literature) and what temporal considerations can bring to our understanding of the dialectical relationships between the ecosystem and everyday practices. Employing Bourdieu's (1986, 2005) concept of the 'field' may bring advantages for theorising the role of social structure in shaping (and being shaped by) social entrepreneurship practices. Indeed, the 'rules of the field' could relate to the legal and regulatory frameworks seen in different ecosystems (or social norms); whilst the 'habitus' of actors (organisms to continue the use of our biological vernacular) and the resources they hold (economic, social and political capital, to name a few) would align with the factors that we see at play in social enterprise 'ecosystems'. But how do we capture this flux, including in relation to how the various forms of capital – whether financial, social or cultural – are mobilised, allocated or enacted in such contexts? And do such processes ameliorate or reinforce forms of structural inequality that social enterprises often exist to address? How are such 'fields' structured by power (and class) relations, to lean further on Bourdieu's work (ibid.) and borrow from Weberian ideas of social action (Weber 1978)? These are all questions that might help shape a research agenda for social entrepreneurship ecosystems looking forward.

Through the use of the 'ecosystem' metaphor, knowledge of the conditions in which social entrepreneurship can thrive is growing all the time, but we should not be afraid to challenge and remain critical of biological metaphors being employed to explain social processes. We should use them when they are useful, discard them when they are not, and certainly not employ them to obfuscate the fact that our focus is upon social processes and structures, which can be changed if they are found to be harmful or work counter to what they were designed to do; there is nothing inherently 'natural' about these forms of ecosystem, after all. In sum, we should never forget about the 'social' in social enterprise!

References

Alvedalen, J. and R. Boschma (2017), 'A Critical Review of Entrepreneurial Ecosystems Research: Towards a Future Research Agenda', *European Planning Studies*, **25** (6), 887–903.

Arthur, L., T. Keenoy, M. Scott-Cato and R. Smith (2006), 'Where is the "Social" in Social Enterprise?', in D. Fuller, A. E. Jonas and R. Lee (eds), *Interrogating Alterity: Alternative Economic and Political Spaces*, Aldershot: Ashgate Publishing, pp. 207–22.

Bacq, S. and F. Janssen (2011), 'The Multiple Faces of Social Entrepreneurship: A Review of Definitional Issues Based on Geographical and Thematic Criteria', *Entrepreneurship and Regional Development*, **23** (5–6), 373–403.

Ban, C. (2016), *Ruling Ideas: How Global Neoliberalism Goes Local*, New York, NY: Oxford University Press.

Biggeri, M., E. Testi, M. Bellucci, R. During and H. T. R. Persson (eds) (2019), *Social Entrepreneurship and Social Innovation: Ecosystems for Inclusion in Europe*, Abingdon: Routledge.

Bourdieu, P. (1986), 'The Forms of Capital', in J. Richardson (ed.), *Handbook of Theory and Research for the Sociology of Education*, Westport, CT: Greenwood Press, pp. 241–58.

Bourdieu, P. (2005), *The Social Structures of the Economy*, Cambridge, UK; Malden, MA: Polity Press.

Buckingham, H., S. Pinch and P. Sunley (2012), 'The Enigmatic Regional Geography of Social Enterprise in the UK: A Conceptual Framework and Synthesis of the Evidence', *Area*, **44** (1), 83–91.

Cairney, P., S. Russell and E. St Denny (2016), 'The "Scottish Approach" to Policy and Policymaking: What Issues Are Territorial and What Are Universal?', *Policy & Politics*, **44** (3), 333–50.

Deloitte LLP (2016), Social Enterprise Ecosystem Toolkit - User Guidance Note, accessed 4 October 2018 at https://www.innovationpolicyplatform.org/system/files/Social%20Enterprise%20Ecosystem%20Toolkit%20-%20User%20Guidance%20Note.pdf.

Dey, P. (2014), 'Governing the Social through "Social Entrepreneurship": A Foucauldian View of "the Art of Governing" in Advanced Liberalism', in H. Douglas and S. Grant (eds), *Social Entrepreneurship and Enterprise: Concepts in Context*, Melbourne: Tilde University Press, pp. 55–72.

Dey, P. and S. Teasdale (2016), 'The Tactical Mimicry of Social Enterprise Strategies: Acting "As If" in the Everyday Life of Third Sector Organizations', *Organization*, **23** (4), 485–504.

Di Domenico, M., H. Haugh and P. Tracey (2010), 'Social Bricolage: Theorizing Social Value Creation in Social Enterprises', *Entrepreneurship Theory and Practice*, **34** (4), 681–703.

Doherty, B. (2018), 'Research in the Social Enterprise Journal – from the Margins to the Mainstream', *Social Enterprise Journal*, **14** (1), 108–16.

During, R., H. T. R. Persson, M. Biggeri, E. Testi and M. Bellucci (2019), 'Research Background, Theoretical Frameworks and Methodologies for Social Entrepreneurship', in M. Biggeri, E. Testi, M. Bellucci, R. During and H. T. R. Persson (eds), *Social Entrepreneurship and Social Innovation: Ecosystems for Inclusion in Europe*, Abingdon: Routledge.

During, R., R. Van Dam, I. Salverda and M. Duineveld (2016), *Using Evolutionary Theory for Pluralism in Social Policies*, Belfast, accessed 6 September 2018 at http://www.social-policy.org.uk/news/2016-conference/.

Esping-Andersen, G. (1990), *The Three Worlds of Welfare Capitalism*, Cambridge, UK: Polity Press.

Gough, I., G. Runciman, R. Mace, G. Hodgson and M. Rustin (2008), 'Darwinian Evolutionary Theory and the Social Sciences', *Twenty-First Century Society*, **3** (1), 65–86.

Grassl, W. (2012), 'Business Models of Social Enterprise: A Design Approach to Hybridity', *ACRN Journal of Social Entrepreneurship Perspectives*, **1** (1), 37–60.

Hazenberg, R., M. Bajwa-Patel, M. Mazzei, M. J. Roy and S. Baglioni (2016), 'The Role of Institutional and Stakeholder Networks in Shaping Social Enterprise Ecosystems in Europe', *Social Enterprise Journal*, **12** (3), 302–21.

Hazenberg, R., M. Bajwa-Patel, M. J. Roy, M. Mazzei and S. Baglioni (2016), 'A Comparative Overview of Social Enterprise "Ecosystems" in Scotland and England: An Evolutionary Perspective', *International Review of Sociology*, **26** (2), 205–22.

Hoyos, A. and D. F. Angel-Urdinola (2018), 'Assessing International Organizations' Support to Social Enterprise', *Development Policy Review*, accessed 6 September 2018 at https://doi.org/10.1111/dpr.12378.

Kerlin, J. A. (2013), 'Defining Social Enterprise across Different Contexts: A Conceptual Framework Based on Institutional Factors', *Nonprofit and Voluntary Sector Quarterly*, **42** (1), 84–108.

Mazzei, M. (2017), 'Understanding Difference: The Importance of "Place" in the Shaping of Local Social Economies', *VOLUNTAS: International Journal of Voluntary and Nonprofit Organizations*, **28** (6), 2763–84.

Moore, J. F. (1993), 'Predators and Prey: A New Ecology of Competition', *Harvard Business Review*, **71** (3), 75–83.

Muñoz, S.-A. (2010), 'Towards a Geographical Research Agenda for Social Enterprise', *Area*, **42** (3), 302–12.

Roy, M. J., N. McHugh, L. Huckfield, A. Kay and C. Donaldson (2015), '"The Most Supportive Environment in the World"? Tracing the Development of an Institutional "Ecosystem" for Social Enterprise', *VOLUNTAS: International Journal of Voluntary and Nonprofit Organizations*, **26** (3), 777–800.

Spigel, B. (2017), 'The Relational Organization of Entrepreneurial Ecosystems', *Entrepreneurship Theory and Practice*, **41** (1), 49–72.

Stam, E. (2015), 'Entrepreneurial Ecosystems and Regional Policy: A Sympathetic Critique', *European Planning Studies*, **23** (9), 1759–69.

Teasdale, S. (2012), 'What's in a Name? Making Sense of Social Enterprise Discourses', *Public Policy and Administration*, **27** (2), 99–119.

Weber, M. (1978), *Economy and Society: An Outline of Interpretive Sociology*, Berkeley, CA: University of California Press.

3 Spectres of marketization? The prospect of the National Disability Insurance Scheme in Australia

Chris Mason

Introduction

In this chapter, I explore the presence of marketization in debates concerning welfare market reform. Specifically, I examine how debates on marketization often frame reforms as inimical to the longevity of charity and non-profit providers (as 'third sector organisations' or TSOs), while social enterprises remain rather enigmatic in these discourses. My aim is to present two main arguments. The first relates to the apparent fact that marketization haunts welfare market reform through the medium of quasi-markets in the sense that marketization appears an implicit and necessary condition of welfare market reform. In other words, we cannot reform our markets without a degree of marketization impacting upon organizations in the market.

Thus framed, I discuss how marketization is presented in the literature and ask: *how can marketization invoke new debate on the neoliberal agenda in welfare reform?*

In response, firstly I focus more deeply on the place of social enterprise in the marketization debate. From this, I draw out the dual role of social enterprise in welfare market reform. On the one hand, social enterprise has often been assumed to be the politically preferred model for TSOs to mimic, in order to survive welfare reform. On the other, I consider that social enterprises are also *subjected to* marketization and likely to experience similar tension and anxiety as a consequence of market reforms. Consequently, social enterprises occupy a critical and liminal space in marketization discourses, being symptomatic of the threat while also subjected to the effects of welfare market reforms.

Secondly, I use the case study of the National Disability Insurance Scheme (NDIS) in Australia to try to illustrate how marketization could 'haunt' a reformed welfare market space. While the NDIS quasi-market has been implemented to increase personalization and service user choice while also encouraging new entrant service providers, social enterprise has received a lot of attention from policy makers in the implementation process. Based on the NDIS case, I explore whether marketization will haunt both the quasi-market and also social enterprise, with the latter often framed as a threat to existing charity or non-profit providers already operating in the market. I suggest that the social enterprises are portrayed as both the signifiers of marketization while also being adversely affected by it.

The rise of marketization

Salamon (1993, p.17) describes marketization as 'the penetration of essentially market-type relationships into the social welfare sector'. Writing on the increasing trend of marketization through the 1980s social welfare system in the United States, he concluded that marketization had resulted in 'nonprofit organisations being sucked increasingly into market-type relations and for-profit firms have steadily expanded their market niche' (Salamon 1993, p.36). Thus, marketization goes beyond the creation of different kinds of relationships and rather is a process of organizational transformation, observing the changing logics of value production in social welfare systems due to shifting external conditions. Such organizational re-engineering as a response to external market reforms has been largely caused by prevailing programmatical shifts over the past 30 years or more. Indeed, acute awareness of marketization arose following the advent of New Public Management (NPM) and latterly New Public Governance (NPG) in several jurisdictions, such as the United States, Australia and United Kingdom.

As Hood (1995, p.94) noted on NPM, it removed 'differences between the public and the private sector and [shifted] the emphasis from process accountability towards a greater element of accountability in terms of results'. This emboldened a keener appreciation of the complex sub-processes involved in the deployment of public policy while reframing the taken-for-granted assumptions about how such processes might involve multiple stakeholder participation. Understandably, this all brought on a sharper emphasis on market reforms in the public sector and re-drawing relationships between public and private markets and providers.

NPG emerged, at least in scholarly circles, through a dawning realization that NPM was rather a 'partial theory' (Osborne 2006, p.380) of public management in practice. Strong critique of NPM focused on its limited paradigmatic forms (Ferlie et al. 1996) and its strong Anglo-American ideological infusion (Borins 2002; Osborne 2006). In other words, such a partial paradigm could not fulfil the aim of radically overhauling how public administration was conceptualized, legitimized and implemented for the public benefit. In contrast, NPG is framed differently (while building on the bureaucratic overhauls already accomplished through NPM agendas), for example by focusing on services outcomes over outputs and relational contracts over the market (Osborne 2006). NPG is a more pluralistic theory of public management, drawing from disparate knowledge and practice-bases to understand how best to facilitate inter-organizational relationships in the modern welfare state.

With this in mind, both NPM and NPG provided the programmatic platform from which reforms could be rationalized to the public sphere and marketization could arise and persist. Rhetorically, for governments to enact reforms to social welfare markets they must address the seeming inadequacies of existing providers. The perception was (and perhaps still is) that charities and non-profits operating in such markets are inefficient based on an assumption that they could be more effective in resourcing themselves to deliver services (McKay et al. 2015). In other words, becoming more 'business-like' is a neoliberal refrain that resonates in much social and public policy discourse to the present day (Dempsey and Sanders 2010; Maier et al. 2016; Sanders and McClellan 2014).

Typically, these reforms have taken the guise of quasi-markets, which are situations where government reduces its role as both direct funder and provider of public services (for example Le Grand 1991). Implementing quasi-markets allows governments to rationalize and engineer intensified competition into welfare service markets while retaining a high level of oversight over the awarding of service contracts, minimum service quality standards and compliance to the system more generally.

An example of quasi-markets in action is the Job Network in Australia (1998–2009), an employment assistance programme that operated for approximately 10 years both during NPM and in the advent of NPG. The Job Network was developed because of 'the perceived inflexibility of the previous state-run labour exchange' (McDonald and Marston 2008, p.104). To which end, the government contracted with agencies to deliver employment services to the unemployed, aiming to improve the quality of outcomes (finding more sustainable employment opportunities) while alleviating the cost and administration burden of providing these services. While some have argued the programme increased the 'pursuit of innovation through the use of non-bureaucratized structures . . . and the state's role in directing and ensuring the delivery of basic welfare services' (Considine et al. 2011, p.812), others have demurred (for example McDonald and Marston 2008). Nevertheless, quasi-markets are a common model for implementing welfare market reforms and where the impact of marketization on TSOs has been most often explored. In the next section I explore a narrower point of focus, the role of social enterprise in these spaces.

Problematizing marketization, again

As might be expected, the scholarly reflex to marketization has been to reveal its debilitating influence on TSOs and to offer a critically engaged resistance to a pervasive neoliberalism. Research often uses quasi-markets as a framing device to show how social welfare market reforms act as the harbinger of pressure to marketize TSOs (Spall and Zetlin 2004). This pressure appears to jeopardize the viability of many existing providers (Carey 2008). As a result, scholars have challenged marketization from a range of disciplinary and analytical angles.

At a broad level of critique, research has explored how marketization has made a lasting impact on the quality of welfare service provision. Bevir and Rhodes (2003, p.57) argued that, based on the UK experience of public sector reforms in the

1990s and early 2000s, 'marketization can undermine standards of service quality'. Presaging the later focus on NPG, they showed that public sector departments did not manage service development with a long-term view. Rather, the public sector pragmatically embraced short-term contracting instead, a simpler process containing very little (if any) joined-up governing.

Alongside the impact on service users has been the impact marketization has had on organizational composition and viability in the reformed market. A strong body of evidence, covering many different social welfare areas, has shown how TSOs have been destabilized by marketization. For example, Eikenberry and Kluver (2004) argued that the adoption of private sector values erodes the potential for non-profits to maintain a strong civil society in the US. Increasing trends towards commercialization and public sector support for social entrepreneurship (SE) in traditional public sector domains undermine non-profits in their own missions to serve for the public benefit. Subsequently, these claims struck a chord with several scholars. Evans et al. (2005) used evidence from Canada to show how neo-liberal market structures enforce a rationalization and professionalization on non-profits, thereby diminishing autonomy and advocacy while increasing dependency on competing for contracts. Similarly, Irvine (2007) showed how corporate creep has become a pervasive and insidious problem for all kinds of TSOs in Australia. She argued that professional consultants are cast as agents of institutional change, bringing private sector terminologies and practices from the private to the non-profit sector. This brings increasing pressure on TSOs to adapt to survive in a prevailing climate of being business-like.

Social enterprises as 'double agents'

Although there is a strong current of scholarly concern regarding marketization and its impact on TSOs, I turn now to consider how social enterprises are treated in the same discourse. An interesting aspect of this research is how social enterprises can feature in both sides of the discourse. On the one hand, the rise of social enterprises (and SE) in policy making is sometimes seen as symptomatic of the marketization problem, particularly among those advocating for TSOs to resist the entrenched neoliberal ideology in the public sector. Cardy (2010, p.435) used the context of reforms to social work practices in the UK to argue that social enterprise was used 'in isolation to any debates about social enterprises and public services . . . not ideologically or politically positioned within the co-operative movement but instead within contemporary neo-liberalism'. In an abstract sense, social enterprise was used as a 'middle-ground' option for social work practices, along with a TSO model and a private sector model. Buckingham (2009) also suggested an increase in competition for homelessness service provision contracts arising from social enterprises, as distinctive from traditional voluntary providers.

In some jurisdictions, such as the UK, social enterprise has been used overtly by policy makers to usher in new, hybrid organizational models that (at least in theory) manage the competing logics required of non-profit organizations in reformed welfare markets (Mason and Moran 2018; Teasdale 2012). In effect, TSOs have been subjected to regimes of enforced hybridity in order to remain competitive for welfare service contracts, a situation that does not sit comfortably with many TSOs and may even be inimical to their stated mission or public benefit (Hall et al. 2012). All of which leads to an increasing sense of precarity for those operating in welfare markets, which is doubly tragic given that many service users may not desire changes to their current provider options (Mason et al. 2017). Rather, these enforced changes are often the consequence of political imperatives as discussed above. Nevertheless, the potential for severe organizational suspicion and service user disruption make it challenging for TSOs to either attempt mimicking social enterprise models (Dey and Teasdale 2013) or seek out mergers and acquisitions to cope with precarity. Arguably, this shifting of models assumes that social enterprises '*can* embrace the pressures of mission drift and hybridisation' (Hall et al. 2012, p.735; italics added). And yet, there remains no comprehensive evidence base indicating the veracity of this assumption over time. This lack is exacerbated by the plenitude of social enterprise models, business lifecycle stages and the intricacies and instabilities of the markets in which they operate. Still, social enterprise has quite successfully been deployed partly as symbolic of welfare market reform, an idea shaped to reflect hybrid characteristics of business and non-profit (Brandsen et al. 2005).

At the same time, social enterprises (and social entrepreneurs) are also victims of marketization in much the same way as other TSOs. Dempsey and Sanders (2010) used the autobiographies of social entrepreneurs to understand how marketization influences perceptions of meaningful work. They argue that marketization fosters the kind of unhealthy practices that detract from a sense of meaningful work. In a similar vein, Sanders and McClellan (2014) explored how being business-like is articulated and negotiated alongside a non-profit's social mission, arguing that suppressed conflicts in the meaning of non-profit work deny the articulation of other possible meanings.

This leads us to conclude that the challenges arising from marketization apply across the spectrum of TSOs, including social enterprises. Furthermore, marketization is only symptomatic of the sway neoliberalism has over public policy making. The real cause of disruption experienced by TSOs is the existence and role of the (quasi) market, meaning that all organizations operating in these markets are prone to the same destabilizing forces.

However, social enterprises *per se* exist in an interesting conceptual space compared to other TSOs. Nicholls and Teasdale (2017) argued that social enterprise not only operates as a challenge to neoliberalism but also reflects neoliberalism by stealth. In a sense, social enterprises can be cast as double agents and this is apparent in how they have been portrayed specifically in the marketization debate. No matter how welfare markets are reformed and reconstructed, marketization will forever haunt them because the process is imbued with the neoliberal agenda (Nicholls and Teasdale 2017).

In the absence of a viable or realizable alternative, the *spectre* of marketization haunts any attempts to reform welfare markets to the benefit of civil society and citizens who rely on them. Indeed, there is seemingly no 'new' way to reform these markets that will avoid marketization and make conditions better for all parties involved: TSOs will always benefit, at least in order to satisfy the claims of other, more prominent players in the neoliberal political agenda. What remains under-appreciated in the scholarly literature is precisely if and how marketization creates a double role for social enterprise in these reforms and the impact this has on embedding marketization and/or resisting it.

To return to the context at hand, in the following section, I describe and discuss the recent development of the NDIS in Australia. This recently implemented scheme holds significant potential (and disruption) for TSOs of all kinds. I use current work in this space to consider how marketization might influence social enterprises in this new market.

Discussion: Spectres of marketization?

In this section, I consider the likely impact of marketization on social enterprise on a new quasi-market, the National Disability Insurance Scheme (NDIS) in Australia. In so doing, I consider the potential new terrain for scholars seeking to deepen our knowledge of the interactions between hybrid organizations and hybrid systems and institutions.

For background, the NDIS is a care personalization scheme 'designed to change the way that support and care are provided to people with permanent and significant disability (a disability that substantially reduces their functional capacity or psychosocial functioning)' (Australian Productivity Commission 2017, p.3). The NDIS was launched in 2013 and was firstly trialled in a small number of sites in Australia. The scheme will be fully implemented across Australia by 2019–2020. Current estimates are that 475 000 people will be served by the scheme, at an annual cost of approximately A$22 billion in the first full year of implementation (Australian Productivity Commission 2017).

The development of quasi-markets has become so ingrained as the *de facto* arrangement for welfare market reform and marketization has become implicit, even accepted, as a necessary consequence of reform. For example, consider Hall et al.'s (2012, p.747) analysis of the Social Enterprise Investment Fund in the UK, where they argue that the 'marketization of public services [is not] flawed or unachievable'. Rather the mechanisms for supporting 'a diverse market of alternative providers [do] not make one' (Hall et al. 2012). In other words, the devil is in the detail and not in the capacity for re-imagining alternate possible realities, thus ways of making welfare reform more effective and sustainable, without neoliberalism (Dey and Mason 2018). Some recent work has argued for the scale of re-thinking that might happen, for example considering a place for a

Polanyian political economy in contrast to the current ideology (Roy and Hackett 2016).

And yet, there are certainly some interesting nuances in the debates over the role of social enterprise in such quasi-markets that are likely to apply in this context. In so doing, I return to the question posed in the Introduction: *how can marketization invoke new debate on the neoliberal agenda in welfare reform?* In this final section, I draw out three linked areas where the NDIS could be used to extend scholarship on marketization using social enterprise as a principal point of study. These areas are interlinked and also intended to be informed by a plurality of theoretical and empirical approaches, underpinned by challenging epistemological and ontological positions.

Challenging assumptions about social enterprise in the quasi-market

The NDIS offers a rich, if still emerging, case from which to explore the above question more precisely. To begin, it is worth considering whether social enterprise has featured in any discourse surrounding the development of the NDIS. In similar schemes overseas (such as the NHS in the UK and reforms in northern Europe), social enterprises have featured more prominently in the mix of public, private and third sector organizations operating at different levels in the system (Hall et al. 2012).

However, from a relatively early stage it was notable how social enterprise was *absent* from the Productivity Commission's reports on the NDIS (Australian Productivity Commission 2017). The encouragement and emergence of social enterprises in the NDIS is rather implicit, perhaps as a natural consequence of marketization and reflecting what has happened in similar schemes overseas. In a sense, this also mirrors the relatively low-key approach to social enterprise given by the Australian federal government more generally. Reviews of federal programmes, policies and the social enterprise sector each attest to this (Mason and Barraket 2015; Mason and Moran 2018). As the effects of marketization begin to be felt by existing providers, this could also be the moment to test assumptions about marketization in jurisdictions with traditionally weak track records relating to social enterprise policy. Indeed, given the scale and scope of the NDIS, the haunting presence of marketization is perhaps rather unknown for social enterprises, as it is seemingly certain for other third sector service providers.

In order to challenge the assumption of social enterprise growth in the NDIS, there are at least two angles to challenge the implicit shift in ontology brought about through marketization. The first relates to the readiness of social enterprise to engage appropriately, legitimately and meaningfully into the quasi-market. For example, if a social enterprise enters the NDIS as a new provider, then we cannot assume they will be 'fit for purpose'. Indeed, the high level of compliance and service quality expected of NDIS providers is likely to make it even harder for social enterprises to match the work already being offered by existing providers. On the flipside, they would also be at a competitive disadvantage to private sector suppliers who may be able to attract professions and skilled workforce based on opportunities for advancement and remuneration. For social enterprise, how much demand is there for this type of service, in a way that differs from existing third sector providers? The lack of true scope of demand is also complicated by consumer inertia; that service users, despite their newly found budgetary control, do not exercise their right to switch to new suppliers due to the perceived transactional costs of moving. Social enterprise would have to offer a significant incentive for users to switch, especially for service users with long-standing working relationships with existing providers. Marketization might still be felt through changing structural/market conditions, where third sector providers struggling to deliver ongoing services creates new opportunities for market entrants.

The second is the inverse of the first: how ready is the NDIS for social enterprise? A central assumption of marketization is that the rise of 'corporate creep' will see corporate norms become newly contestable norms of thinking and practice in the NDIS (Irvine 2007). However, as we already know from the social enterprise literature, their strong social (and moral) focus, combined with their organizational hybridity, can pose some challenges for control through market mechanisms. Social enterprise might seem to be an ideal solution to the quasi-market, meeting both social and economic logics but the evidence (thus the transferability across policy domains) is equivocal at best.

There are direct and indirect organizational impacts as a consequence of rapid marketization being introduced into the market. One aspect that sets the NDIS apart from personalization schemes in other jurisdictions is the speed of its national implementation. As noted above, the scale and scope of provision in a geographically vast country and serving people with a wide range of disabilities accentuates the strain on both the system and more specifically those involved in the delivery of services (Mason et al. 2017). In effect, we are witnessing a rapid deployment of marketization on service providers largely ill-equipped to deal with significant changes to their operating environment. Research is already beginning to show how important these reforms have been in shaping how services are provided. Indeed, there is a degree of scepticism that the scheme has reformed not just the market but rehabilitated the spectre of marketization that has haunted other schemes.

Both of the scenarios create interesting lines of inquiry that would challenge some assumptions about marketization and social enterprise in quasi-markets. Dealing with the significant knowledge gap concerning the market-level demand for social enterprise in the NDIS represents a first challenge. The second is to address the 'readiness factor': are particular models of social enterprises more likely to enter into the NDIS than others? Where will this activity likely occur? What are the issues concerning structuring service delivery and building and maintaining legitimate relationships with networks of supporting organizations, communities and families that often take a long time to build? Indeed, how well set up is the NDIS to handle increasing numbers of social enterprises alongside the lower barriers to entry for private, for-profit providers?

Hybrid systems for hybrid organizations

A second area for exploration is the confluence of hybrid systems with hybrid organizations. I have already acknowledged the scale of the NDIS implementation: a complex environment dealing with rapid, transformational change. As marketization looms into view, however, it would also be worthwhile to interrogate how it will come to bear on hybrid organizations, such as social enterprises, working in a hybrid system (Skelcher and Smith 2015). This would further extend our knowledge of how pervasive marketization can be in reformed markets that transgress traditional public/private boundaries. The speed and scale of implementation also complicate the picture: how has this implementation created uneven reform through the scheme and has marketization thus impacted some areas, organizations and communities more than others?

From an early stage, as Malbon et al. (2018) argue, several issues of accountability (or dilemmas) have arisen in the NDIS. Notable among them is the notion that the NDIS confronts hybrid logics (or care and choice) which are in tension. During implementation, these competing logics have accentuated the need for government to retain a strong and visible accountability role in the scheme.

Alongside this is the complexity of hybrid organizing (Barraket et al. 2016). A key conceptual aspect of social enterprise is that they represent a hybrid organization – where competing logics are managed to achieve multiple outcomes. In the case of social enterprise, the principal outcome is to deliver social impact while navigating the operational imperative to produce market-ready, competitive services and making creating use of the resources at hand to achieve this, in other words bricolage (Di Domenico et al. 2010).

There may be some significant impacts of marketization on hybrid organizations that are intensified by working amidst plural rationalities. These impacts might enforce structural changes on existing providers or shifts in their operational focus to try to adhere to new market expectations and pre-empt/respond to new competitors entering the market. For example, some charity and non-profit providers have felt sufficiently concerned to entertain the prospect of staff retrenchment and/or organizational restructuring (Gilchrist 2017). Further concerns have been raised about the impact the scheme will have on the working conditions, especially for 'front-line' workers. Macdonald and Charlesworth (2016) note that similar 'cash-for-care' schemes are highly dependent on cost control and the NDIS is likely to increase the pool of informal workers in the sector (via the recognition of in-home family carers), while potentially compromising commitments to quality of service standards.

Thus, marketization could be viewed as creating less effective 'real' outcomes for service users, where an over-riding concern of cost-control leads to increasing organizational pressure to adapt in the hybrid system. In theory at least, hybrid organizations are often presumed to be adept at handling the spaces in-between traditional sectoral boundaries.

Tracing ideological shifts among providers in the NDIS

The third and final area for further exploration is the ideological foundations that underpin current and future service provision in the NDIS. Capturing both the intensity and scale of social enterprise activity in the NDIS alongside the impacts of hybridity in such a large quasi-market could lead to a third, final challenge for marketization. As prior scholarship has noted, social enterprise has been used as a tactical response to the pressure brought on by changing market conditions (Mason et al. 2017). An interesting angle to this line of thought is how profoundly marketization shapes the ideological basis for existing providers in the market, whether this is temporary or lasting and if social enterprises also experience resistance from service users as a response to marketization. In other words, does the trace of marketization come into conflict with other ideologies present at organizational and individual levels? Increasing marketization will fundamentally shift perceptions of which organizational models are deemed legitimate.

We know that marketization is already being felt by incumbent providers. Extant evidence suggests that TSOs involved in the NDIS space are feeling the strain of systemic reform to the way they operate (Gilchrist 2017). Typically, some organizational responses have included seeking mergers to consolidate business models in order to maintain financial viability to ensure continuity of service for the communities they serve (Mason et al. 2017). To what extent does the enforced marketization create pockets of resistance among both current providers and service users? How do these responses interact with the market and the personalization agenda? Responding to both of these questions could pave the way to a deeper critical research stream that makes use of the complexity and ambition of the NDIS project.

In pushing this idea further, scholars could question the ideological foundations from a highly critical standpoint, invoking non-traditional analytical approaches to reveal the multiple realities experienced by social enterprises, commissioners, policy makers and of course service users. To illustrate, one approach could be to reveal the seemingly hidden but also present nature of marketization over markets, organizations and citizens. Jacques Derrida's concept of 'hauntology' could be usefully deployed here. Derrida (1993) coined the term in his text *Spectres of Marx*, using to it explain how Marxism will forever haunt capitalism no matter how stridently history seeks to erase it. Hauntology, a portmanteau of 'haunting' and 'ontology', offers interesting potential to studies of quasi-markets and marketization because the latter haunts quasi-markets and the organizations that operate in them. As the current third sector literature has it, marketization is inimical to the sustainability of traditional charities and non-profits, forcing them into becoming quasi-businesses that ill-suit their structure and their pro-social purposes

(Eikenberry and Kluwer 2004). For policy makers, we might begin to wonder if the development of quasi-markets is just a symptom of being nostalgic for a failed public market revolution. More critically informed scholars might use concepts to re-frame the debate: if we can't have market reforms without marketization, what alternative social imaginaries are possible? To this end, closer attention to the infusion of marketization in social policies and related texts, as well as the ideologies of policy makers, would shed new light on how this 'haunting' persists.

Conclusion

The aim of this chapter was to re-assert the potential for more critical research around marketization. To argue as such, I have used a short case example of the recent full implementation of the NDIS in Australia as a fruitful context for further inquiry. Without doubt, social enterprise has become a much more visible presence in the delivery of welfare services in Australia, in keeping with similar trends in like jurisdictions. However, the NDIS experience offers a glimpse into how marketization interacts with rapid transformational change, combined with hybrid systems, organizational logics and a highly complex personalization agenda for service users. Indeed, rather than accepting the inevitability of marketization on reformed welfare markets, we need a broader conceptual scope to confront challenges, such as the nature of the supposed double-agency of social enterprise and the impacts of rapid policy implementation, especially regarding the development of the skilled workforce amid all of these changes. This potentially volatile admixture promises to broaden and enliven the potential for marketization as a constant threat to organizations working in quasi-markets.

References

Australian Productivity Commission (2017), *Disability Care and Support: Productivity Commission Inquiry Report*, Melbourne, Victoria: Productivity Commission.

Barraket, J., V. Archer and C. Mason (2016), 'The effects of hybridity on local governance: The case of social enterprise', in G. Carey, C. Landvogt and J. Barraket (Eds), *Creating and Implementing Public Policy: Cross-sectoral Debates*, London: Routledge, pp. 169–184.

Bevir, M. and R. Rhodes (2003), 'Searching for civil society: Changing patterns of governance in Britain', *Public Administration*, **81** (1), 41–62.

Borins, S. (2002), 'Leadership and innovation in the public sector', *Leadership and Organization Development Journal*, **23** (8), 467–476.

Brandsen, T., W. Van de Donk and K. Putters (2005), 'Griffins or chameleons? Hybridity as a permanent and inevitable characteristic of the third sector', *International Journal of Public Administration*, **28** (9–10), 749–765.

Buckingham, H. (2009), 'Competition and contracts in the voluntary sector: Exploring the implications for homelessness service providers in Southampton', *Policy and Politics*, **37** (2), 235–254.

Cardy, S. (2010), '"Care Matters" and the privatization of looked after children's services in England and Wales: Developing a critique of independent "social work practices"', *Critical Social Policy*, **30** (3), 430–442.

Carey, G. (2008), 'Conceptualising the Third Sector: Foucauldian insights into the relations between the Third Sector, civil society and the State', *Third Sector Review*, **14** (1), 9.

Considine, M., J.M. Lewis and S. O'Sullivan (2011), 'Quasi-markets and service delivery flexibility following a decade of employment assistance reform in Australia', *Journal of Social Policy*, **40** (4), 811–833.

Dempsey, S.E. and M.L. Sanders (2010), 'Meaningful work? Nonprofit marketization and work/life imbalance in popular autobiographies of social entrepreneurship', *Organization*, **17** (4), 437–459.

Derrida, J. (1993), *Spectres of Marx: The State of the Debt, the Work of Mourning and the New International*, London: Routledge.

Dey, P. and C. Mason (2018), 'Overcoming constraints of collective imagination: An inquiry into activist entrepreneuring, disruptive truth-telling and the creation of "possible worlds"', *Journal of Business Venturing*, **33** (1), 84–99.

Dey, P. and S. Teasdale (2013), 'Social enterprise and dis/identification', *Administrative Theory and Praxis*, **35** (2), 248–270.

Di Domenico, M.L., H. Haugh and P. Tracey (2010), 'Social bricolage: Theorizing social value creation in social enterprises', *Entrepreneurship Theory and Practice*, **34** (4), 681–703.

Eikenberry, A. and J. Kluver (2004), 'The marketization of the nonprofit sector: Civil society at risk?', *Public Administration Review*, **64** (2), 132–140.

Evans, B., T. Richmond and J. Shields (2005), 'Structuring neoliberal governance: The nonprofit sector, emerging new modes of control and the marketisation of service delivery', *Policy and Society*, **24** (1), 73–97.

Ferlie, E., L. Fitzgerald and A. Pettigrew (1996), *The New Public Management in Action*, Oxford: Oxford University Press.

Gilchrist, D. (2017), 'NDIS pricing – new research confirms risks to service users', *Pro Bono Magazine*, accessed 2 July 2018 at probonoaustralia.com.au/news/2017/09/ndis-pricing-new-research-confirms-risks-service-users/.

Hall, K., P. Alcock and R. Millar (2012), 'Start up and sustainability: Marketisation and the social enterprise investment fund in England', *Journal of Social Policy*, **41** (4), 733–749.

Hood, C. (1995), 'The "new public management" in the 1980s: Variations on a theme', *Accounting, Organizations and Society*, **20** (2/3), 93–109.

Irvine, H. (2007), 'Corporate creep: An institutional view of consultancies in a non-profit organisation', *Australian Accounting Review*, **17** (41), 13–25.

Le Grand, J. (1991), 'Quasi-markets and social policy', *The Economic Journal*, **101** (408), 1256–1267.

Macdonald, F. and S. Charlesworth (2016), 'Cash for care under the NDIS: Shaping care workers' working conditions?', *Journal of Industrial Relations*, **58** (5), 627–646.

Maier, F., M. Meyer and M. Steinbereithner (2016), 'Nonprofit organizations becoming business-like: A systematic review', *Nonprofit and Voluntary Sector Quarterly*, **45** (1), 64–86.

Malbon, E., G. Carey and H. Dickinson (2018), 'Accountability in public service quasi-markets: The case of the Australian National Disability Insurance Scheme', *Australian Journal of Public Administration*, **77** (3), 468–481.

Mason, C. and J. Barraket (2015), 'Understanding social enterprise model development through discursive interpretations of social enterprise policymaking in Australia (2007–2013)', *Social Enterprise Journal*, **11** (2), 138–155.

Mason, C., J. Barraket, R. Simnett and A. Elmes (2017), 'A year in the life of Western Australia's social enterprises', *Bankwest Foundation Social Impact Series No. 7*, Perth, Western Australia: Bankwest Foundation.

Mason, C. and M. Moran (2018), 'Social enterprise and policy discourse: A comparative analysis of the United Kingdom and Australia', *Policy and Politics*, **46** (4), 607–626.

McDonald, C. and G. Marston (2008), 'Re-visiting the quasi-market in employment services: Australia's Job Network', *Asia Pacific Journal of Public Administration*, **30** (2), 101–117.

McKay, S., D. Moro, S. Teasdale and D. Clifford (2015), 'The marketisation of charities in England and Wales', *VOLUNTAS: International Journal of Voluntary and Nonprofit Organizations*, **26** (1), 336–354.

Nicholls, A. and S. Teasdale (2017), 'Neoliberalism by stealth? Exploring continuity and change within the UK social enterprise policy paradigm', *Policy and Politics*, **45** (3), 323–341.

Osborne, S.P. (2006), 'The new public governance?', *Public Management Review*, **8** (3), 377–387.

Roy, M.J. and M.T. Hackett (2016), 'Polanyi's "substantive approach" to the economy in action? Conceptualising social enterprise as a public health "intervention"', *Review of Social Economy*, **75** (2), 89–111.

Salamon, L.M. (1993), 'The marketization of welfare: Changing nonprofit and for-profit roles in the American welfare state', *Social Service Review*, **67** (1), 16–39.

Sanders, M.L. and J.G. McClellan (2014), 'Being business-like while pursuing a social mission: Acknowledging the inherent tensions in US nonprofit organizing', *Organization*, **21** (1), 68–89.

Skelcher, C. and S.R. Smith (2015), 'Theorizing hybridity: Institutional logics, complex organizations, and actor identities: The case of nonprofits', *Public Administration*, **93** (2), 433–448.

Spall, P. and D. Zetlin (2004), 'Third sector in transition – A question of sustainability for community service organizations and the sector?', *Australian Journal of Social Issues*, **39** (3), 283–298.

Teasdale, S. (2012), 'What's in a name? Making sense of social enterprise discourses', *Public Policy and Administration*, **27** (2), 99–119.

4 Social enterprises and democracy in countries with transitional or authoritarian regimes

Angela M. Eikenberry

Introduction

It has been 15 years since scholars first raised concerns about the impact of social enterprise and entrepreneurship on democracy (Dart 2004b; Eikenberry and Kluver 2004). Since then, this critique has become partially mainstreamed (Ebrahim et al. 2014; Nicholls and Teasdale 2017), but questions remain, particularly around democratization in the context of transitional and authoritarian regimes. Scholars studying in these countries find that commercialization may help organizations to become more independent and emancipate themselves from the state, thereby facilitating their ability to expand democracy and develop civil society (Vaceková et al. 2017; Yu and Chen 2018). Scholarly work on social enterprise and entrepreneurship suggests that they are contextually dependent (Defourny and Nyssens 2010; Defourny and Kim 2011; Kerlin 2009, 2012; Teasdale 2012b), so it is important to examine both in various political environments. The focus of this chapter is to examine to what degree, in the context of transitional or authoritarian political regimes, social enterprise might lead to democratization of (civil) society more broadly. As we witness a growing number of authoritarian regimes around the world, it is increasingly important to understand the mechanisms and tools that might enable us to counter and resist this development. Could social enterprise help to this end?

Social enterprises in transitional and authoritarian contexts

There is no clear consensus on the definition of social enterprise and its meaning and practice appear to vary by place and perspective (Teasdale 2012b). In its broadest sense, social enterprise involves the use of market-based strategies to achieve social goals (Kerlin 2009). As Peattie and Morley (2008) note in a review of literature, the social enterprise field is comprised of a plethora of organizational types that vary by size, function, legal and ownership structures, funding arrangements, motivations and purposes, and degree of profit distribution permitted. Many now distinguish between US and European conceptualizations of social enterprise (e.g. Defourny and Nyssens 2010; Kerlin 2006) and observe that, in Anglo-American conceptions, nonprofit organizations (NPOs) are encouraged to grow social enterprise strategies to create new business ventures that supposedly meet double or triple bottom lines. As in the UK, social enterprise in the USA has clearly been linked to efforts to roll back the state and privatize social welfare.

In contrast, social enterprise was traditionally thought of as part of the social and/or solidarity economy tradition in many places throughout the world, predominantly in continental Europe, Francophone Canada and Latin America (Defourny et al. 2014). For example, there is a long history of solidarity, mutual-help organizations, foundations and cooperatives in the Czech Republic; however, with their association with the Communist regime, these eroded and so today, social enterprise is "connected with the implementation of projects supported by the European Structural Funds" and mainly connected "with the employment of disabled people" and others who are socially disadvantaged (Dohnalová et al. 2015, pp. 6–7). In East Asia, the emergence of social enterprises is associated with socio-economic change during the late 1990s and the growing role of nongovernmental organizations as social service providers. In China particularly, social enterprises emerged in the context of market transition, with the role of the state as social provider shrinking and the market economy expanding (Yu 2011; Defourny and Kim 2011).

There has been a good deal of attention paid to the potentially problematic democratic effects of social entrepreneurship/enterprise (e.g. Dey and Steyaert 2010; Edwards 2008; Eikenberry and Kluver 2004; Lundqvist and Williams Middleton 2010; Parkinson and Howorth 2008); however, much of this work has focused on the USA and other Western democracies. The same concerns may not be relevant in countries such as the Czech Republic and China, which are undergoing democratic transition (Vaceková et al. 2017) or are "gradually liberalizing but still highly controlled authoritarian countries" (Yu and Chen 2018, p. 1). The effect of social enterprise/entrepreneurship and other forms of marketization may have a different effect in these countries because, it is argued, they may help create more space for the growth of civil society in transitional and authoritarian regimes. Scholars studying in these countries find, for example, that commercialization may help organizations to become more independent from the state, by, for example, alleviating fund-seeking pressure and thereby facilitating their ability to develop civil society (Vaceková et al. 2017; Yu and Chen 2018).[1] For example, Vaceková et al. (2017) observe that in the Czech Republic, "while historically well-established in the Western hemisphere, the Czech nonprofit sector had to undergo a difficult process of emergence and formation in the last quarter of the century as the Czech Republic itself was overcoming the totalitarian past and evolving into a parliamentary democracy," and the government has been a "monopoly provider of educational, cultural, social, health, and other services that constitute the premier activity fields" (p. 2110). In this context, Czech nonprofit organizations and the government both see commercialization as a positive step toward greater sustainability and toward independence.

Similarly, Yu and Chen (2018) state that in China marketization within the nonprofit sector has been growing over the past 20 years, as China has been undertaking a transformation from a planned economy to a market-oriented economy. They note that an increasing number of organizations "have employed market values and methods in their practices" (p. 6), including marketization through organizational management, commercialization of service delivery, and funding relationships such as through government contracting. These have:

- facilitated the growth of grassroots NPOs by alleviating their fund-seeking pressure and helping them create a network of social trust around NPOs bearing different backgrounds and clients;
- encouraged organizations to break away from governmental control and demand citizen participation and helped emphasize the market values of autonomy, openness, and transparency; and
- counterbalanced the controlling power of the authoritarian government, thus freeing up space for the nonprofit sector to perform policy advocacy.

These claims unfortunately lack supporting empirical data; nevertheless, they make a good theoretical argument, importantly pointing out that the narrow focus of the marketization critiques to date ignore a large part of the world.

Social enterprises and an independent civil society

Vaceková et al.'s (2017) and Yu and Chen's (2018) assertions about the importance of having an independent, autonomous social sector rest on a widely held assumption that this is essential for democratization in transitional and authoritarian regimes. However, as Kasfir (1998) challenges, this view is based on a western model that does not hold up well in many other parts of the world. Newer research takes issue with the conventional view of nongovernmental organizations as "ontologically distinct from the state and as a location of resistance to political hegemony" (Lewis 2013, p. 326). As Lewis (2013) summarizes:

> non-governmental associations and the state are enmeshed together in a complex and multilayered network of material transactions, personal connections, and organizational linkages . . . Scholars . . . view this close relationship between state and civil society organizations as an inevitable or natural outcome of particular cultural or social structures, or as reflecting the dynamics of particular patterns of state formation processes. (p. 326)

Scholars increasingly recognize nongovernmental organizations and civil society as inherently dependent on the wider political environment—they are *interdependent* with the state (Cavatorta 2013; Shieh and Deng 2011). We know in the case of the UK, for example, that the majority of social enterprises still rely heavily on grant income and/or service-level contracts with the government (Amin et al. 2002; Teasdale 2012a). Likewise, in China, social enterprises often collaborate with the government (Hsu 2017) and many nonprofit or nongovernmental organizations are established by the government or have significant government backing (Hsu et al. 2017). Yu (2011) notes that under the Chinese legislative framework, nonprofits are "under close government supervision at the registration threshold and through annual inspection" (p. 27).

Thus, Lewis (2013) writes, "far from challenging the authoritarian state, civil society organizations reaffirm, legitimize, and reproduce elements of authoritarian structures, behaviours, and discourses" (p. 328). Nongovernmental organizations are limited in what they can do to resist this. If they operate within the legal framework, they must generally align with the state, regardless of resources. If they do not, they must operate illegally or outside of the country altogether (Heiss 2017); or otherwise face limitations in engaging in "controversial political advocacy" (Hsu et al. 2017, p. 1175). Warnecke (2018) writes that: "Chinese social enterprises are unlikely to focus on political reforms or issues that would be considered an overt challenge to the communist party leadership, as this would jeopardize their survival" (p. 371).

The argument for an autonomous civil society also assumes that organizations operating in this realm are inherently good and aimed toward a common and democratically progressive change agenda. Yet, many such organizations and associations may intentionally support authoritarian rule and its ideology. That is, "civil" society action can just as easily be targeted toward "divisive and destructive causes that can motivate hateful gatherings" (Janoski 2010, p. 113; see also Chambers and Kopstein 2001; Kaufman 2002) as it can work towards more progressive democratic ends. For example, Berman (1997) shows in her examination of 'Civil Society and the Collapse of the Weimar Republic' that the Nazis seized power by taking advantage of civil society's dense associational networks, through creating local party chapters whose members also belonged to occupational, sports, and fraternal groups. The Nazis also infiltrated other groups to spread their political views.

Democratizing in transitional and authoritarian contexts

This leaves us to sort out what nongovernmental organizations can do to bring about democratization in transitional or authoritarian contexts. Following Wischermann et al. (2018), if we understand authoritarianism as fundamentally repudiating individual and collective self-determination and autonomy, then democratization does the opposite by bringing about collective and individual self-determination and autonomy. Here "autonomy means that individuals—both individually and collectively—hold their interests with due consideration, and are able to provide reasons for holding them" (Wischermann et al. 2018, pp. 99–100). We also must address the problem of the potential for 'bad civil society' or organizations that align themselves with illiberal causes. Social enterprises might address these issues by, at the least, providing and supporting individuals with opportunities for meaningful and empowering democratic participation and by helping individuals to broaden their identification with others. There are no doubt additional ways to help with democratization, but these seem the most foundational/basic (and feasible) to addressing the issues noted above.

Meaningful democratic participation involves the degree to which members (and those affected by a decision) have equal opportunities to participate in and learn the skills of agenda setting, deliberation, and decision-making in organizations. A democratic society depends on associational and organizational democracy (Eckstein 1966; Pateman 1970). For a group to be democratic, it must be inclusive; that is, those significantly affected by the decisions of the group ought to have full membership in the group and have the opportunity to have a voice in the governance of the group (Gastil 1992). Participation in agenda setting, deliberation, and decision-making are essential elements of such democratic governance. Members should have influence over what is discussed, and a voice in the final decisions and outcomes of the group. Finally, participation should be meaningful in the sense of engaging individuals routinely in civic relationships over time and that builds social capacity. Tocqueville and others looked to participation in associations as a way for citizens to practice governance and to achieve the virtues necessary for democratic citizenship: trust, moderation, compromise, reciprocity, and the skills of democratic discussion and organization (Newton 1997).

Participation in and of itself is not enough, however, as Berman and others show. Social enterprises need to also link individuals to one another across social, cultural, and economic differences to enhance identification with others. This assumes that democracy is possible where people are able to understand each other and come to some notion of the common good (Dahl 1989). Organizations need to help build bridging social capital (Putnam 2000). Putnam defines social capital as the "features of social organization such as networks, norms, and social trust that facilitate coordination and cooperation for mutual benefit" (p. 67). Forms of social capital that are inward looking and tend to reinforce exclusive identities and homogeneous groups are *bonding* social capital; social capital that is outward looking and encompasses people across diverse social cleavages is *bridging* social capital. Bridging is more likely to consist of less intimate, or even 'weak,' ties, and focuses on relationships that span different groups, linking these groups together as a means of strengthening the larger society. Bridging social capital points to the value of transcending social differences, including identity (race, ethnicity, religious tradition, sexual preference, and national origin) and status (vertical arrangements of power, influence, wealth, and prestige) differences (Wuthnow 2002).

To what degree then can social enterprise help in bringing about democratization by providing individuals with opportunities for meaningful democratic participation and broadening individuals' identification with others? There is not much work to draw on to try to address these questions in a transitional or authoritarian context. For now, we can draw on work done in other parts of the world, mostly in the western, Anglo-American democratic context, and tentatively assume that some of these may apply.

Regarding meaningful participation, Maier et al. (2016) find in their systematic literature review of nonprofit organizations becoming business-like that theoretical arguments point toward negative community effects of commercialization; although empirical evidence regarding these is scarce (e.g. Galaskiewicz et al. 2006). In addition, they note that typically, commercialization "entails the use of more paid work and unchanged amounts of voluntary work, as well as a qualitative change of volunteering in the sense of volunteers being involved in ancillary tasks, whereas central tasks are performed by paid staff (e.g., Geoghegan and Powell 2006)" (Maier et al. 2016, p. 76), suggesting fewer opportunities for meaningful participation for volunteers or members. Others find that being business-like leaves little space for structurally anchored organizational democracy (e.g. Hvenmark 2013) and self-organization at the grassroots level (e.g. Eizenberg 2012). Cooney (2006) and Dart (2004a) showed how social enterprise activities impact negatively on organizations' ability to create spaces for civic action and engagement, particularly contributions to public goods and prosocial values.

Regarding identification with others, Maier et al. (2016, p.77), find that "becoming business-like affords privilege to certain types of knowledge such as instrumental rationality, while devaluing substantive rationalities based on empathy, religion, aesthetics, feminism, and so on (e.g. Bromley, 2010; Keevers et al., 2012; Treleaven and Sykes, 2005)." Eikenberry and Kluver (2004) expressed concerns about nonprofits becoming social enterprises and leading to a focus on bottom line instead of strengthening social capital. Nevertheless, the literature also suggests social enterprises may have an important impact on building social capital, infrastructure, and engagement (Bertotti et al. 2012; Smallbone et al. 2001). Teasdale (2010) found in several case studies, for example, that social enterprises can help to build participation, social interaction, political engagement and bonding social capital and sometimes help individuals escape exclusion altogether. In addition, in their examination of seven case studies of the 'most successful' social enterprises, Alvord et al. (2004) show that some social enterprises build social movements to deal with powerful actors and shape activities of decision-makers and some transform economic circumstances and increase voice of marginalized groups. Four of the cases they examined—Bangladesh Rural Advancement Committee, Grameen Bank, Self-Employment Women's Association, and Highlander Research and Education Center—were characterized as high reach and high transformational impact (p. 280).

However, there is a noted challenge in balancing the competing demands of economic and social outcomes within social enterprises (Dart 2004a; Teasdale 2010; Garrow and Hasenfeld 2014). Balancing social and commercial goals is very difficult over the longer term (Teasdale et al. 2013) and organizations tend to go toward one end of the spectrum or the other (Young et al. 2012). Thus, if social enterprise organizations were to lean more toward social goals, or rejuvenating the 'sociality' or relational ethic of social entrepreneurship (SE) (Bull et al. 2010; Dey and Steyaert 2010; Hjorth 2009; Humphries and Grant 2005; Steyaert and Hjorth 2006) and emphasizing emancipatory social enterprises as processes that empower and contribute to changing the social order (Haugh and Talwar 2016), they might be more likely to support meaningful participation and identification with others.

Warnecke (2018), Yu and Chen (2018), Vaceková et al. (2017) and others suggest that social enterprises in transitional and authoritarian regimes offer significant opportunities for social change. Can more be done to enhance the sociality of social enterprises in these political contexts and would it be enough to create democratic change? Future research should examine these questions and the connections between social enterprise and active participation and identification, as well as other means of democratization, in transitional and authoritarian countries. Or consider that perhaps democratization would be more likely through other means. For example, there is citizen participation work being done in China, but not necessarily due to or supported by socially entrepreneurial activities (Shieh and Deng 2011; Hsu et al. 2017).

Conclusion

The focus of this chapter was to examine to what degree, in the context of transitional or authoritarian political regimes, social enterprise might lead to democratization of (civil) society more broadly. The literature suggests that we might expect social enterprises to have limited independence in such a context; thus, the best we might hope for is to encourage social enterprises to provide meaningful participation and identification with others—the minimum necessary to resist authoritarianism and lead to democratization. Theories and empirical evidence is limited mostly to western, democratic countries, but suggests that social enterprises may be able to do this to some degree if they emphasize their sociality or relational and emancipatory aspects over commercial goals.

NOTE

1 These authors do not define what they mean by civil society. Their discussion implies a definition of civil society as one of three sectors and largely made up of nonprofit or nongovernmental organizations.

References

Alvord, S. H., D. L. Brown and C. W. Letts (2004), 'Social entrepreneurship and societal transformation: An exploratory study', *Journal of Applied Behavioral Science*, **40** (3), 260–82.

Amin, A., A. Cameron and R. Hudson (2002), *Placing the Social Economy*, London, UK and New York, USA: Routledge.

Berman, S. (1997), 'Civil society and the collapse of the Weimar Republic', *World Politics*, **49** (3), 401–29.

Bertotti, M., A. Hardin, A. Renton and K. Sheridan (2012), 'The contribution of a social enterprise to the building of social capital in a disadvantaged urban area of London', *Community Development Journal*, **47** (2), 168–83.

Bromley, P. (2010), 'The rationalization of educational development: Scientific activity among international nongovernmental organizations', *Comparative Education Review*, **54**, 577–601.

Bull, M., R. Ridley-Duff, D. Foster and P. Seanor (2010), 'Conceptualising ethical capital in social enterprise', *Social Enterprise Journal*, **6** (3), 250–64.

Cavatorta, F. (2013), 'Civil society activism under authoritarian constraints', in F. Cavatorta (ed.), *Civil Society Activism Under Authoritarian Rule*, London, UK: Routledge, pp. 1–2.

Chambers, S. and J. Kopstein (2001), 'Bad civil society', *Political Theory*, **29** (6), 837–65.

Cooney, K. (2006), 'The institutional and technical structuring of nonprofit ventures: Case study of a U.S. hybrid organization caught between two fields', *Voluntas*, **17** (2), 143–61.

Dahl, R. A. (1989), *Democracy and Its Critics*, New Haven, USA: Yale University Press.

Dart, R. (2004a), 'Being "business-like" in a nonprofit organization: A grounded and inductive typology', *Nonprofit and Voluntary Sector Quarterly*, **33** (2), 290–310.

Dart, R. (2004b), 'The legitimacy of social enterprise', *Nonprofit Management and Leadership*, **14** (4), 411–24.

Defourny, J., L. Hulgård and V. Pestoff (2014), *Social Enterprise and the Third Sector: Changing European Landscapes in a Comparative Perspective*, London, UK and New York, USA: Routledge.

Defourny, J. and S-Y. Kim (2011), 'Emerging models of social enterprise in Eastern Asia: A cross-country analysis', *Social Enterprise Journal*, **7** (1), 86–111.

Defourny J. and M. Nyssens (2010), 'Conceptions of social enterprise and social entrepreneurship in Europe and the United States: Convergences and divergences', *Journal of Social Entrepreneurship*, **1** (1), 32–53.

Dey, P. and C. Steyaert (2010), 'The politics of narrating social entrepreneurship', *Journal of Enterprising Communities*, **4** (1), 85–110.

Dohnalová, M., D. Guri, J. Hrabětová, K. Legnerová and V. Šlechtová (2015), 'Social Enterprise in the Czech Republic', ICSEM Working Papers, No. 24, Liege, Belgium: The International Comparative Social Enterprise Models (ICSEM) Project.

Ebrahim, A., J. Battilana and J. Mair (2014), 'The governance of social enterprises: Mission drift and accountability challenges in hybrid organizations', *Research in Organizational Behavior*, **34**, 81–100.

Eckstein, H. (1966), *Division and Cohesion in Democracy: A Study of Norway*, Princeton, USA: Princeton University Press.

Edwards, M. (2008), *Just Another Emperor? The Myths and Realities of Philanthrocapitalism*, New York, USA: Demos and the Young Foundation.

Eikenberry, A. M. and J. D. Kluver (2004), 'The marketization of the nonprofit sector: Civil society at risk?' *Public Administration Review*, **64** (2), 132–40.

Eizenberg, E. (2012), 'The changing meaning of community space: Two models of NGO management of community gardens in New York City', *International Journal of Urban and Regional Research*, **36**, 106–20.

Galaskiewicz, J., W. Bielefeld and Dowell, M. (2006). Networks and organizational growth: A study of community based nonprofits. *Administrative Science Quarterly*, **51**, 337–80.

Garrow, E. E. and Y. Hasenfeld (2014), 'Social enterprises as an embodiment of a neoliberal welfare logic', *American Behavioral Scientist*, **58** (1), 1475–93.

Gastil, J. (1992), 'A definition of small group democracy,' *Small Group Research*, **23**, 278–301.

Geoghegan, M. and F. Powell (2006), 'Community development, partnership governance and dilemmas of professionalization: Profiling and assessing the case of Ireland', *British Journal of Social Work*, **36**, 845–61.

Haugh, H. M. and A. Talwar (2016), 'Linking social entrepreneurship and social change: The mediating role of empowerment', *Journal of Business Ethics*, **133** (4), 643–58.

Heiss, A. (2017), 'Amicable contempt: The strategic balance between dictators and international NGOs', Dissertation. Duke University, Durham, USA.

Hjorth, D. (2009), 'Entrepreneurship, sociality and art: Re-imagining the public', in R. Ziegler (ed.), *An Introduction to Social Entrepreneurship: Voices, Preconditions, Contexts*, Cheltenham, UK and Northampton, USA: Edward Elgar Publishing, pp. 207–27.

Hsu, C. (2017), 'Social entrepreneurship and citizenship in China: The rise of NGOs in the PRC', *Asia-Pacific Journal*, **15** (3), 1–15.

Hsu, J. Y. J., C. L. Hsu and R. Hasmath (2017), 'NGO strategies in an authoritarian context, and their implications for citizenship: The case of the People's Republic of China', *Nonprofit and Voluntary Sector Quarterly*, **28** (3), 1157–79.

Humphries, M. and S. Grant (2005), 'Social enterprise and re-civilization of human endeavors: Re-socializing the market metaphor or encroaching of the lifeworld?', *Current Issues in Comparative Education*, **8** (1), 41–50.

Hvenmark, J. (2013), 'Business as usual? On managerialization and the adoption of the balanced score-card in a democratically governed civil society organization', *Administrative Theory & Praxis*, **35** (2), 223–47.

Janoski, T. (2010), 'The dynamic processes of volunteering in civil society: A group and multi-level approach', *Journal of Civil Society*, **6**, 99–118.

Kasfir, N. (1998), 'Civil society, the state and democracy in Africa', *Commonwealth & Comparative Politics*, **36** (2), 123–49.

Kaufman, J. A. (2002), *For the Common Good? American Civic Life and the Golden Age of Fraternity*, Oxford, UK: Oxford University Press.

Keevers, L., L. Treleaven, C. Sykes and M. Darcy (2012), 'Made to measure: Taming practices with results-based accountability', *Organization Studies*, **33**, 97–120.

Kerlin, J. A. (2006), 'Social enterprise in the United States and Europe: Understanding and learning from the differences', *Voluntas*, **17** (3), 247–63.

Kerlin, J. A. (ed.) (2009), *Social Enterprise: A Global Comparison*, Lebanon, USA: University Press of New England.

Kerlin, J. A. (2012), 'Considering context: Social innovation in comparative perspective', in A. Nicholls and A. Murdock (eds.), *Social Innovation*, London, UK: Palgrave Macmillan, pp. 66–88.

Lewis, D. (2013), 'Civil society and the authoritarian state: Cooperation, contestation and discourse', *Journal of Civil Society*, **9** (3), 325–40.

Lundqvist, M. A. and K. L. Williams Middleton (2010), 'Promises of societal entrepreneurship: Sweden and beyond', *Journal of Enterprising Communities: People and Places in the Global Economy*, **4** (1), 24–36.

Maier, F., M. Meyer and M. Steinbereithner (2016), 'Nonprofit organizations becoming business-like: A systematic review', *Nonprofit and Voluntary Sector Quarterly*, **45** (1), 64–86.

Newton, K. (1997), 'Social capital and democracy', *American Behavioral Scientist*, **40**, 575–86.

Nicholls, A. and S. Teasdale (2017), 'Neoliberalism by stealth? Exploring continuity and change within the UK social enterprise policy paradigm', *Policy & Politics*, **45** (3), 323–41.

Parkinson, C. and C. Howorth (2008), 'The language of social entrepreneurs', *Entrepreneurship & Regional Development*, **20** (3), 285–309.

Pateman, C. (1970), *Participation and Democratic Theory*, London, UK: Cambridge University Press.

Peattie, K. and A. Morley (2008), *Social Enterprises: Diversity and Dynamics, Contexts and Contributions*, London, UK: Social Enterprise Coalition.

Putnam, R. D. (2000), *Bowling Alone: The Collapse and Revival of American Community*, New York, USA: Simon & Schuster.

Shieh, S. and G. Deng. (2011), 'An emerging civil society: The impact of the 2008 Sichuan earthquake on grass-roots associations in China', *The China Journal*, **65**, 181–94.

Smallbone D., M. Evans, I. Ekanem and S. Butters (2001), *Researching Social Enterprise: Final Report to the Small Business Service*, London, UK: Centre for Enterprise and Economic Development Research, Middlesex University. Accessed 12 August 2014 at http://www.mbsportal.bl.uk/secure/subjareas/smlbusentrep/bis/120401file38361.pdf.

Steyaert, C. and D. Hjorth (2006), 'Introduction: What is social in social entrepreneurship?', in C. Steyaert and D. Hjorth (eds.), *Entrepreneurship as Social Change: A Third Movements of Entrepreneurship Book*, Cheltenham, UK and Northampton, USA: Edward Elgar Publishing, pp. 1–18.

Teasdale, S. (2010), 'How can social enterprise address disadvantage? Evidence from an inner city com-munity', *Journal of Nonprofit & Public Sector Marketing*, **22** (2), 89–107.

Teasdale, S. (2012a), 'Negotiating tensions: How do social enterprises in the homelessness field balance social and commercial considerations?', *Housing Studies*, **27** (4), 514–32.

Teasdale, S. (2012b), 'What's in a name? Making sense of social enterprise discourses', *Public Policy and Administration*, **27** (2), 99–119.

Teasdale, S., J. Kerlin, D. Young and J. In Soh (2013), 'Oil and water rarely mix: Exploring the relative stability of nonprofit revenue mixes over time', *Journal of Social Entrepreneurship*, **4** (1), 69–87.

Treleaven, L. and C. Sykes (2005), 'Loss of organizational knowledge: From supporting clients to serving head office', *Journal of Organizational Change Management*, **18**, 353–68.

Vaceková, G., V. Valentinov and J. Nemec (2017), 'Rethinking nonprofit commercialization: The case of the Czech Republic', *Voluntas*, **28** (5), 2103–23.

Yu, J. and K. Chen (2018), 'Does nonprofit marketization facilitate or inhibit the development of civil society? A comparative study of China and the USA', *Voluntas* (online).

Yu, X. (2011), 'Social enterprise in China: Driving forces, development patterns and legal framework', *Social Enterprise Journal*, **7** (1), 9–32.

Warnecke, T. (2018), 'Social entrepreneurship in China: Driving institutional change', *Journal of Economic Issues*, **52** (2), 368–77.

Wischermann, J., B. Bunk, P. Köllner and J. Lorch (2018), 'Do associations support authoritarian rule? Evidence from Algeria, Mozambique, and Vietnam', *Journal of Civil Society*, **14** (2), 95–115.

Wuthnow, R. (2002), 'The United States: Bridging the privileged and the marginalized?' in Robert D. Putnam (ed.), *Democracies in Flux: The Evolution of Social Capital in Contemporary Society*, Oxford, UK: Oxford University Press, pp. 59–102.

Young, D., J. Kerlin, S. Teasdale and J. In Soh (2012), 'The dynamics and long term stability of social enterprise', in J. Kickul and S. Bacq (eds.), *Patterns in Social Entrepreneurship Research*, Cheltenham, UK and Northampton, USA: Edward Elgar Publishing, 217–40.

5 Measuring impact in social entrepreneurship: developing a research agenda for the 'practice turn' in impact assessment

Jarrod Ormiston and Erin Castellas

Introduction

Social enterprises, along with nonprofits, foundations and corporations, are under increasing pressure to measure and report their impact in order to overcome criticisms of whether they are actually having an impact on the social problems they claim to address (Ebrahim & Rangan 2014; Kania & Kramer 2011). However, Rawhouser, Cummings and Newbert (2017) claim that the measurement of social impact for social entrepreneurs is highly underdeveloped both theoretically and empirically. The literature exhibits inconsistent terminology around the focus (e.g. outputs, outcomes, impact), domains (e.g. social, environmental, cultural), and activities (e.g. accounting, assessment, measurement, management, evaluation) of impact assessment, resulting in a wide range of terms describing what is essentially the same phenomenon: impact assessment, impact measurement, outcome measurement, performance evaluation, performance measurement, social accounting, social and environmental reporting (Ormiston forthcoming).

This chapter adopts the broader term 'impact assessment' to encompass the diversity of perspectives. 'Impact assessment' refers to the processes involved in understanding, measuring, and reporting the anticipated or actual contribution of actions focused on tackling persistent social problems (Ebrahim & Rangan 2014; Jäger & Rothe 2013). This includes: activities, tools and frameworks for thinking about impact; methods for data gathering and analysis; artefacts such as reports, data sets, models, and forms of evidence; and standards which aim to deliver common approaches to impact assessment across similar sectors (Ormiston forthcoming).

A multitude of impact assessment approaches have emerged in recent years, with some sectors and fields converging on particular approaches (Mulgan 2010). For example: in the social sector, logic models have become the accepted standard for many large institutional players (Ebrahim & Rangan 2010); in development circles, randomised controlled trials (RCTs) have been proposed as the gold standard for impact assessment, despite considerable debate about their efficacy (Liket, Rey-Garcia & Maas 2014); and, in impact investment, Social Return on Investment

(SROI) and Impact Reporting and Investment Standards (IRIS) have been viewed as global benchmarks (Antadze & Westley 2012).

Despite the myriad of approaches, theory has not sufficiently addressed the complex nature of impact assessment and how it is experienced within everyday organisational activities. The literature on impact assessment has been dominated by conceptual studies, with relatively limited empirical studies on impact assessment (Antadze & Westley 2012; Lecy, Schmitz & Swedlund 2012; Nicholls 2009). Theory development in impact assessment research has been characterised by conceptual studies and a reliance on small -*n* case studies focused at an organisational level. This has resulted in an under-theorised field in which academic studies are trailing behind advancements in the practitioner literature (Ebrahim & Rangan 2014; Rawhauser et al. 2017). And Benjamin (2008) emphasises the need to consider how impact assessment influences organisational activities. In response, this chapter aims to promote a practice turn in studies of impact assessment in social entrepreneurship (SE) to understand how practitioners cope with the complexity of impact assessment in their everyday activities.

A practice lens (Miettinen, Samra-Fredericks & Yanow 2009; Nicolini 2012; Whittington 1996) encourages a focus on the everyday sayings and doings of impact assessment. Adopting a practice lens allows for:

1. a re-evaluation of the significance of everyday human activity that permeates organisational life (Schatzki 2001; Whittington 2011) to shift focus from abstract notions of measures, reports and impact accounts to the simple actions of measuring, reporting and accounting;
2. a reframing to understand how impact assessment plays out across levels of organisational ecosystems between *micro* (individual sayings and doings), *meso* (organisational routines) and *macro* (institutions) (Miettinen et al. 2009; Whittington 2011);
3. the potential to overcome Cartesian dualism by exploring the relations between subject/object, mind/body, person/world rather than their separateness, thereby appreciating the sociomaterial nature of impact assessment (Miettinen et al. 2009; Orlikowski 2007; Sandberg & Dall'Alba 2009); and
4. an understanding of how practitioners cope with impact assessment in their everyday actions (Chia & Holt 2006; Zundel & Kokkalis 2010).

The next section reviews the impact assessment literature, including: a focus on tools, frameworks, and reports; confusion around the purpose of impact assessment; and a limited exploration of the multiple actors involved in impact assessment. The following sections highlight the 'practice turn' in impact assessment. The final section outlines a research agenda for expanding the turn to practice in studies of impact assessment in SE.

The impact assessment literature

The main academic fields studying impact assessment include SE; development studies; nonprofit studies; public administration; and business and management. The following sub-sections review the themes that emerge from a review of these streams of literature, highlighting the need for a turn to practice.

Metrics and frameworks, challenges and constraints

The impact assessment literature is heavily focused on metrics, tools, frameworks, and reports (see Table 5.1). While the large majority of studies have focused on the use of individual tools and frameworks, critics have argued against the use of single standardised metrics, especially the use of financial proxies, instead calling for a combination of qualitative and quantitative data to understand impact (Arena, Azzone & Bengo 2014; Hudon & Sandberg 2015; Lecy et al. 2012; Nicholls 2009). Other scholars have focused on the appropriateness of various frameworks, with multiple studies questioning the utility and applicability of different approaches to impact assessment. Most of these critiques have centred on methodological and philosophical issues with current approaches, decrying the use of practices from accounting and economics disciplines that are not well-suited to evaluating non-financial impact (Antadze & Westley 2012; Marée & Mertens 2011; Mulgan 2010; Nicholls 2009; Pathak & Dattani 2014).

Studies have also considered the challenges of measurement and organisational constraints that impede impact assessment activities, including: questions of incommensurability due to diverse operating contexts; the heterogeneity of social interventions; subjectivity; non-quantifiability; multi-causality; and temporality (Barraket & Yousefpour 2013; Carnochan, Samples, Myers & Austin 2013; Harji & Jackson 2018; Kroeger & Weber 2014; Mayhew 2012; Mulgan 2010; Nicholls 2009; Willems, Boenigk & Jegers 2014). The organisational constraints of impact assessment include: competing commitments, lack of financial and human resources, cultural openness to measurement, and the perceived complexity of measurement (Barman & MacIndoe 2012; Barraket & Yousefpour 2013; Carnochan et al. 2013; Kroeger & Weber 2014; Mayhew 2012; Molecke and Pinkse 2017; Moxham & Boaden 2007; Thomson 2010; Willems et al. 2014). Future research can extend this literature by exploring: how the multitude of approaches to impact assessment influence organisational activities; and how individuals and organisations cope with the challenges in their everyday impact assessment activities.

The purpose of impact assessment

Studies on the purpose of impact assessment have generally focused on its importance for accountability or its utility in enhancing impact (Ebrahim & Rangan 2014; Edwards & Hulme 1995; Jepson 2005; Nicholls 2010; see Table 5.2). This corresponds to both the top-down promotion of performance measurement, which

Table 5.1   A focus on the tools, frameworks, and reports

Theme	Exemplar studies	Research opportunities
Individual tools and frameworks	Willems et al. (2014), Keevers et al. (2012), Gasper (2000), Nicholls (2010), Lodhia (2015)	Multiple formal and informal approaches to impact assessment utilised by organisations
Dissatisfaction with single and/or aggregated metrics	Nicholls (2009), Mulgan (2011), Hudon and Sandberg (2015), Lecy et al. (2012), Arena et al. (2014), Zappala and Lyons (2009), Desa and Koch (2014), Jäger and Rothe (2013), Carnochan et al. (2013)	Both qualitative and quantitative measures in impact assessment
Critiques of the appropriateness of various approaches	Kroeger and Weber (2014), Antadze and Westley (2012), Marée and Mertens (2011), Mouchamps (2014), Pathak and Dattani (2014), Gasper (2000), Lee and Nowell (2015), Moxham and Boaden (2007), Willems et al. (2014)	Multiple informal/formal, qualitative/quantitative approaches to impact assessment used by organisations and how their shortcomings are experienced
Challenges and constraints of doing impact assessment	Kroeger and Weber (2014), Barraket and Yousefpour (2013), Harji and Jackson (2018), Nicholls (2009), Mulgan (2011), Carnochan et al. (2013), Mayhew (2012), Willems et al. (2014), Barman and MacIndoe (2012), Moxham and Boaden (2007), Molecke and Pinkse (2017)	How organisations cope with the challenges and constraints of impact assessment in their everyday activities

focuses heavily on accountability, particularly in the context of funding relationships (Grimes 2010); and the bottom-up approach to performance management, which focuses on stakeholder engagement and the strategic use of impact assessment practices to enhance impact (Nicholls 2009). Beyond accountability and enhanced performance, studies also explore how impact assessment can inform strategy, organisational learning, employee motivation, stakeholder relations, marketing, and gaining legitimacy (see Table 5.2).

Some studies have begun to explore the link between these multiple rationales, considering the interplay between strategy, accountability and legitimacy (Jäger & Rothe 2013; Mouchamps 2014; Saj 2013) and learning, strategy and accountability (Liket et al. 2014). Given the breadth of potential purposes for impact assessment, there is an opportunity for future research to explore the extent to which these multiple purposes are experienced in the everyday activities of organisations. Following calls from Mayhew (2012) and Lecy et al. (2012), future research should cross disciplinary divides to empirically explore how organisations engage with the multiple purposes of impact assessment.

Table 5.2   Conflicted understandings of the purpose of impact assessment

Purpose	Elements	Articles
Accountability	• Accountability • Measuring performance • Transparency • Control	Edwards & Hulme (1995), Nicholls (2010), Grimes (2010), Bagnoli and Megali (2009), Mouchamps (2014), Ebrahim and Rangan (2014), Campbell et al. (2012), Jepson (2005), Lee and Nowell (2015), Antadze and Westley (2012), Beamon and Balcik (2008), Molecke and Pinkse (2017)
Strategy	• Developing strategy • Improving performance • Informing decision-making • Accessing resources	Nicholls (2009), Zappala and Lyons (2009), Mouchamps (2014), Ebrahim and Rangan (2014), Campbell et al. (2012), Benjamin and Misra (2006), Liket et al. (2014), Sawhill and Williamson (2001), Nicholls (2010), Antadze and Westley (2012), Bagnoli and Megali (2009), Liket et al. (2014), Willems et al. (2014), Barraket and Yousefpour (2013)
Broader purposes	• Organisational learning • Employee motivation • Stakeholder dialogue • Marketing • Legitimacy	Barraket and Yousefpour (2013), Buckmaster (1999), Liket et al. (2014), Arvidson and Lyon (2014), Benjamin and Misra (2006), Jäger and Rothe (2013), Sawhill and Williamson (2001), Nicholls (2010), Grimes (2010), Seelos and Mair (2005), Jepson (2005), Willems et al. (2014), Lee and Nowell (2015)
Multiple purposes	• Strategy & Accountability • Accountability & Legitimacy • Learning & Budgeting	Saj (2013), Mouchamps (2014), Jäger and Rothe (2013), Liket et al. (2014), Mayhew (2012)

Source: Adapted from Ormiston (forthcoming).

Actors in impact assessment

The majority of the impact assessment literature has considered the role of impact assessment from an organisational perspective. Despite the management of relationships across inter-organisational networks being perceived as a key component of impact assessment (Lee & Nowell 2015), very few studies have considered how the phenomenon is enacted across organisational boundaries (Barraket & Yousefpour 2013). Table 5.3 highlights the multiple actors in impact assessment, beyond the funded organisation.

Considerations of inter-organisational aspects of impact assessment have failed to go beyond dyadic relationships between funders and social sector organisations. There is a dearth of studies that consider how impact assessment is enacted

Table 5.3 Multiple actors in impact assessment

Actor	Role	Studies
Funders (Government, Investors, Philanthropists)	Accountability	Grimes (2010), Nicholls (2010), Ebrahim and Rangan (2014), Chell et al. (2010), Jäger and Rothe (2013), Benjamin (2008)
	Decision-making	Schmitz et al. (2012), Thomson (2011), Nicholls (2009), Ebrahim and Rangan (2014)
Employees	Implementation	Chell et al. (2010), Lee (2004)
Clients	Beneficiary voice	Smith and Stevens (2010), Ebrahim (2005), Jäger and Rothe (2013)
External evaluators	Providing expertise and promoting specific approaches	Harji and Jackson (2018), Ospina et al. (2002), André (2012), Ruff and Olsen (2018)

across broader ecosystems encompassing diverse inter-organisational relationships (Barraket & Yousefpour 2013; Ebrahim 2003). The role of stakeholders beyond funders in driving impact assessment has been scarcely discussed, despite indications that employees (Grimes 2010), policymakers and government agencies (Chell et al. 2010), clients (Ebrahim 2005; Smith & Stevens 2010), beneficiaries (Jäger & Rothe 2013), institutional supporters (Ospina, Diaz & O'Sullivan 2002), and external evaluators (André 2012; Harji & Jackson 2018; Ruff & Olsen 2018) play an important role in impact assessment. There is an opportunity for future research to investigate the broader ecosystem of stakeholders involved in impact assessment (Barraket & Yousefpour 2013) and their relational dynamics.

A research agenda for the practice turn in impact assessment

A review of the impact assessment literature reveals a preoccupation with the tools and frameworks for impact assessment, confusion about the purposes of impact assessment, and a narrow focus on organisational perspectives and experiences. To date, little research has been undertaken on how impact assessment tools, frameworks, and purposes are experienced in the everyday activities of individuals and organisations (Ebrahim & Rangan 2010; Nicholls 2009).

At the heart of practice theory is an attention to the everyday doings and sayings of people and things (Sandberg & Dall'Alba 2009). The dominant themes of practice theory include: positioning human agency and activity at the core of practice (Sandberg & Dall'Alba 2009; Whittington 2011); appreciating the embodied nature of practice which is mediated by non-human material objects and artefacts (Miettinen et al. 2009; Nicolini 2012; Sandberg & Dall'Alba 2009; Schatzki 2001; Whittington 2011); and emphasising that practice is social and that the interconnectedness of social practice is central to theorising human activity (Heidegger

[1927] 1962; Jarzabkowski & Seidl 2008; Nicolini 2012; Schatzki 2001; Whittington 2011; Wittgenstein 1967). Schatzki describes practices as "embodied, materially mediated arrays of human activity centrally organized around shared practical understandings" (2001, p. 11). The practice 'turn' has been documented across fields, including sociology, anthropology, history, education, cultural theory, gender studies, philosophy, science, and technology (Schatzki 2001).

This chapter advocates the adoption of the practice 'turn' in impact assessment. Understanding 'impact assessment as practice' requires a focus on the everyday activities involved in assessing, measuring, evaluating and reporting impact rather than focusing on the impact tools, measures and reports utilised and produced by organisations. Whittington's (2006) practices-praxis-practitioners framework provides a useful foundation for theorising impact assessment practice (Ormiston forthcoming).

'Practices' refer to "shared routines of behavior, including traditions, norms and procedures for thinking, acting, and using 'things'" (Whittington 2006, p. 619). Within the strategy-as-practice literature, practices can refer to strategy tools (e.g. SWOT and Five Forces), strategic planning documents, visual tools (e.g. PowerPoints), and strategy workshops (Vaara & Whittington 2012). It is important to note the distinction between the higher order concept of *practice* and this element of practice – *practices* (Sandberg & Dall'Alba 2009). Within the context of impact assessment, practices refer to formal and informal, qualitative and quantitative, tools, frameworks, and reports involved in assessing impact such as logics models, expected return frameworks (e.g. SROI, CBA), randomised control trials, participatory frameworks and standardised metrics (e.g. IRIS, GRI), along with workshops and meetings. Beyond these formal practices, informal norms of impact assessment are also relevant (Ormiston forthcoming).

'Praxis' refers to what practitioners do in their work, in their everyday activities (Whittington 2006). Within the strategy-as-practice literature, praxis refers to "episodes or sequences of strategy-making" (Vaara & Whittington 2012, p. 298), which include conversations, interactions between employees and managers, individual interpretations of strategy, and activities at both the centre and periphery of organisations. In the context of impact assessment, praxis refers to the everyday enactment of impact assessment through activities such as measuring, evaluating, and reporting in conversations, interactions, and individual activities (Ormiston forthcoming).

'Practitioners' refers to those who actually carry out the activities of the practice. They are the link between practices and praxis (Whittington 2006). Within the strategy-as-practice literature, practitioners often include senior management, middle management, employees, strategy directors, and strategy consultants (Vaara & Whittington 2012). Within the context of impact assessment practice, practitioners refer to the multiple players in the ecosystem, including funders, investors, government representatives, managers, employees, consultants, clients, beneficiaries, and community members who are engaged in assessing impact (Ormiston forthcoming).

Whilst some studies have begun to employ a practice lens to understand impact assessment (Ormiston forthcoming), these studies have predominantly focused on negative implications of impact assessment for organisational practices. These studies have highlighted how impact assessment can lead to gaming (Bevan & Hood 2006), mission drift (Ormiston & Seymour 2011; Ramus & Vaccaro 2017), trade-offs (United Way of America 2000; Willems et al. 2014), and create barriers to learning (Barraket & Yousefpour 2013; Gasper 2000; Mayhew 2012).

There have also been studies exploring the potential negative implications stemming from impact assessment practice. For example, studies have explored: funding measurement activities at the expense of services; overloading accounting and record-keeping systems; the vulnerability of outcomes targets to gaming approaches; placing too much weight on unreliable metrics and proxies; and valuing accountability to funders over service improvement (Bevan & Hood 2006; Ebrahim & Rangan 2014; Kramer, Graves, Hirschhorn & Fiske 2007; Torjman 1999; United Way of America 2000).

Other studies have shown that impact assessment can create tensions within organisations by illuminating incongruity around the relative importance of social, environmental, and economic goals and their respective emphasis for different stakeholders (Smith, Gonin & Besharov 2013; Stevens et al. 2015). Research has explored the nexus between mission and impact assessment, revealing the potential for mission drift where mission and impact assessment are misaligned (Ormiston & Seymour 2011; Ramus & Vaccaro 2017). In their reviews of impact assessment in the microfinance industry, Khavul (2010), along with Datar, Epstein and Yuthas (2008), derided the prioritisation of organisational longevity and profitability over impact on clients. Their work provides insights into the negative implications of this goal misalignment for organisational decision-making.

One of the cited benefits of impact assessment is organisational learning (Arvidson & Lyon 2014; Barraket & Yousefpour 2013; Buckmaster 1999; Liket et al. 2014). Studies on how impact assessment practice influences everyday activities have questioned its potential contribution to organisational learning. For example, Barraket and Yousefpour (2013) found no evidence that organisational learning was used to pursue mission-related goals. Rather, impact assessment was predominantly employed to appease funders and attract external funding support. Gasper (2000) drew a similar conclusion in a review of logical frameworks, noting that the overt focus on intentional actions and effects encouraged a problematic prioritisation of audit over learning, in which unintended benefits were not valued or incorporated into future decision-making. Mayhew (2012) neatly captured the conflict between enhancing impact and promoting accountability, showing that failure was discouraged in the latter, which, when excluded, detracted from the potential for learning and program improvement. In contrast to these studies, Sawhill and

Table 5.4   A research agenda for understanding impact assessment as practice

Theme	Research questions
Tools/frameworks (Practices)	• How do organisations adopt a multitude of formal/informal, qualitative/quantitative, impact assessment approaches? • How do organisations cope with the challenges and constraints of impact assessment in their everyday activities?
Purposes/rationale (Praxis)	• What are the potential purposes and benefits of impact assessment beyond accountability and strategy? • How do organisations engage with the multiple purposes of impact assessment?
Multiple actors (Practitioners)	• How does the presence of multiple funders from diverse sectors, with potentially competing demands, influence impact assessment practice? • How is impact assessment incorporated within a broader ecosystem of stakeholders and inter-organisational activities?

Williamson (2001) in their study of 30 US nonprofits, elucidated that impact assessment was perceived as useful for learning and improving outcomes when measures were mission-aligned, simple and communicable. They also found that outcome measurement was a powerful tool for marketing to funders and useful in everyday decision-making and long-term strategic planning, thus suggesting the potential for multiple influences of impact assessment in practice (Sawhill & Williamson 2001).

These studies highlight the more nuanced understanding of impact assessment through a practice lens. They move beyond perceived benefits and challenges of impact assessment to consider how stakeholders experience the practice. Building on these studies, Table 5.4 offers some key future research questions to better understand impact assessment as practice. These research questions illustrate how a practice lens allows an understanding of: practices, what resources are used (e.g. the impact assessment tools and frameworks); praxis, the activities of impact assessment and how they take place (e.g. measuring, evaluating, and reporting for accounting, strategising, decision-making); and practitioners, appreciating the social nature of practice and who is involved (e.g. the multiple actors in the ecosystem).

References

André, R. (2012), 'Assessing the Accountability of the Benefit Corporation: Will This New Gray Sector Organisation Enhance Corporate Social Responsibility?', *Journal of Business Ethics*, **110** (1), 133–150.

Antadze, N. and F. R. Westley (2012), 'Impact Metrics for Social Innovation: Barriers or Bridges to Radical Change?' *Journal of Social Entrepreneurship*, **3** (2), 133–150.

Arena, M., G. Azzone and I. Bengo (2014), 'Performance Measurement for Social Enterprises', *Voluntas: International Journal of Voluntary and Nonprofit Organisations*, **26** (2), 649–672.

Arvidson, M. and F. Lyon (2014), 'Social Impact Measurement and Non-profit Organisations: Compliance, Resistance, and Promotion', *VOLUNTAS: International Journal of Voluntary and Nonprofit Organisations*, **25** (4), 869–886.

Bagnoli, L. and C. Megali (2009), 'Measuring Performance in Social Enterprises', *Nonprofit and Voluntary Sector Quarterly*, **40** (1), 149–165.

Barman, E. and H. MacIndoe (2012), 'Institutional Pressures and Organisational Capacity: The Case of Outcome Measurement', *Sociological Forum*, **27** (1), 70–93.

Barraket, J. and N. Yousefpour (2013), 'Evaluation and Social Impact Measurement Amongst Small to Medium Social Enterprises: Process, Purpose and Value', *Australian Journal of Public Administration*, **72** (4), 447–458.

Beamon, B. M. and B. Balcik (2008). 'Performance Measurement in Humanitarian Relief Chains', *International Journal of Public Sector Management*, **21** (1), 4–25.

Benjamin, L. M. (2008), 'Account Space: How Accountability Requirements Shape Nonprofit Practice', *Nonprofit and Voluntary Sector Quarterly*, **37** (2), 201–223.

Benjamin, L. M. and K. Misra (2006), 'Doing Good Work: Implications of Performance Accountability for Practice in the Nonprofit Sector', *International Journal of Rural Management*, **2** (2), 147–162.

Bevan, G. and C. Hood (2006), 'What's Measured is What Matters: Targets and Gaming in the English Public Health Care System', *Public Administration*, **84** (3), 517–538.

Buckmaster, N. (1999), 'Associations between Outcome Measurement, Accountability and Learning for Non-profit Organisations', *International Journal of Public Sector Management*, **12** (2), 186–197.

Campbell, D., K. Lambright and L. Bronstein (2012), 'In The Eyes of the Beholders: Feedback Motivations and Practices among Nonprofit Providers and Their Funders', *Public Performance & Management Review*, **36** (1), 7–30.

Carnochan, S., M. Samples, M. Myers and M. J. Austin (2013), 'Performance Measurement Challenges in Nonprofit Human Service Organisations', *Nonprofit and Voluntary Sector Quarterly*, **43** (6), 1014–1032.

Chell, E., K. Nicolopoulou and M. Karataş-Özkan (2010), 'Social Entrepreneurship and Enterprise: International and Innovation Perspectives', *Entrepreneurship & Regional Development*, **22** (6), 485–493.

Chia, R. and R. Holt (2006), 'Strategy as Practical Coping: A Heideggerian Perspective', *Organisation Studies*, **27** (5), 635–655.

Datar, S. M., M. J. Epstein and K. Yuthas (2008), 'In Microfinance, Clients Must Come First', *Stanford Social Innovation Review*, **6** (1), 38–45.

Desa, G. and J. L. Koch (2014), 'Scaling Social Impact: Building Sustainable Social Ventures at the Base-of-the-Pyramid', *Journal of Social Entrepreneurship*, **5** (2), 146–174.

Ebrahim, A. (2003), 'Making Sense of Accountability: Conceptual Perspectives for Northern and Southern Nonprofits', *Nonprofit Management and Leadership*, **14** (2), 191–212.

Ebrahim, A. (2005), 'Accountability Myopia: Losing Sight of Organizational Learning', *Nonprofit and Voluntary Sector Quarterly*, **34** (1), 56–87.

Ebrahim, A. and V. K. Rangan (2010), 'The Limits of Nonprofit Impact: A Contingency Framework for Measuring Social Performance', *Working Paper*. Cambridge, MA: Harvard Business School.

Ebrahim, A. and V. K. Rangan (2014), 'What Impact? A Framework for Measuring the Scale and Scope of Social Performance', *California Management Review*, **56** (3), 118–141.

Edwards, M. and D. Hulme (1995), 'NGO Performance and Accountability in the Post-Cold War World', *Journal of International Development*, **7** (6), 849–856.

Gasper, D. (2000), 'Evaluating the "Logical Framework Approach" towards Learning-oriented Development Evaluation', *Public Administration and Development*, **20** (1), 17–28.

Grimes, M. (2010), 'Strategic Sensemaking within Funding Relationships: The Effects of Performance Measurement on Organisational Identity in the Social Sector', *Entrepreneurship: Theory and Practice*, **34** (4), 763–783.

Harji, K. and E. T. Jackson (2018), 'Facing Challenges, Building the Field: Improving the Measurement of the Social Impact of Market-Based Approaches', *American Journal of Evaluation*, Online First.

Heidegger, M. (1927/1962), *Being and Time* (J. Macquarrie and E. Robinson, Trans.), Oxford: Blackwell.

Hudon, M. and J. Sandberg (2015), 'The Ethical Crisis in Microfinance: Issues, Findings, and Implications', *Business Ethics Quarterly*, **23** (4), 561–589.

Jäger, U. P. and M. D. Rothe (2013), 'Multidimensional Assessment of Poverty Alleviation in a Developing Country: A Case Study on Economic Interventions', *Nonprofit Management and Leadership*, **23** (4), 511–528.

Jarzabkowski, P. and D. Seidl (2008), 'The Role of Meetings in the Social Practice of Strategy', *Organization Studies*, **29** (11), 1391–1426.

Jepson, P. (2005), 'Governance and Accountability of Environmental NGOs', *Environmental Science & Policy*, **8** (5), 515–524.

Kania, J. and M. Kramer (2011), 'Collective Impact', *Stanford Social Innovation Review*, **9** (1), 36–41.

Keevers, L., L. Treleaven, C. Sykes and M. Darcy (2012), 'Made to Measure: Taming Practices with Results-based Accountability', *Organization Studies*, **33** (1), 97–120.

Khavul, S. (2010), 'Microfinance: Creating Opportunities for the Poor?' *The Academy of Management Perspectives*, **24** (3), 58–72.

Kramer, M., R. Graves, J. Hirschhorn and L. Fiske (2007), *From Insight to Action: New Directions in Foundation Evaluation Research*, Boston, MA: FSG Social Impact Advisors.

Kroeger, A. and C. Weber (2014), 'Developing a Conceptual Framework for Comparing Social Value Creation', *Academy of Management Review*, **39** (4), 513–540.

Lecy, J. H. Schmitz and H. Swedlund (2012), 'Non-Governmental and Not-for-Profit Organisational Effectiveness: A Modern Synthesis', *VOLUNTAS: International Journal of Voluntary and Nonprofit Organisations*, **23** (2), 434–457.

Lee, C. and B. Nowell (2015), 'A Framework for Assessing the Performance of Nonprofit Organisations', *American Journal of Evaluation*, **36** (3), 299–319.

Lee, M. (2004), 'Public Reporting: A Neglected Aspect of Nonprofit Accountability', *Nonprofit Management and Leadership*, **15** (2), 169–185.

Liket, K. C., M. Rey-Garcia and K. Maas (2014), 'Why Aren't Evaluations Working and What to Do About It: A Framework for Negotiating Meaningful Evaluation in Nonprofits', *American Journal of Evaluation*, **35** (2), 171–188.

Lodhia, S. (2015), 'Exploring the Transition to Integrated Reporting Through a Practice Lens: An Australian Customer Owned Bank Perspective', *Journal of Business Ethics*, **129** (3), 585–598.

Marée, M. and S. Mertens (2011), 'The Limits of Economic Value in Measuring the Performance of Social Innovation'. In A. Nicholls and A. Murdock (Eds.), *Social Innovation: Blurring Boundaries to Reconfigure Markets*, Basingstoke, UK: Palgrave Macmillan, pp. 114–136.

Mayhew, F. (2012), 'Aligning for Impact: The Influence of the Funder–Fundee Relationship on Evaluation Utilization', *Nonprofit Management and Leadership*, **23** (2), 193–217.

Miettinen, R., D. Samra-Fredericks and D. Yanow (2009), 'Re-Turn to Practice: An Introductory Essay', *Organisation Studies*, **30** (12), 1309–1327.

Molecke, G. and J. Pinkse (2017). 'Accountability for Social Impact: A Bricolage Perspective on Impact Measurement in Social Enterprises', *Journal of Business Venturing*, **32** (5), 550–568.

Mouchamps, H. (2014), 'Weighing Elephants with Kitchen Scales: The Relevance of Traditional Performance Measurement Tools for Social Enterprises', *International Journal of Productivity and Performance Management*, **63** (6), 727–745.

Moxham, C. and R. Boaden (2007), 'The Impact of Performance Measurement in the Voluntary Sector', *International Journal of Operations & Production Management*, **27** (8), 826–845.

Mulgan, G. (2010), 'Measuring Social Value', *Stanford Social Innovation Review*, **8** (3), 38–43.

Mulgan, G. (2011), 'The Theoretical Foundations of Social Innovation'. In A. Nicholls and A. Murdock (Eds.), *Social Innovation: Blurring Boundaries to Reconfigure Markets*, Basingstoke, UK: Palgrave Macmillan, pp. 33–65.

Nicholls, A. (2009), '"We Do Good Things, Don't We?": "Blended Value Accounting" in Social Entrepreneurship', *Accounting, Organisations and Society*, **34** (6–7), 755–769.

Nicholls, A. (2010), 'The Functions of Performance Measurement in Social Entrepreneurship: Control, Planning and Accountability'. In K. Hockerts, J. Mair and J. Robinson (Eds.), *Values and Opportunities in Social Entrepreneurship*, New York: Palgrave Macmillan, pp. 241–272.

Nicolini, D. (2012), *Practice Theory, Work, and Organisation: An Introduction*, Oxford: Oxford University Press.

Orlikowski, W. J. (2007), 'Sociomaterial Practices: Exploring Technology at Work', *Organisation Studies*, **28** (9), 1435–1448.

Ormiston, J. (forthcoming), 'Blending Practice Worlds: Impact Assessment as a Transdisciplinary Practice', *Business Ethics: A European Review*.

Ormiston, J. and R. Seymour (2011), 'Understanding Value Creation in Social Entrepreneurship: The Importance of Aligning Mission, Strategy and Impact Measurement', *Journal of Social Entrepreneurship*, **2** (2), 125–150.

Ospina, S., W. Diaz and J. F. O'Sullivan (2002), 'Negotiating Accountability: Managerial Lessons from Identity-Based Nonprofit Organizations', *Nonprofit and Voluntary Sector Quarterly*, **31** (1), 5–31.

Pathak, P. and P. Dattani (2014), 'Social Return on Investment: Three Technical Challenges', *Social Enterprise Journal*, **10** (2), 91–104.

Ramus, T. and A. Vaccaro (2017), 'Stakeholders Matter: How Social Enterprises Address Mission Drift', *Journal of Business Ethics*, **143** (2), 307–322.

Rawhouser, H., M. Cummings and S. L. Newbert (2017), 'Social Impact Measurement: Current Approaches and Future Directions for Social Entrepreneurship Research', *Entrepreneurship Theory and Practice*, Online First.

Ruff, K. and S. Olsen (2018), 'The Need for Analysts in Social Impact Measurement: How Evaluators Can Help', *American Journal of Evaluation*, Online First.

Saj, P. (2013), 'Managing Multiple Accountabilities: Balancing Outputs, Inputs and Behaviours to Implement Strategy in a Large Australian Charity', *Third Sector Review*, **19** (2), 51–78.

Sandberg, J. and G. Dall'Alba (2009), 'Returning to Practice Anew: A Life-World Perspective', *Organisation Studies*, **30** (12), 1349–1368.

Sawhill, J. and D. Williamson (2001), 'Mission Impossible? Measuring Success in Nonprofit Organisations', *Nonprofit Management & Leadership*, **11** (3), 371–386.

Schatzki, T. R. (2001), 'Introduction: Practice Theory'. In T. R. Schatzki, K. K. Cetina and E. von Savigny (Eds.), *The Practice Turn in Contemporary Theory*, London: Routledge, pp. 10–23.

Schmitz, H. P., P. Raggo and T. Bruno-van Vijfeijken (2012), 'Accountability of Transnational NGOs: Aspirations vs. Practice', *Nonprofit and Voluntary Sector Quarterly*, **41** (6), 1175–1194.

Seelos, C. and J. Mair (2005), 'Social Entrepreneurship: Creating New Business Models to Serve the Poor', *Business Horizons*, **48** (3), 241–246.

Smith, B. R. and C. E. Stevens (2010), 'Different Types of Social Entrepreneurship: The Role of Geography and Embeddedness on the Measurement and Scaling of Social Value', *Entrepreneurship & Regional Development*, **22** (6), 575–598.

Smith, W. K., M. Gonin and M. L. Besharov (2013), 'Managing Social-Business Tensions: A Review and Research Agenda for Social Enterprise', *Business Ethics Quarterly*, **23** (3), 407–442.

Stevens, R., N. Moray and J. Bruneel (2015), 'The Social and Economic Mission of Social Enterprises: Dimensions, Measurement, Validation, and Relation', *Entrepreneurship: Theory & Practice*, **39** (5), 1051–1082.

Thomson, D. E. (2010), 'Exploring the Role of Funders' Performance Reporting Mandates in Nonprofit Performance Measurement', *Nonprofit and Voluntary Sector Quarterly*, **39** (4), 611–629.

Thomson, D. (2011), 'The Role of Funders in Driving Nonprofit Performance Measurement and Use in Strategic Management', *Public Performance & Management Review*, **35** (1), 54–78.

Torjman, S. (1999), *Are Outcomes the Best Outcome?* Ottawa, Canada: Caledon Institute of Social Policy.

United Way of America (2000), *Agency Experiences with Outcome Measurement: Survey Findings*, Alexandria, VA: United Way of America.

Vaara, E. and R. Whittington (2012), 'Strategy-as-Practice: Taking Social Practices Seriously', *The Academy of Management Annals*, **6** (1), 285–336.

Whittington, R. (1996), 'Strategy as Practice', *Long Range Planning*, **29** (5), 731–735.

Whittington, R. (2006), 'Completing the Practice Turn in Strategy Research', *Organization Studies*, **27** (5), 613–634.

Whittington, R. (2011), 'The Practice Turn in Organisation Research: Towards a Disciplined Transdisciplinarity', *Accounting, Organisations & Society*, **36** (3), 183–186.

Willems, J., S. Boenigk and M. Jegers (2014), 'Seven Trade-offs in Measuring Nonprofit Performance and Effectiveness', *VOLUNTAS: International Journal of Voluntary and Nonprofit Organisations*, **25** (6), 1–23.

Wittgenstein, L. (1967), *Philosophische Untersuchungen. Philosophical Investigations; Translated by GEM Anscombe. Reprinted*, Malden, MA: Blackwell Publishing.

Zappala, G. and M. Lyons (2009), 'Recent Approaches to Measuring Social Impact in the Third Sector: An Overview', *CSI Background Paper*, Vol. 5. Sydney: The Centre for Social Impact.

Zundel, M. and P. Kokkalis (2010), 'Theorizing as Engaged Practice', *Organisation Studies*, **31** (9/10), 1209–1227.

6 When form follows function: governing for good

Deborah Burand

Much of the legal scholarship taking place in the field of social entrepreneurship (SE) has concentrated on critiquing and comparing the legal forms available to enterprises that seek to achieve both profits for owners and positive impacts for a broader range of stakeholders who may or may not own shares of these ventures (Ball, 2016, p. 924). While this scholarship usefully catalogues the laws in the United States and elsewhere that have been enacted recently to permit a range of legal forms to house SE activities, it is time to advance a broader, legal scholarship agenda in the field of SE – one that prioritizes function over form, grounds theoretical observations in empirical research, and examines the role that corporate governance plays in the evolution of the SE field.

I am not alone in calling for an expanded legal agenda in the field of SE. Professors Dana Brakman Reiser and Steven A. Dean in their recent book note that "new thinking from the legal community" is necessary to help lower the risk that social enterprises fail to deliver on their commitments to blend mission and profit (Brakman Reiser and Dean, 2017, pp. 4–5).

Some of that new thinking is likely to come from legal practitioners as they represent social enterprises and those who invest in social enterprises. But there is also an important role for legal scholars to play. Namely, by extending legal scholarship beyond existing critiques of the necessity and efficacy of creating new legal forms for enterprises that plan to engage in SE, legal scholars can contribute to this nascent field by assisting in the development of more robust legal infrastructures that support and advance SE wherever it may be housed – in nonprofit organizations, in start-up for-profit organizations, or even in existing corporations (both those whose shares are privately held and those whose shares are publicly traded). One important outgrowth of this broader agenda for legal scholarship is to come to a more informed view as to what "good governance" looks like in the social enterprise context, not only for the social enterprise but also for those who invest in social enterprises.

Current state of legal scholarship

Why has legal scholarship to date focused on the legal *forms* that companies engaged in SE take while paying less attention to how and why companies devoted to blending profit and purpose *function* as they do?

One obvious answer is that the enactment of new laws opens new areas of inquiry for legal scholarship. Accordingly, the recent focus of scholarship on the legal forms available to social enterprises is understandable given the last decade's proliferation of social enterprise statutes that have created new legal forms in the United States and beyond. For example, during the period starting with the state of Vermont's recognition of the low-profit limited liability company (L3C) in 2008 and ending on 31 December 2017, 38 jurisdictions in the United States had enacted at least one form of a social enterprise statute (Jones et al., 2018, p. 9; Social Enterprise Law Tracker[1]).

Enactment of social enterprise statutes that create new legal forms to house social entrepreneurial activities is gaining traction outside the United States too. For example, in 2005, the United Kingdom created the community interest company (CIC). The CIC is now the "legal form of choice" for social enterprises in the United Kingdom that adopt the business model required of CICs (Regulator of Community Interest Companies, 2018, p. 5). And Italy, in 2015, was the first country outside of the United States to adopt benefit corporation legislation (Societa Benefit, 2015).

Another likely reason that legal scholarship has focused on the new legal forms being created for social enterprises can be found in that old joke about why a man looking for lost keys at night limited his search to the ground under the one bright streetlight on his block. When asked if this was the spot where he lost his keys, the man replied, "Probably not, but this is the only place where I can see." Similarly, legal scholars may be challenged in finding data that can support a broader line of legal inquiry beyond analyzing laws and regulations that are publicly available. Restricting legal inquiry to data that is easily available, however, will limit legal scholars' usefulness to this field just as much as a search that is confined to only the spot illuminated by a streetlight limits the likelihood of finding lost keys.

Governing for good

The legal issues that surround the corporate governance of social enterprises have both philosophical and practical underpinnings. At the heart of this discussion is a longstanding debate over the very purpose of corporations in society (Murray, 2012, p. 16). The answer to this question has practical implications as it informs the extent to which corporate directors are required to place the interests of shareholders above all else.

It is one thing to say that shareholder interests should come before other interests in shaping the decisions of corporate directors (Strine, 2015, p. 768). It is quite another thing, however, to suggest, as Milton Friedman famously espoused in 1970, that shareholder wealth maximization is the *primary* purpose of corporations. Although a chorus of legal scholars led by Professor Lynn Stout has argued that maximizing shareholder wealth has never been legally required of corporations incorporated in the United States (Stout, 2008, pp. 168–176), the Friedman view that corporations must seek to maximize shareholder wealth not only persists but "commands wide acceptance among both economists and lawyers today" (Hart and Zingales, 2017, p. 248).

This debate over corporate purpose has spilled over to the SE field fueled, in part, by those who worry that shareholder primacy considerations will constrain corporations (particularly corporate directors) from giving significant weight to other societal interests when making decisions. At the risk of oversimplifying their position, proponents of some of the new legal forms for corporations that are being adopted in the United States, such as benefit corporations, argue that these new forms provide necessary legal protections so that directors of social enterprises can include and even prioritize social and environmental considerations when making decisions. Without the express benefit mandates set forth in social enterprise statutes, so the argument goes, the duty to maximize profits will limit the ability of directors and officers to consider broader social benefits if such considerations risk reducing corporate profits.

On the other side of this debate are those who take the position that many of the traditional legal corporate forms in the United States can accommodate a blending of profit and purpose. They worry that the new legal forms for social enterprises are unnecessary at best, and, at worst, reinforce an overly narrow delineation of the fiduciary duties of corporate directors in more traditional private and public companies. They point to the unhelpful complexity arising as varying jurisdictions impose different statutory obligations under the social enterprise statutes. They also point to the lack of certainty about how these obligations will be interpreted by courts.

Eventually the debate over the necessity of creating new legal forms for enterprises intent on delivering profits and social impact should resolve itself as both new and more traditional legal forms are tested in the marketplace and in the courts. To support that process, however, more empirical data is needed about the adoption rates and adherence to mission taking place within and outside of the new legal forms as enterprises seek to embed both profit and purpose into their business models.

According to some scholars, a "theoretical landscape of social enterprise governance is emerging," but they also observe that empirical research, which tests the performance and appropriateness of various governance mechanisms, lags behind these theoretical groundings (Mason and Royce, 2007, pp. 59–63). Therefore, legal scholarship that contributes to developing a theory of how to "govern for good" and bolsters that theory with empirical evidence should be in high demand and relevance long after the dust settles among those arguing over which legal forms social enterprises should take.

There are a range of governance models that companies that are intent on blending purpose and profit might employ. At one end of the spectrum are those who argue that social enterprises should adopt a shareholder-centric approach to corporate governance. Proponents of this view look at shareholders as residual owners of companies and argue that the interests of shareholders, therefore, should deserve the greatest attention (and protections) of corporate law.

At the other end of the spectrum are those who are of the view that social enterprises should adopt a stakeholder approach to corporate governance, called here the "participatory governance" model. This model would seek legal protections and create enforceable rights for certain groups of stakeholders even if they hold no ownership interest in the social enterprise. These stakeholders might include local communities, employees, beneficiaries/customers, or environmental interests. Some are going even a step beyond participatory governance and are advancing a stewardship governance model, whereby companies are controlled by autonomous steward owners. Under the stewardship governance model, governance rights are separated from dividend rights in order to eliminate financial incentives that otherwise might distract the governing body of a company (its steward owners) from furthering the company's intended social impacts.

Somewhere in the middle between the shareholder-centric and participatory/ stewardship models is yet a third way, called here the "enlightened shareholder value" model, whereby non-shareholder interests may be taken under consideration to the extent that advancing such interests is believed to generate shareholder wealth over the long term. This enlightened shareholder model, while putting shareholders' interests at the center of corporate decision making, makes room for corporate decision makers to entertain courses of action that take into consideration broader societal goals so long as these actions are believed to advance shareholder interests over the long term.

All three of these governance models are wrestling with interrelated questions – first, defining what a corporation should do, and, second, determining who should hold the corporation accountable for meeting that intended purpose. Here it is worth looking at other sources of legal standing that could be used to strengthen corporate accountability in the conduct of social entrepreneurial activities. This could include rights of action arising out of deceptive advertising claims or other forms of consumer protections. At least one country has taken this tack. Italy's benefit corporation legislation authorizes the Italian Competition Authority to fine those Italian benefit companies that do not adhere to their stated pursuit of social benefits (Societa Benefit, 2015 – see Article 6, Italian Competition Authority's competences). Further legal scholarship and analysis could be very helpful in this area, particularly as other jurisdictions consider expanding the legal toolbox, beyond laws aimed at enterprise incorporation, to strengthen the accountability of the SE field.

The law, as should be evident from the above discussion, plays an important role in directing corporate behavior. Yet, much of the substance of corporate governance typically is not mandated by statutes, case law, or regulation. Rather, corporate governance more often is influenced by norms than by legal requirements. These norms frequently take shape in the form of "internal corporate law" as evidenced by charter documents, corporate policies and procedures.

Accordingly, it is worth asking if corporate charters (whether required by legislation or contracted privately) can lock social missions durably into place. More to the point, will a mission-oriented, charter lock survive pressure from future shareholders who later may want to change the charter so as to shift or lower the primacy of the social mission? Similarly, which structural governance mechanisms – such as staggered board terms, dual classes of stock, founder locks, perpetual (self-nominating) boards, golden shares, steward owners, to name a few – best protect the mission of a social enterprise? Currently social enterprises around the world are experimenting with these and other governance mechanisms. More empirical research is necessary, however, to evaluate how well these governance mechanisms withstand changing shareholder interests or leadership successions.

Norms are not limited to individual companies, however. They also can be "transfirm" – that is, they reach across firms within an industry or sector (Ball, 2016, p. 959, citing Rock and Wachter, 2001). Accordingly, a point of legal inquiry for further scholarly investigation is to identify the sources and efficacy of transfirm norms that are emerging in the SE field. Are the new social enterprise statutes filling this norm-setting role or are there other sources of transfirm norms, such as external pressures from the marketplace or funders of social enterprises, that are more influential in shaping the corporate governance and, hence, decision making of social enterprises?

There is at least anecdotal evidence that benefit corporation legislation may be starting to generate transfirm norms in the SE field. As a result, even where social enterprises do not incorporate formally as a benefit corporation, some are including language in their charter documents or are adopting governance structures that reflect much of what one finds mandated in benefit corporation legislation. Before we celebrate the emergence of transfirm norms within the SE field, however, more empirical research is required to understand what these norms are, where they are coming from, and how they are being used to shape corporate behavior.

Beyond corporate governance of the social enterprise

Some legal scholars and practitioners have dared to ask whether this emphasis on the constructs of governance within social enterprises may be misplaced. If, as some argue, "reliance on enforcement from within" is unwarranted given the reluctance of corporate directors to sue each other or jurisdictional limitations on the extent to which shareholders and other stakeholders have access to judicial remedies to hold social enterprises accountable to their social missions (Brakman Reiser and Dean, 2017, p. 73), are there other legal tools that can help to enforce the durable blending of profit and purpose?

One obvious source of legal tools can be found in the private contracting that is taking place among social enterprises and their funders. More specifically, some impact investors and their lawyers are creating new financial products or modifying investment structures used in venture capital to give social entrepreneurs more long-term control over the social missions of their enterprises. The effectiveness of new financial products and investment structures to preserve and support mission goals remains to be seen, but certainly warrants further exploration and investigation by legal scholars.

But this is not simply about creating new financial products and contractual relationships. The governance structures of those institutions that invest in social enterprises also deserve more study. This call for more scholarly attention to the governance of investors in social enterprises comes against a backdrop of the changing world of corporate finance. In the decades since Friedman's wealth maximization pronouncement, there have been dramatic shifts in the ownership of public companies (Hart and Zingales, 2017, pp. 264–265, citing Zingales, 2009). Yet the story does not end there for one can observe another shift taking place among investors. Some investors are choosing to invest in portfolio companies based on the extent of alignment with their social values; still others are seeking to shape portfolio company behavior so as to generate more social value alignment as a result of their investments.

It remains to be seen how investor interest in generating social as well as financial returns plays out in the marketplace. Is it, as some argue, "virtually impossible" for investors to affect the behavior of publicly traded firms by buying and selling their shares in the secondary market (Brest et al., 2018, p. 6)? Or do socially oriented investors need to join forces with other stakeholders to shift portfolio company behavior? Even for companies whose shares trade in private markets, to what extent can socially oriented investors shape portfolio company behavior? Does this require a trade-off between non-concessionary and concessionary financial terms? And, if so, how does such a trade-off square with the duties an institutional investor or a foundational investor owes to those whose money it manages?

Answering these questions is complicated by the differing (and evolving) approaches taken by various jurisdictions and regulatory regimes regarding investor behavior. Uncertainty about what the law requires of different types of investors may be having a chilling effect on both the amount and sources of capital flowing to social enterprises. Not surprisingly, impact investing advocates like the Global Impact Investing Network (GIIN) have begun to call for enhanced policy and regulation to catalyze growth in impact investing by creating a supportive regulatory environment for investors as well as for their portfolio companies (Bouri et al., 2018, p. 7). To create conducive policy and regulatory frameworks, however, requires further study and understanding about the governance structures of those that might consider investing in social enterprises.

Conclusion

This is a call to advance a broader, legal scholarship agenda in the field of SE – one that prioritizes function over form, grounds theoretical observations in empirical research, and highlights the increasingly important role that corporate governance is likely to play in the evolution of the SE field. In my view, corporate governance is likely to prove a more useful tool for ensuring the durable blending of purpose and profit than do the legal forms that house social entrepreneurial activities. But it is not only the corporate governance of social enterprises that matters. Governance structures of those that invest in social enterprises matter too. Legal scholarship that focuses exclusively on how social enterprises are formed and governed runs the risk of overlooking another important driver of corporate behavior – that is, the investors that are mobilizing and aggregating sources of capital for companies engaged in SE. This is an area that also is ripe for further legal inquiry and analysis.

NOTE

1 Social Enterprise Law Tracker, Grunin Center for Law and Social Entrepreneurship at NYU School of Law, accessed 21 July 2018 at www.socentlawtracker.org.

References

Ball, A. (2016), 'Social Enterprise Governance', *University of Pennsylvania Journal of Business Law*, **18**, 919–984.

Bouri, A., Mudalia, A., Schiff, H., Bass, R. and Dithrich, H. (2018), *Roadmap for the Future of Impact Investing: Reshaping Financial Markets*, Global Impact Investing Network – GIIN, accessed 1 September 2018 at https://thegiin.org/assets/GIIN_Roadmap%20for%20the%20Future%20of%20Impact%20Investing.pdf.

Brakman Reiser, D. and Dean, S. (2017), *Social Enterprise Law: Trust, Public Benefit, and Capital Markets*, New York, NY, USA: Oxford University Press.

Brest, P., Gilson, R.J. and Wolfson, M.A. (2018), 'How Investors Can (and Can't) Create Social Value', *ECGI Working Paper Series in Law*, Working Paper No. 394/2018, 1–27.

Hart, O. and Zingales, L. (2017), 'Companies Should Maximize Shareholder Welfare Not Market Value', *Journal of Law, Finance, and Accounting* **2**, 247–274.

Jones, R., Suh, M. and Thai, A. (2018), *Mapping the State of Social Enterprise and the Law, 2017–2018*, New York, NY, USA: Grunin Center for Law and Social Entrepreneurship at NYU School of Law.

Mason, C. and Royce, M. (2007), 'Fit for Purpose – Board Development for Social Enterprise', *Journal of Finance and Management in Public Services* **6**, 57–67.

Murray, J.H. (2012), 'Choose Your Own Master: Social Enterprise, Certifications, and Benefit Corporation Statutes', *American University Business Law Review* **2**, 1–53.

Regulator of Community Interest Companies (2018), Annual Report 2017–2018, accessed 1 September 2018 at https://www.gov.uk/government/publications/cic-regulator-annual-report-2017-to-2018.

Social Enterprise Law Tracker, Grunin Center for Law and Social Entrepreneurship at NYU School of Law, accessed 21 July 2018 at www.socentlawtracker.org.

Societa Benefit, LEGGE 28 December 2015, n. 208.

Stout, L. (2008), 'Why We Should Stop Teaching Dodge v. Ford', *Virginia Law and Business Review* **3**, 163–190.

Strine, L. (2015), 'The Dangers of Denial: The Need for a Clear-Eyed Understanding of the Power and Accountability Structure Established by the Delaware General Corporation Law', *Wake Forest Law Review* **50**, 761–793.

7 Community perspectives on social entrepreneurship

Helen Haugh and Andrew Brady

Introduction

Community entrepreneurship (CE) describes the process of creating a business venture in which ownership and control is vested in a community of some kind (Somerville and McElwee, 2011). CE has long been present in the economies and societies of developed and developing countries, whether in the 19th century cooperative movement and the Rochdale Pioneers, or the sometimes overlooked, communal provisioning traditions of communities in developing countries and indigenous communities (Peredo and MacLean, 2013). This chapter identifies the common ground shared by social and CE and distils four distinctive characteristics of CE. Community perspectives on mission and business models are then considered and a theory-rich CE research agenda is developed in five distinct areas: networks, social capital, social innovation, impact and sustainability.

Entrepreneurial diversity

Entrepreneurship refers to any "activity that produces or aims to produce value that can be expressed in monetary terms" (Somerville and McElwee, 2011, p. 319). Entrepreneurial goals range from profit to social orientation (Austin et al., 2006; Thompson et al., 2000). While commercial entrepreneurs pursue profit, social entrepreneurs pursue multiple goals (Borch et al., 2008), for example to satisfy basic, long-standing needs, create benefits for society (Tracey et al., 2005) and advance social change (Thompson et al., 2000; Mair and Marti, 2006; Urban, 2008).

Community enterprise and social enterprise

CE describes the collective processes involved in working for sustainable regeneration through a mix of economic, environmental, cultural and social activities. One result of this process is the creation of community enterprises: independent, not for private profit organizations, locally accountable and committed to involving local people in the process of community development. A community enterprise is thus a type of social enterprise (Nwankwo et al., 2007), and the two models share several common characteristics.

In the UK context, 31% of social enterprises describe themselves as community businesses (SEUK, 2017), and two of the common legal structures for social enterprise – Community Interest Companies and Community Benefit Societies – make an explicit link to communities in their names. The most common social objective for this broader population of social enterprises is 'improving a particular community', and over half involve the community in their decision making (SEUK, 2017).

In common with all forms of social enterprise, community enterprises are concerned with trading for a social purpose (Nwankwo et al., 2007). While both social and community enterprises emphasize trading activity as their primary source of income, in contrast to traditional charitable funding (such as donations, grants or legacies), Pearce (2003) places community enterprises in an overlapping space in the social economy, between social enterprises and those charities which trade to generate part, rather than all, of their income.

Another similarity between social enterprises and community enterprises is that, in addition to the economic impact of trading, both types of organization attempt to create social or environmental value. As Peattie and Morley (2008) suggest, social or environmental aims are the primary drivers for social enterprises, with trading being the mechanism by which they are achieved rather than an end in themselves. For community enterprises, these aims can encompass political, economic, social or environmental objectives, for the relevant locality (Somerville and McElwee, 2011).

Multiple goals imply a need to find new ways of measuring performance, as traditional financial measures are only of limited use (Costa and Pesci, 2016). This has led to a trend towards adopting tools to "assess impact on the communities in which they are embedded: their workforce, customers, service users and physical environment" (Ridley-Duff and Bull, 2016, p.132). These tools include Social Return on Investment and Social Accounting and Audit, the latter in particular having a focus on organizations as part of their communities. More recently, as proposed by Bailey (2012), specific methodologies to assess *community* impact for community enterprises have been piloted (see Willis et al., 2017).

Social enterprises have common features, but are diverse in business model (Alter, 2007; Teasdale, 2012), area of operation, legal structure, and industrial sector (SEUK, 2017). Similarly, community enterprises comprise a range of organizations and operate in diverse industries and contexts (Bailey, 2012), with UK examples including football clubs, hydroelectric schemes and community pubs (BLF, 2018).

Community entrepreneurship

The core concepts of CE are, first, community and, second, entrepreneurship. A community is a small basic administrative area, preferably as homogenous as possible (Borzaga and Defourny, 2001). In practice a community comprises aspects of both people and place. The relationships between people in communities are substantial contributors to economic and social well-being (OECD, 2001), and the significance of place connects people, history and attachment. Entrepreneurship is anchored in resource acquisition, opportunity recognition and value creation. CE is produced when community and entrepreneurship work together.

The literature suggests that distinguishing characteristics of CE lie in people, place, participation and governance. First, community enterprise purpose is inseparable from a defined population or sub-group (Bailey, 2012; Vestrum, 2014). While SE is rooted in individualism and often overlooks collective forms of entrepreneurship (Peredo and Chrisman, 2006; Austin et al., 2006; Urban, 2008; Wren Montgomery et al., 2012), CE is enacted by a defined group of people. Although a social entrepreneur may be the figurehead, for example Greg Macleod (Cape Breton Island), Jose Maria Arizmendiarreta (Mondragon, Basque) and Muhammed Yunus (microfinance), CE sustainability is dependent on community embeddedness.

Communities are in themselves constructed from shared understandings, values and practices that are continuously re-negotiated as people relate to everyday life (Johannisson, 2007). Communities are also socialization sites: through socialization a community moulds individual character towards acceptable norms of behaviour and interests coalesce around shared understandings of issues and actions. For example, Community Land Trusts emerged in the 1960s as a mechanism to acquire and hold in perpetuity land on which to provide affordable homes to people on low incomes (Peredo et al., 2017).

Second, CE embodies strong connections to place (Vidal and Keating, 2004; Bailey, 2012; Vestrum, 2014), which may be a physical or virtual locality. The conditions under which a community enterprise is created are often unique (Bailey, 2012): they arise in response to a defined neighbourhood need and orientate activities to meet the needs of local people and businesses (Bailey, 2012). The politics of place is inseparable from the political dimension of CE, empowerment and asset ownership (Clark et al., 2007), and from policy makers' attempts to build local capacity as a strategy to assist impoverished communities in becoming self-reliant (Peredo and Chrisman, 2006). For example, Community Development Corporations (CDC) are community-based organizations that aim to foster asset development (Vidal and Keating, 2004). Their primary activity is to conduct "revenue-generating business as a means of producing substantial economic and social progress in their immediate environment" (Block, 1971, p. 176). In doing so CDCs have also catalysed growth of private business in depressed areas (Vidal and Keating, 2004).

Third, CE requires community participation (Kerlin, 2006; Nwankwo et al., 2007; Bailey, 2012; Vestrum, 2014). While the deceptively benign notion of community participation has a universal appeal (Clark et al., 2007), the practical implications of securing and maintaining community participation are many. Community enterprises, by definition, have democratic structures that allow members of the community or constituency they serve to participate in the management of the organization (Tracey et al., 2005; Kerlin, 2006). Productive community participation can foster a sense of local ownership and bring about important insights into how entrepreneurial action can build from an area's existing strengths (Haughton, 1998; Smith, 2012).

Community organizations give people an active identity in society through enabling participation in local development rather than more passive roles such as bystanders or consumers, voters, and other functions ascribed to them by those in more powerful positions (Nel and Binns, 2000; MacIntyre, 2003). The community enterprise approach works because activism is community-led from below and inside (Smith, 2012). For example, the legislation for the Community Interest Company requires that activities are carried out for the benefit of a community and that a report of community engagement activities is provided annually to the government regulator (Haugh and Peredo, 2012).

Finally, community enterprises take a variety of legal forms in which commercial operations make a return on investment to the community (Adams and Hess, 2010). Unlike social enterprises, community enterprises are expected to adopt structures that allow community members to participate in organizational governance (Pearce, 2003). Practical governance actions include community election of trustees or directors who are expected to consult with stakeholders and make strategic decisions on the basis of community priorities (Nwankwo et al., 2007). For example, cooperative societies are businesses that are owned and run by their members and all members have an equal voice in determining what the business does. All cooperative societies share the values of self-help, democracy, equality and solidarity, underpinned by principles such as democratic member control, supporting other cooperatives and helping communities (Huybrechts and Haugh, 2018). It is through member governance that cooperative societies advance economic and social emancipation.

Community perspectives on social entrepreneurship

Turning now to consider community perspectives on SE, this section reviews community enterprise missions and business models.

Community enterprise mission

Community enterprise mission is grounded in the recognition that there are possibilities for communities to act, and community issues to address. The opportunities for community enterprise, however, are neither sufficiently profitable to attract the private sector nor politically strategic enough to warrant direct state provision (Hudson, 2009).

Stimulating economic development

This occurs as community enterprises identify existing markets and engage with them (Berkes and Davidson-Hunt, 2007). The community is the motivating force for stimulating enterprise and enterprising behaviour (Smith, 2012). The principle is that community owned and managed organizations are vehicles for advancing economic development. Indigenous communities have unique heritages, languages, cultural practices and spiritual beliefs (Johnstone, 2008) which can be brought into play in the local economy. Community enterprises may expand beyond the local to mainstream markets, for example by developing new lines of activity and trading in broader markets (Hudson, 2009), serving, and drawing resources from, a market beyond the local community and its economy (Block, 1971). CE is the process of mobilizing resources to develop new ventures in the form of activities, services and institutions for the common good of a community (Johannisson and Nilsson, 1989; Austin et al., 2006; Borch et al., 2008).

Community provisioning

This is the process of using local knowledge to create small-scale organizations to advance development and social change. The services provided vary between communities, depend significantly on location (Bailey, 2012) and may encompass a range of entrepreneurial actions, such as providing goods and services to local people that otherwise would not be provided to those that need them most (Hudson, 2009), for example community food banks.

Fostering community cohesion

The sites of CE are not restricted to lagging areas, depleted regions and poor people, and its principles can be applied universally. Community cohesion is about relationships between people and how they can be made more fruitful and mutually beneficial in a specific place (MacIntyre, 2003). The flexibility that community enterprises have in terms of self-governance (Bailey, 2012) enables them to offer social dividends to community members (Berkes and Davidson-Hunt, 2007).

Empowering communities

Many community enterprises advance empowerment by enabling communities to gain control of their local natural resources (Berkes and Davidson-Hunt, 2007) and creating enterprises that are under local political control (Kuuder et al., 2013). The uniqueness of communities means that each possesses distinctive characteristics, niches and resources (Wallace, 1999) and communities may look inwards to their own resources and potential to carve out some form of future for themselves and their families (Nel and Binns, 2000). Community enterprises also seek to change wider political policies, such as advocating for the community right to acquire assets from the state (Bailey, 2012).

Sustainable communities

Sustainable community economic development broadly concerns the development of stronger local economies by engaging with local communities in shaping their own destinies, taking responsibility for local strategies which seek long-term, durable solutions to addressing economic regeneration (Haughton, 1998). The strong area focus of community economic development is based on action to foster local self-help and long-term community self-reliance.

Community enterprise business models

Setting up a community enterprise may be challenging. However, a bigger task is to find a business model that is sustainable and effective in the community context. A business model generally refers to the configuration of a resource set to achieve the goals of an enterprise (George and Bock, 2011). Although use of the term 'business model' is widespread in the practice literature, we use it here to describe the main approaches to community entrepreneurial action.

Asset-based development business model

This business model describes the use of community assets to generate income and achieve impact (Hart, 2002). The assets may historically belong to the indigenous community (Berkes and Adhikari, 2006) or be acquired from other sources, such as transfer from central or local government, other government agencies, negotiations through the planning system, or purchased using acquisition grants and loans from a variety of public, private and charitable sources (Hart, 2002; Aiken et al., 2008; Bailey, 2012). The assets form the basis of strategies to provide various local services (Bailey, 2012; Kuuder et al., 2013).

Trading business model

Financial sustainability and autonomy is dependent on generating unrestricted income from sales. Examples of the types of goods sold by community enterprises include food (Austin and Garnett, 2011) and energy generation (Cato et al., 2008); in the service sector examples span tourism and cultural attractions (Borch et al., 2008; Kuuder et al., 2013) as well as theatre and events (Borch et al., 2008; Vestrum, 2014). The catalyst for formation may be dissatisfaction with current market provision. The football club FC United of Manchester was founded in 2005 by fans of Manchester United who were unhappy at the leveraged buyout of their club. The new club is owned by the community, regularly consults its member owners on ticket prices and delivers an extensive community programme involving 300 volunteers (Supporters Direct, 2017).

Community-based enterprise (CBE) business model

The CBE involves the whole community acting cooperatively to further economic and social development (Peredo and Chrisman, 2006). The CBE is an innovative response to impoverishment that is oriented around business-based community development arising from within the community itself, with common goals based directly on local economic, cultural, social and environmental needs. This business model combines traditional organizational and participatory skills with new processes and systems to respond to market challenges, an approach which has led, for example, to Choctaw Enterprises (started by the indigenous people of the Mississippi) establishing a number of businesses which now employ over 8,000 people in an area previously blighted by 80% unemployment (Welsch and Kuhns, 2002).

Employment training business model

Community enterprise business models may be specifically established to create secure jobs for people disadvantaged in the labour market (Alter, 2007). The work integration social enterprise (WISE) has been the subject of substantial research (Borzaga and Defourny, 2001; Pache and Santos, 2013). Employment training community enterprises have been noted in horticultural services (Handy et al., 2011) and the hospitality industry (Vestrum, 2014).

Public service business model

Revenue is generated from delivering public sector contracts to provide services to citizens (Hudson, 2009). Community-based organizations are held to bring additional benefits, for example in understanding need and co-designing services with commissioners. These enterprises may previously have been part of the public sector, before 'spinning out' as autonomous entities with structures designed to involve staff and communities more effectively. For example, Provide Community Interest Company now runs as a co-operative delivering community health care initiatives in the East of England (Provide CIC, 2017, p. 6).

Partnership business model

Community enterprises work in partnership with the public and private sectors, and provide a range of services to meet economic, social and environmental needs (Bailey, 2012). Communities are complex and heterogeneous, multilevel and include competing groups with different interests whose voices need to be heard, considered and responded to (Berkes and Davidson-Hunt, 2007; Block, 1971). The diversity is reflected in the different members' views on the use of community assets. Research has noted how local rivalries between place-based communities affected both policies for community engagement and opportunities for local partnership working (Clark et al., 2007).

Research agenda

Building on the review of community enterprise mission and business models, in this section a theory-rich research agenda is mapped out. In much of the entrepreneurship literature, communities have been treated as a contextual part of the environment and it was not until SE rose to prominence that the importance of social and cultural issues was noted. In CE, however, people and place are central.

Community perspectives on social networks

All economic activity is socially embedded and social networks are central to entrepreneurial processes (Birley, 1985; Witt, 2004). A social network describes and maps the type and extent of relationships that an actor, such as a community enterprise, is embedded within. Social network analysis gathers information about the connections between network members. For a community enterprise this is likely to include the local population and organizations. In addition, network analysis maps the content, frequency and value of exchange between network members (Kilduff and Tsai, 2003).

Prior research has found that social networks have been used to gain access to resources more cheaply than using market transactions, and to acquire resources that would not be available via market transactions (Witt, 2004). Networking is a central element of CE (Johannisson and Nilsson, 1989) and the networks are used to access knowledge, technology, capital and access to markets (Berkes and Davidson-Hunt, 2007). Social networks are thus an important element in the entrepreneurial process (Birley, 1985) in that the acquisition of resources is contingent on the ways that social structure brings people together (Burt, 1987).

While social networks have been fostered by CE (Gliedt and Parker, 2007), and have also been correlated with economic growth (OECD, 2001) and quality of health (Kawachi et al., 1997), we do not know the extent to which network characteristics determine the efficacy and sustainability of CE. Further research that investigated the structure, density and content of community entrepreneur and community enterprise networks would advance knowledge of community perspectives on SE, and may shed light on the different processes at work for individual social ventures and group-based community enterprises.

Community perspectives on social capital

Related to social networks is the concept of social capital, pioneered by Bourdieu (1986). Social capital describes the actual and potential resources embedded in network relationships (Bourdieu, 1986; Nahapiet and Ghoshal, 1998). Bonding social capital links members of the same community (Putnam, 2000) and can be leveraged to source labour and other resources for the community enterprise (Austin and Garnett, 2011; Somerville and McElwee, 2011). Bridging social capital links communities with others outside their community (Putnam, 2000) and has been used, for example, to find external partners (Berkes and Davidson-Hunt, 2007).

The role of community organizations that either formally or informally connect people together was noted most prominently by Putnam (2000). These connections build social capital, promote healthy democracies and contribute to well-being and prosperity. The more social capital a place has, the greater the capacity of its residents to overcome personal hardships, access economic opportunities and ensure effective governance. For example, social capital is important in the case of the jasmine growers of Karnataka (Handy et al., 2011). Producers and buyers are involved in repeated face-to-face interactions and reputation was essential for continued participation.

To advance knowledge on the determinants, creation and impact of social capital on community perspectives on SE, further research to investigate the formation, strength and durability of community social capital would be worthwhile. Comparisons of community enterprise performance where the community is strong in bridging social capital but weaker in bonding social capital, or vice versa, would also shed light on what may prove an important success factor.

Community perspectives on social innovation

Innovation describes the development and implementation of an idea that is new to an organization and that gives rise to a new set of activities to solve problems (Seelos and Mair, 2012). The definition of innovation is broad and extends to innovation in products, services, business models and organizational processes. There is a long tradition of innovation research (Rogers, 1983) and innovation processes in the private sector (Cohen and Levinthal, 1990). More recently interest in public and social sector innovation has increased (Jaskyte, 2011; Seelos and Mair, 2012; Osborne et al., 2008).

Social innovation refers broadly to new products, services and processes that solve societal and environmental problems (Moulaert et al., 2013) and has emerged as a new variant of innovation in which the aim is to generate new products, processes or services with social and environmental impacts (Adams and Hess, 2010; van der Have and Rubulcaba, 2016). Despite some definitional ambiguity (Adams and Hess, 2010), the potential of social innovation to resolve social and environmental problems has led to an increased interest from researchers (Brown and Wyatt, 2010; Young, 2011).

Country-level data about company innovative performance has accumulated; for example in the UK annual innovation data is published (e.g., DTI, 2003; BIS, 2010). We know less however, about community-level social innovation (Borch et al., 2008; Adams and Hess, 2010). Further research that investigated the capacity and willingness of communities to participate in and support innovative activity would advance knowledge about community perspectives of SE.

Community perspectives on social impact

Turning now to CE impact, prior research has noted that there are multiple impacts of community participation, building capacity at three levels. Individual-level impacts measure outcomes as they affect people's lives. Positive impact is reflected in better physical and mental health, higher educational achievement and better employment outcomes (Adams and Hess, 2010). Individuals may also profit from focussing on community and community welfare (and family) aspirations as opposed to material or financial ones (Dana and Hipango, 2011). Community-level impacts include lower crime rates, decreases in maltreatment of children and increased capacity for the community to respond to threats and interventions (Adams and Hess, 2010). Societal benefits concern poverty alleviation, reducing inequality, discrimination and social exclusion, enhancing social justice, and improved environmental awareness and management (e.g., Williams and Windebank, 2000; Handy et al., 2011; Teerakul et al., 2012). Cost savings on other types of intervention (such as incarceration, or hospital treatment) may also accrue as a result of the impact on individuals and communities (see Ridley-Duff and Bull, 2016).

The assessment of impact requires gathering data on mission, outputs, outcomes and societal change. For examples, CE is more likely to be empowering when relationships within communities are altered, creating new forms of democratic participation as well as economic activity (Clark et al., 2007) and power is devolved to local citizens (Hudson, 2009). Some community-based organizations are concerned only to improve the quality of life within their localities, for example by encouraging local democracy (MacIntyre, 2003), and so have little interest in influencing activity outside these very specific places. In other cases, the aim is to advocate that the voices of the poor and marginalized are heard in the policy-making process (Wallace, 1999).

There are many opportunities for further CE research to investigate impact conducted at specific levels and the connections between levels. For example, the community right to own and control land and other resources might be connected to a more radical agenda of self-determination (Aiken et al., 2008). How might participation in CE contribute to changing institutionalized structures and practices?

Community perspectives on sustainability

Economic growth is of little enduring value if it progressively erodes the environment, promotes inequality and exclusion, creates unhappiness or displaces social functions into the marketplace (Hart, 2002). The community enterprise is not pursued for capital growth alone, although profit is a necessary requirement for community enterprises to survive (Berkes and Davidson-Hunt, 2007; Block, 1971). Survival is also dependent on the ability of the community enterprise to meet the social mandate of the community to whom it is accountable.

Prior research has identified key constructs of sustainable CE. First, community enterprises foster the survival of local economies by creating local structures that serve the needs of communities and also act as development catalysts (Nel and Binns, 2000; Hart, 2002). Second, CE supports local communities to identify, collate and leverage local resources, skills and indigenous knowledge (Nel and Binns, 2000; Hart, 2002) and is thus based on ecologically sound and sustainable principles. Third, CE emphasizes cooperation rather than competition between groups (Smith, 2012) and thus avoids wasting resources and duplication. Fourth, community participation is fundamental because for community enterprise to be sustainable, the ideas must develop from within the community (Haugh and Pardy, 1999). And finally, CE shifts the community mindset from dependence and passivity to community action and enterprise (Block, 1971; Urban, 2008) and self-determination.

Further research that examined the relationships between community, context and growth would advance theory and practice of sustainable CE. For example, brico-lage and effectuation theories have been developed to explain how entrepreneurs make the best use of resources to hand, and it would be rewarding to extend our understanding of such resource acquisition processes in a community context, and to explore how local conditions influence the sustainability of different com-munity enterprise business models. Improved knowledge of community enterprise strategies for acquiring resources and exploiting opportunities would contribute to advancing both theory and practice.

Conclusion

Community perspectives on SE centre on the greater prominence given to people, place, participation and governance. Community enterprises situate people and place at the forefront of resource acquisition and opportunity recognition, crea-tion and exploitation. As their governance structures are designed to be directly accountable to local people, to develop strategies in response to community needs, they have greater local legitimacy than imposed, top-down solutions to community deficiencies. Examples of successful CE provide a road map for sustainable and context-sensitive growth from which all organizations, irrespective of mission, business model and legal structure, can learn.

Acknowledgement

The authors thank the Edmond de Rothschild Foundations and the Isaac Newton Trust for funding the Social Enterprise Productivity and Sustainability project on which this chapter is based.

References

Adams, D. and M. Hess (2010), 'Social innovation and why it has policy significance', *The Economic and Labour Relations Review*, **21**, 139–156.

Aiken, M., B. Cairns and S. Thake (2008), *Community Ownership and Management of Assets*, York: Joseph Rowntree Foundation.

Alter, S.K. (2007), *Social Enterprise Typology*, Virtue Ventures LLC.

Austin, B.J. and S.T. Garnett (2011), 'Indigenous wildlife enterprise. Mustering swamp buffalo (Bubalis bubalis) in northern Australia', *Journal of Enterprising Communities*, **5**, 309–323.

Austin, J, H. Stevenson, and J. Wei-Skillern (2006), 'Social and commercial entrepreneurship: Same, different or both?', *Entrepreneurship Theory and Practice*, **30**, 1–22.

Bailey, N. (2012), 'The role, organization and contribution of community enterprise to urban regeneration policy in the UK', *Progress in Planning*, **77**, 1–35.

Berkes, F. and T. Adhikari (2006), 'Development and conservation: Indigenous businesses and the UNDP Equator Initiative', *International Journal of Entrepreneurship and Small Business*, **3**, 671–690.

Berkes, F. and I.J. Davidson-Hunt (2007), 'Communities and social enterprises in the age of globalization', *Journal of Enterprising Communities*, **1**, 209–221.

Birley, S. (1985), 'The role of networks in the entrepreneurial process', *Journal of Business Venturing*, **1**, 107–117.

BIS (2010), *Annual Innovation Report*, London: Department of Business Innovation and Skills.

BLF (2018), 'What is a Community Enterprise?', available at www.biglotteryfund.org.uk (accessed 27 June 2018).

Block, C.E. (1971), 'Marketing techniques for the community-based enterprise', *Law and Contemporary Problems*, **36**, 173–190.

Borch, O.J., A. Forde, L. Ronning, I.K. Vestrum and G.A. Alsos (2008), 'Resource configuration and creative practices of community entrepreneurs', *Journal of Enterprising Communities*, **2**, 100–123.

Borzaga, C. and J. Defourny (2001), *The Emergence of Social Enterprise*, London: Routledge.

Brown, T. and J. Wyatt (2010), 'Design thinking for social innovation', *Stanford Social Innovation Review*, Winter, 30–35.

Bourdieu, P. (1986), 'The forms of capital', in J.G. Richardson (ed.), *Handbook for Theory and Research for the Sociology of Education*, Westport, CT: Greenwood Press, pp. 241–258.

Burt, R.S. (1987), 'Social contagion and innovation: Cohesion versus structural equivalence', *American Journal of Sociology*, **92**, 1287–1335.

Cato, M.S., L. Arthur, T. Keenoy and R. Smith (2008), 'Associative entrepreneurship in the renewable energy sector in Wales', *International Journal of Entrepreneurial Behaviour and Research*, **14**, 313–329.

Clark, D., R. Southern and J. Beer (2007), 'Rural governance, community empowerment and the new institutionalism: a case study of the Isle of Wight', *Journal of Rural Studies*, **23**, 254–266.

Cohen, W.M. and D.A. Levinthal (1990), 'Absorptive capacity: A new perspective on learning and innovation', *Administrative Science Quarterly*, **35**, 128–152.

Costa, E. and C. Pesci (2016), 'Social impact measurement: Why do stakeholders matter?' *Sustainability Accounting, Management and Policy Journal*, **7** (1), 99–124.

Dana, L.-P. and W. Hipango (2011), 'Planting seeds of enterprise. Understanding Maori perspectives on the economic application of flora and fauna in Aotearoa (New Zealand)', *Journal of Enterprising Communities*, **5**, 199–211.

DTI (2003), *Competing in the global economy. The Innovation Challenge*, London: DTI.

George, G. and A.J. Bock (2011), 'The business model in practice and its implications for entrepreneurship research', *Entrepreneurship, Theory and Practice*, **35**, 83–111.

Gliedt. T and P. Parker (2007), 'Green community entrepreneurship: Creative destruction in the social economy', *International Journal of Social Economics*, **34**, 538–553.

Handy, F., R.A. Cnaan, G. Bhat and L.C.P.M. Meijs (2011), 'Jasmine growers of coastal Karnataka: Grassroots sustainable community based enterprise in India', *Entrepreneurship and Regional Development*, **23**, 405–417.

Hart, L. (2002), *Asset-Based Development for Community-Based Regeneration Organizations*, London: Development Trusts Association.

Haugh, H. and W. Pardy (1999), 'Community entrepreneurship in north east Scotland', *International Journal of Entrepreneurial Behaviour and Research*, **5**, 163–172.

Haugh, H. and A.-M. Peredo (2012), 'Critical narratives of the origins of the community interest company', in R. Hull, J. Gibbon, O. Branzei and H. Haugh (eds), *Critical Perspectives of the Third Sector. Dialogues in Critical Management Studies*, Volume 1, London: Emerald, pp. 7–27.

Haughton, G. (1998), 'Principles and practice of community economic development', *Regional Studies*, **32**, 872–877.

Hudson, R. (2009), 'Life on the edge: Navigating the competitive tensions between the "social" and the "economic" in the social economy and its relations to the mainstream', *Journal of Economic Geography*, **9**, 493–510.

Huybrechts, B. and H. Haugh (2018), 'The roles of networks in institutionalizing new hybrid organizational forms: Insights from the European Renewable Energy Cooperative Network', *Organization Studies*, **39**, 1085–1108.

Jaskyte, K. (2011), 'Predictors of administrative and technological innovations in nonprofit organizations', *Public Administration Review*, **71**, 77–86.

Johannisson, B. (2007), 'Enacting local economic development – theoretical and methodological challenges', *Journal of Enterprising Communities*, **1**, 7–26.

Johannisson, B. and A. Nilsson (1989), 'Community entrepreneurs: Networking for local government', *Entrepreneurship and Regional Development*, **16** (3), 217–233.

Johnstone, H. (2008), 'Membertou First Nation indigenous people succeeding as entrepreneurs', *Journal of Enterprising Communities*, **2** (2), 140–150.

Kawachi, I., B.P. Kennedy, K. Lochner and D. Prothrow-Stith (1997), 'Social capital, income inequality and mortality', *American Journal of Public Health*, **87**, 1491–1498.

Kerlin, J.A. (2006), 'Social enterprise in the United States and Europe: Understanding and learning from the differences', *Voluntas*, **17**, 247–263.

Kilduff, M. and W. Tsai (2003) *Social Networks and Organizations*, London: Sage Publications.

Kuuder, C.-J.W., E. Bagson and I.O. Aalangdong (2013), 'Livelihood enhancement through ecotourism: A case of Mognori Ecovillage near Mole National Park, Damongo, Ghana', *International Journal of Business and Social Science*, **4**, 128–137.

MacIntyre, G.A. (2003), 'The third option: Linking top-down and bottom-up efforts in community-based development', *Humanomics*, **19**, 5–11.

Mair, J. and I. Marti (2006), 'Social entrepreneurship research: A course of explanation, prediction and delight', *Journal of World Business*, **41**, 36–44.

Moulaert, F., D. MacCallum, M. Mehmood and A. Hamdouch (2013), *The International Handbook on Social Innovation*, London: Edward Elgar.

Nahapiet, J. and S. Ghoshal (1998), 'Social capital, intellectual capital and the organizational advantage', *Academy of Management Review*, **23** (2), 242–266.

Nel, E. and T. Binns (2000), 'Rural self-reliance in South Africa: Community initiatives and external support in the former black homelands', *Journal of Rural Studies*, **16** (3), 367–377.

Nwankwo, E., N. Phillips and P. Tracey (2007), 'Social investment through community enterprise: The case of multinational corporation involvement in the development of Nigerian water resources', *Journal of Business Ethics*, **73** (1), 91–101.

OECD (2001), *The Well-Being of Nations. The Role of Human and Social Capital*, Paris: OECD.

Osborne, S., C. Chew and K. McLaughlin (2008), 'The once and future pioneers? The innovative capacity of voluntary organizations and the provision of public services: A longitudinal approach', *Public Management Review*, **10**, 51–70.

Pache, A.C. and F. Santos (2013), 'Inside the hybrid organization. Selective coupling as a response to competing institutional logics', *Academy of Management Journal*, **56**, 972–1001.

Pearce, J. (2003), *Social Enterprise in Anytown*, Portugal: Gulbenkian Foundation.

Peattie, K. and A. Morley (2008), *Social Enterprises: Diversity and Dynamics, Contexts and Contributions*, Cardiff: ESRC/Brass Research Centre.

Peredo, A.-M. and J. Chrisman (2006), 'Toward a theory of community-based enterprise', *Academy of Management Journal*, **31**, 309–328.

Peredo, A.-M., H. Haugh and M. McLean (2017), 'Uncommon forms of prosocial organizing', *Journal of Business Venturing*, **33**, 591–602.

Peredo, A.-M. and M. McLean (2013), 'Indigenous communities and the cultural captivity of entrepreneurship', *Business and Society*, **52**, 592–620.

Provide CIC (2017), 'Annual Report and Financial Statements', Colchester, Provide CIC.

Putnam, R. (2000), *Bowling Alone: The Collapse and Revival of American Community*, New York: Simon and Shuster.

Ridley-Duff, R. and M. Bull (2016), *Understanding Social Enterprise: Theory and Practice*, London: Sage Publications.

Rogers, E.M. (1983), *Diffusion of Innovations*, London: Free Press.

Santos, F.M. (2012), 'A positive theory of social entrepreneurship', *Journal of Business Ethics*, **111** (3), 335–351.

Seelos, C. and J. Mair (2012), *What Determines the Capacity for Continuous Innovation in Social Sector Organizations?* Rockefeller Foundation Report. Stanford Centre on Philanthropy and Civil Society.

SEUK (2017), *The Future of Business: State of Social Enterprise Survey 2017*, London: Social Enterprise UK.

Smith, R. (2012), 'Developing and animating enterprising individuals and communities. A case study from rural Aberdeenshire, Scotland', *Journal of Enterprising Communities*, **6**, 57–83.

Somerville, P. and G. McElwee (2011), 'Situating community enterprise: a theoretical explanation', *Entrepreneurship and Regional Development*, **23** (5–6), 317–330.

Supporters Direct (2017), 'Case Study: FC United', available at https://supporters-direct.org/articles/case-study-fc-united (accessed 4 July 2018).

Teasdale, S. (2012), 'What's in a name? Making sense of social enterprise discourses', *Public Policy and Administration*, **27** (2), 99–119.

Teerakul, N., R.A. Villano, F.Q. Wood and S.W. Mounter (2012), 'A framework for assessing the impacts of community-based enterprises on household poverty', *Journal of Enterprising Communities*, **6**, 5–27.

Thompson, J., A. Alvy and A. Lees (2000), 'Social entrepreneurship: A new look at the people and potential', *Management Decision*, **38** (5), 328–338.

Tracey, P., N. Phillips and H. Haugh (2005), 'Beyond philanthropy: Community enterprise as a basis of corporate citizenship', *Journal of Business Ethics*, **58** (4), 327–344.

Urban, B. (2008), 'Social entrepreneurship in Africa. Delineating the construct with associated skills', *International Journal of Entrepreneurial Behaviour and Research*, **14**, 346–364.

van der Have, R.P. and L. Rubalcaba (2016), 'Social innovation research: An emerging area of innovation studies, *Research Policy*, **45** (9), 1923–1935.

Vestrum, I. (2014). 'The embedding process of community ventures: creating a music festival in a rural community', *Entrepreneurship & Regional Development*, **26** (7–8), 619–644.

Vidal, A.C. and D.W. Keating (2004), 'Community development: Current issues and emerging challenges', *Journal of Urban Affairs*, **26**, 125–137.

Wallace, S.L. (1999), 'Social entrepreneurship: The role of social purpose enterprises in facilitating community economic development', *Journal of Developmental Entrepreneurship*, **4**, 153–174.

Welsch, H.P. and Kuhns, B.A. (2002), *Community-Based Enterprises: Propositions and Cases*, Chicago: DePaul University.

Williams, C.C. and J. Windebank (2000), 'Helping people to help themselves: Policy lessons from a study of deprived urban neighbourhoods in Southampton', *Journal of Social Policy*, **29** (3), 355–373.

Willis, D., S. Coutinho, A. Fitzpatrick and J. Williams (2017), 'The impact of community business on local communities: A feasibility study to test new measures based on the Community Life Survey', *Power to Change Research Institute Report No.9*.

Witt, P. (2004), 'Entrepreneur's networks and the success of start ups', *Entrepreneurship and Regional Development*, **16**, 391–412.

Wren Montgomery, A., P.A. Dacin and T.M. Dacin (2012), 'Collective social entrepreneurship: Collaboratively shaping social good', *Journal of Business Ethics*, **111** (3), 375–388.

Young, H.P. (2011), 'The dynamics of social innovation', *Proceedings of the National Academy of Sciences of the United States of America*, **108**, 21285–21291.

8 Collective social entrepreneurship

Roger Spear

Introduction

This chapter challenges some assumptions about the nature of social entrepreneurship (SE) – particularly the commonly held view that SE is based on the activities of heroic individuals. This view receives support through the media's cult of the entrepreneur, and from Western policy to support an enterprise culture. The field of SE has followed a similar path in the work of early popular writers, such as Bornstein (1998) and key academic founding figures in the field, such as Dees (2001). Foundations such as Schwab and Ashoka have also been very influential in promoting this narrative.

An alternative view is that while there are many impressive individuals creating social enterprise, this is not the only model and, in many cases, SE may be better understood as a result of collective action, involving groups of citizens (often with a cast of supporting stakeholders), or organisations, or networks and social movements. This perspective also fits better with European social economy traditions. Early contributors to this view include Spear (2006) and Haugh (2007). There is increasing recognition of this view, including Montgomery, Dacin and Dacin (2012), who define collective social entrepreneurship (CSE) "as collaboration amongst similar as well as diverse actors for the purpose of applying business principles to solving social problems" (p. 376). Note that a limitation of this definition, which reflects a general tendency, is that it emphasises the creation of social enterprise and the application of business principles, rather than social innovation, which encompasses a wider range of organisational and social change processes, practices, rules and regulations, as well as products/services (see Tepsie, 2014). The influential EMES Network[1] goes further in emphasising the collective dimension, stating that social enterprise is "an initiative launched by a group of citizens. Social enterprises are the result of collective dynamics involving people belonging to a community or to a group that shares a well-defined need or aim" (Defourny and Nyssens, 2008, p. 228).

This chapter continues by reviewing some key literature relevant to different types of CSE, and how these are embedded and contextualised and includes a discussion of different approaches. An outline of a future research agenda for CSE follows.

Literature on collective social entrepreneurship

Despite popular understandings of SE focusing on the initial start-up phase, the literature on CSE reveals that there are several relevant entrepreneurial phases:

- New start-up social enterprise;
- Transformation into social enterprise when another organisation, such as from the traditional voluntary sector, decides to adopt a social enterprise pathway by adopting an earned income stream; also includes: public sector spinoffs, and conversions of businesses, due to failure, succession crises, or endowments from philanthropic owners;
- Social growth: where social enterprises engage in scaling or replication.

While there has been considerable emphasis on successful social entrepreneurs, this hasn't given rise to a large number of studies on trait theories; even a recent paper on demographics and social enterprise focused on the influence of consumer demographics on success (Medina Munro and Belanger, 2017). Many studies have implicitly followed the advice of Gartner (1998, p. 11), who emphasises that "'Who is an entrepreneur?' is the wrong question," leading to researchers focusing on stage theories (from opportunity identification, and selection, to establishing a new enterprise; e.g. Haugh, 2007, adapted this model to SE). In contrast to rational economic perspectives, SE can also be considered to involve extended processes of effectuation where opportunities are constructed and shaped in collaboration with a range of actors/stakeholders (Corner and Ho, 2010). Similarly bottom-up grassroots approaches to SE, and social innovation (see Moulaert et al., 2013), argue that close involvement of beneficiaries is essential for addressing their needs.

A number of biases and constraints appear to limit the potential for the development of CSE. The cultural bias towards the heroic entrepreneur reduces the visibility and legitimacy of collective initiatives. This is reinforced by most economic theories which are unable to explain incentives for collective activity. There are legal and fiscal barriers to start-ups (ICF Consulting Services, 2015); and other institutional barriers to many of the transformation models (fiscal, insolvency, etc.); and market failures of investment finance limit the potential for social growth.

Institutional and policy measures supporting SE may also shape its collective dimension; cooperatives require more than one person to be founders; and although it may be possible for one person to set up a charity, they would require a Board of Trustees. And collective dynamics would influence the choice of organisational forms of start-ups and transformations. Theoretically researchers adopting a resource-based perspective have argued that disadvantaged people in particular may need support to establish a social enterprise. This might include financial resources, know-how, social capital, etc.; and alongside resource-based rationales, from an institutional perspective (Dart, 2004; Suchman, 1995) such collective groups may struggle to gain the legitimacy attached to the heroic social entrepreneur for their ventures.

Approaches to collective social entrepreneurship

This section begins by exploring the importance of context, and then outlines types of CSE – coalitions of stakeholders, partnerships, and networks and social movements; and the relationships within which they are embedded. It includes a discussion of the institutional and policy context supporting or constraining these different types.

Importance of context: embeddedness

In a Polanyian perspective (1968), the economy is organised according to three types of transactions: market, reciprocal, redistributive (state); and economic activity through the market is constrained by institutions and social and cultural relations (redistributive and reciprocal); thus the market does not function in an economic vacuum, but is embedded in society. This perspective helps explain how conventional business may seek to position itself purely in the market, and social enterprise may position itself in an embedded hybrid relationship with reciprocity and redistribution institutions – and thereby access a different range of resources, and a different legitimacy. Although there may be varying degrees of embeddedness of different social entrepreneurial initiatives, social relationships and networking are particularly important in place-based SE, such as community entrepreneurship: where the community are the beneficiaries and stakeholders within the community are the drivers of entrepreneurship. Johannisson and Nilsson (1989) argue that the (economic) success of communities is a result of local networking. Parkinson and Howorth (2008) note that the everyday language used by community entrepreneurs and stakeholders to legitimise their activities is in line with local moralities, rather than national policy inspired narratives of heroic social entrepreneurship. And, socially constructed territory identities can form a base for networks of cooperation in the social and solidarity economy (Richez-Battesti, 2018).

This local/territorial context helps shape community responses to local social problems. But there is also the institutional environment of agencies, intermediaries, organisations and regulatory regimes (Mason et al., 2018). These include innovation labs, incubators, social investment markets, including crowdfunding platforms, foundations, which form an ecosystem (see Chapter 2 by Roy and Hazenberg) for co-constructing social entrepreneurial initiatives. These ecosystems, including their policy contexts, are central in supporting or constraining CSE. This is particularly relevant for new-starts, and transformation models (e.g. public sector spinoffs).

Coalitions of stakeholders

Doherty et al. (2014, p. 431) argue "most social enterprises tend to be a coalition of multi-stakeholder groups." This type is commonly found in community entrepreneurship. Haugh (2007; see also Chapter 7 in this book) adapts the stage model of entrepreneurship (opportunity recognition, etc.) to include the mobilisation of stakeholders, noting the importance of two types of support networks: a formal one drawn largely from government provision and a tailor-made one developed for their specific needs. Haugh sees the early networking activity as hidden, and often volunteer supported. Similarly, Peredo and Chrisman (2006) emphasise the community as entrepreneur as well as beneficiary (dual roles), both creating and drawing upon social capital.

Stakeholders in the social entrepreneurs' network play very diverse roles, as economic resources for accessing skill and finance, and as brokers of information and expertise. They are often much more important than an economic resource; they can form important links in social capital networks; help to provide legitimacy in the community; and help to shape the social enterprise as guardians of its social values (cf Aiken, 2002). Managing the involvement of multiple stakeholders demands important process skills, where participation and user involvement are often emphasised, and volunteer input is needed. And Johannisson and Nilsson (1989) argue that networking is even more important for community entrepreneurs than for business entrepreneurs. For transformational and growth phases of social entrepreneurship, negotiation skills and access to higher-level professional expertise become more important.

Partnerships and collaborations

There are wide varieties of partnerships, and collaborations (Tracey, Phillips and Haugh, 2005; Vurro and Dacin, 2014). Some involve activities of mutual interest; others involve developmental roles such as corporate venturing (Agrawal and Sahasranamam, 2016), or NGOs sponsoring social entrepreneurship; and intermediaries can be different kinds of partners, for example universities, trades unions.

Much research on partnerships, rather than focusing on collaboration at the entrepreneurial start-up stage, has focused on established organisations collaborating entrepreneurially to exploit new business opportunities together with social benefits for the social enterprise and/or for the sector, for example fair trade (Huybrechts and Nicholls, 2013; Davies, 2009). Theoretically there tends to be a split between some studies focusing on collaborations leading to efficiency gains based on transaction costs economics, the business and strategy literature, or stakeholder theory (as noted by Huybrechts and Nicholls, 2013); but there is a growing interest in collaboration drawing on legitimacy theory. Huybrechts and Nicholls (2013) develop a staged approach examining how cross-sector collaboration evolves: who is aiming for legitimacy and why, legitimacy issues in the choice of partners, and how legitimacy evolves during the partnership. One clear difference is between same- and cross-sector partnerships.

Same-sector partnerships may offer social enterprise the potential for social growth, including through franchising. But there is evidence to indicate tensions between collaboration and competition (for funding and markets) (see Seanor and Meaton, 2008).

Advocacy partnerships often involve collaborations between social enterprise and advocacy organisations, both to improve market conditions and to increase legitimacy, including through certification systems – fair trade being a prime example. Advocacy may also involve lobbying government to change policy. Advocacy and trading might occur within the same organisation, or in its origins – Fairphone began as an NGO awareness campaign against mining in civil conflict regions, and built an online community, which helped marketing and crowdfunding to produce an ethical mobile phone (Akemu, Whiteman and Kelly, 2016).

Cross-sector partnerships involve collaborations between social enterprises, public and private sector organisations, which often have different interests, and so require distinct skills and strategies to negotiate. A normative literature highlights supposed synergies surrounding notions of complementary resources and mutual interests. However, it is unclear as to whether the rational benefits outweigh transaction costs (Weber et al., 2017), particularly since contradictory institutional logics and power imbalances often rise to the fore (Huybrechts and Nicholls, 2013).

Public–social enterprise collaborations may be at the local level, for example in community services, but also operate at a much larger scale through traditional welfare service provision partnerships. The growth of public service markets has transformed many traditional and local partnerships into mixed economies of service provision, whereby social enterprises compete with private and public sector providers; nonetheless at a smaller scale such partnerships may continue for reasons of mutual advantage, for example recognising the value of building social capital for community development.

Corporate–social enterprise collaborations appear to have been flourishing in recent years (Huybrechts and Nicholls, 2013) in the Global North in sectors such as recycling, community housing, micro-finance, and fair trade. This includes collaborations for competing in public services markets, where, for example, social enterprises have collaborated to support more demanding segments of work integration activities. Here there have been concerns that social enterprises are inadequately compensated due to their weaker position in the partnership between large primary contractors and smaller voluntary and community sector (VCS) providers. In the Global South, partnerships may be driven by interest in bottom of the pyramid markets, for example Grameen Bank's collaborations with Nortel, Danone, and Veolia.

Corporate Social Responsibility (CSR) partnerships: CSR motives clearly underlie many partnerships in the North and South. Tracey et al. (2005) examine the extent to which CSR can be moved from corporate philanthropy through grants and donations towards a corporate partnership where strategies are jointly developed for addressing social problems. They conclude that a partnership approach offers advantages of sustainability and effectiveness, despite the issues of inequality of power and resources.

Pooling and trading resources partnerships: Montgomery et al. (2012) examine same-sector and cross-sector collaborative strategies. Pooling resources within the same sector involves sharing resources and knowledge to increase efficiency and reduce costs. This may be through collaboration in supply chains, the setting up of collectively managed services, as well as alliances for certification, and advocacy. Cross-sector pooling can allow the aggregation of resources, for example Kiva's online platform (non-profit) aggregates donations for providing micro-loans, as well as coordinating micro-finance lenders to monitor and administer such loans. Same-sector trading resources facilitates learning and knowledge exchange as well as joint ventures. Cross-sector trading of resources may also involve sharing knowledge, organising skills and resources to form multi-partner alliances for social change. While these partnership strategies may support social growth and the development of new joint ventures, they also aid resilience.

Networks and movement-based CSE

Networks are a prominent theme in conventional entrepreneurship, both at the micro and meso levels where networks of interlinked firms collaborate for innovation and efficiency. This is based on the view that high trust in social networks facilitates economic transactions; and that specialised institutions supporting a particular business cluster allows the development of important knowledge capabilities. Doherty et al. (2014) argue that social entrepreneurs' network of stakeholders may bridge institutional voids to facilitate resource flows.

Davies (2009), drawing on fair trade examples, identifies several types of collaborative relationships (alliances and networks): networked ownership, networked supply chains, networked retail and distribution, networks for knowledge, information, and ideological development, trading and non-trading partnerships, forums and associations. Dufays and Huybrechts (2014) identify four foci in the literature on social networks and social entrepreneurship: embeddedness, coalition of actors in a collective dynamic, critical skills and mobilising actors in networks, and SE's impacts on social capital. There have been relatively few contributions relating to social movements and SE, including: Smith et al. (2017) and Montgomery et al. (2012). Social movements can be powerful drivers for social change, complementing institutional entrepreneurs and helping create new markets (fairtrade, renewable energy, recycling, ecological products and services, organic foods, hacker spaces and fab labs, etc.). This social movement approach offers a new perspective on the replication of SE and sectoral development. Furthermore, theories of resource mobilisation, together with framing strategies, can be used to explain how collective action can be achieved.

Future research agenda

Haugh (2012) argues that there are three ways for theory development: theory borrowing, theory extension, and theory generation. Dacin, Dacin and Tracey (2011) argue that SE research does not sufficiently build on entrepreneurship theory. However, it could be argued that since SE is on the boundary of several different research fields, it could strengthen its theory by building on these adjoining fields. With reference to CSE, these might include: community development, development studies (including indigenous communities), social movements theory, social innovation, and social and solidarity economy. For example, innovation and social movements theories could be better linked to SE (Smith, Fressoli and Thomas, 2014), since they reveal interesting dynamics around scaling, and the development of niches. And it may be the case that there is a reverse recognition of themes arising from collective social entrepreneurship, which reveal interesting but so far under-researched aspects of conventional entrepreneurship.

Several different theoretical themes are prominent in collective social partnership. Firstly, despite the influence of foundations on the development of social entrepreneurship, the field doesn't seem to have followed conventional entrepreneurship's emphasis on trait theories significantly; instead there are many authors who adopt stage theories, and recognise the collective dimension in social entrepreneurship. Furthermore, although there are competing (pre-)paradigms (Mauksch et al., 2017), there appear to be a core of theories drawn upon business strategy and resources (including social capital and non-market resources); resource mobilisation and utilisation; and legitimacy. And some researchers develop multi-level approaches combining theories. For example, Vestrum (2016) draws upon four sets of theories to study community entrepreneurship: entrepreneurial orientation, social embeddedness, resource dependence theory and legitimacy approaches. And there are broader critical approaches raising issues of ethics, social justice, structural inequality – all of which have a bearing on CSE.

Similarly, this theme could benefit from increasing the greater diversity of research methods. Ethnographic methods have been particularly useful in broadening the emphasis away from an elite group of entrepreneurs to "more encompassing representations," with an emphasis on social entrepreneurship embedded within the community (Mauksch et al., 2017). Going further, this contributes to seeing social enterprise as "a relational space beyond organisational type, a fluctuating network of entangled persons" (p. 121). And as Mauksch et al. (2017) argue, multi-sited ethnographies provide an opportunity for representations which offer new perspectives on partnership and network dynamics through "thick descriptions" of the social entrepreneurs in context. Actor-network theory offers a similarly revealing processual perspective through its constructivist material-semiotic approach, with a focus on distributed agency and collaborative practices for social change (Barinaga, 2017).

Three themes appear particularly relevant for the future development of CSE theory:

Cultural and constructivist perspectives

Nicholls's (2010) much quoted work on the pre-paradigmatic nature of social enterprise discourse emphasised the split between researchers' and foundations' models of SE. Collective social ownership, to a certain extent, has suffered from the dominance of the foundations' emphasis on the heroic social entrepreneur – and policy and ecosystems may also be strongly influenced by individualist models. However, the field of SE is not only constructed by academics and foundations, it is constructed both through (collective) agency and structural/institutional context and through the cognitive cultural dimension of shaping enterprise – narratives and discourses. Indeed Weick (1995) argues that organisations construct a view of the world in interaction with actors in their context; and social entrepreneurship builds its model of the enterprise in association with its stakeholders, networks and community. Thus, it is important to recognise how agency, structures/institutions, and cultural narratives construct and support different trajectories of social entrepreneurial activity. And an interesting research theme is how the collective dynamics in society (social movements, Polanyian double movements, etc.) influence (collective) entrepreneurship models.

Closely linked to the role of cultural narratives in constructing SE is the skill and knowledge required, such as facilitation skills in bottom-up support for CSE, including where supported by intermediaries. Sarpong and Davies (2014) argue that managers use three main strategies to legitimise the enterprise, including using compassionate enterprise narratives (stories) to acquire and support legitimacy claims. Despite an emphasis on business skills in the literature, there has been some consideration of other skills: Battilana and Dorado (2010) examine challenges of combining business with social skills with regard to hiring and socialisation processes. Dufays and Hubrechts (2014) note the skills required for linking and mobilising coalitions of stakeholders. In a similar vein, Montgomery et al. (2012) identified three important processes needed for collaboration: convening, framing, and multi-vocality. Tracey and Phillips (2011) highlight the political skills and connections required for social entrepreneurs to carry out institutional work to support the creation of new hybrid organisational forms. The skills and processes of how narratives are co-constructed, how this might differ from heroic leaders, including through story-telling, offer interesting future research themes.

SE as enterprise vs innovation vs social change

SE is frequently conceptualised as an activity resulting in social enterprise. However, SE is also about achieving social innovation and social change (Barinaga, 2012). Consequently, it is important "to acknowledge the multifaceted nature of entrepreneurship as social change . . . Irrespective of whether it is based on economic activity or not" (Dey and Mason, 2018, p. 85).

Early researchers on social innovation emphasise its collective dimension, user participation, and collective mobilisation for social innovation (Moulaert et al., 2013).

Similarly, social change frequently has a collective and more political dimension for democratising power structures and overcoming social exclusion and inequality. Thus, the development of the social innovation field raises theoretical issues for SE, such as the "institutional externalities" of social structure (Nicholls, 2018).

Additionally, Zasada (2017) argues that not all organisations will be equipped to successfully follow the social enterprise path, without considerable hybrid cultural tensions. Some organisations may be more effective adopting traditional VCS models. Following the same logic might reveal other patterns of entrepreneurial activity based on resistance and contestation – leading to different forms of activism, and alternativism – such as transition movements, advocacy campaigns; and alternative theoretical frameworks which link to the development of grassroots movements (Smith et al., 2017) – such as niches, landscapes, regimes.

Much hybridisation theorising privileges the market logic. But as Doherty et al. (2014, p. 9) assert, hybrid organisations combining different institutional logics are inevitably "sites of contradiction, contestation and conflict," it could be argued that different hybridity pathways might not prioritise the market logic, but give precedence to a social or community or voluntaristic logic. This broader view of CSE could inform hybridity research.

Evolutionary aspects

At the initial entrepreneurial phase, one interesting question is: how are collective dynamics structured into a social enterprise? Then as it becomes established/ transformed/grows, what trajectory it follows over time, and its impacts on context (stakeholders and networks), are further questions.

One outcome from mobilising a coalition of stakeholders for SE is that accountability to these stakeholders may be designed into the governance system, through, for example, multi-stakeholder boards (Spear and Hulgard, 2007; Spear, Cornforth and Aiken, 2009). These may evolve over time, as in the Italian social cooperatives, where insider stakeholders (workers/managers) have tended to increase their presence and influence. But the decision on institutional form (cooperative, non-profit, for profit, social enterprise, legal status) offers some constraints on the changing collective dynamic (level of participation, protection of collective assets). And as Haugh (2007) notes, some stakeholders may only expect temporary involvement in the coalition for SE. Partnerships for social growth (replication and scaling) can result in multi-organisational social enterprise with multi-stakeholder ownership and governance structures (like community development trusts with social enterprise subsidiaries).

These evolutionary aspects of SE are relatively under-researched, even though they are a central part of one SE trajectory: the commercialisation of non-profits (Young, 2013). In social economy organisations there is often a vigorous collective dimension, but degeneration (Michels, 1915), isomorphism, and commodification can lead to its decline. However, there are also studies indicating how the collective dimension may be maintained or regenerated (Aiken, 2002). Life-cycle studies might offer a slightly different evolutionary perspective where growth, scaling, replication, consolidation and failure could be examined; likewise, the multi-organisational character of many social enterprises as they evolve. And on a broader scale, sectoral approaches might offer comparisons with business cluster studies, the evolution of social movements, niche theories, and the symbiotic evolution of an ecosystem.

NOTE

1 www.emes.net.

References

Agrawal, A. and S. Sahasranamam (2016), 'Corporate social entrepreneurship in India', *South Asian Journal of Global Business Research*, **5** (2), 214–233.

Aiken, M. (2002), *Managing values: The reproduction of organisational values in social economy organisations*, PhD thesis, The Open University, UK.

Akemu, O., G. Whiteman and S. Kennedy (2016), 'Social enterprise emergence from social movement activism: The Fairphone case', *Journal of Management Studies*, **53** (5), 846–877.

Barinaga, E. (2012), 'Overcoming inertia: The social question in social entrepreneurship', in D. Hjorth (ed.), *Handbook on Organisational Entrepreneurship*, Cheltenham, UK: Edward Elgar Publishing, pp. 242–256.

Barinaga, E. (2017), 'Tinkering with space: The organizational practices of a nascent social venture', *Organization Studies*, **38** (7), 937–958.

Battilana, J. and S. Dorado (2010), 'Building sustainable hybrid organisations: The case of commercial micro-finance organisations', *Academy of Management Journal*, **53**, (6), 1419–1440.

Bornstein, D. (1998), 'Changing the world on a shoestring', *Atlantic Monthly*, **281** (1), 34–38.

Corner, P. D. and M. Ho (2010), 'How opportunities develop in social entrepreneurship', *Entrepreneurship Theory and Practice*, **34** (4), 635–659.

Dacin, M.T., P.A. Dacin and P. Tracey (2011), 'Social entrepreneurship: A critique and future directions', *Organization Science*, **22** (5), 1203–1213.

Dart, R. (2004), 'The legitimacy of social enterprise', *Nonprofit management and leadership*, **14** (4), 411–424.

Davies, I.A. (2009), 'Alliances and networks: Creating success in the UK fair trade market', *Journal of Business Ethics*, **86** (1), 109–126.

Dees, J.G. (2001), 'The meaning of "social entrepreneurship"', Center for the Advancement of Social Entrepreneurship, Duke University's Fuqua School of Business, USA.

Defourny, J. and M. Nyssens (2008), 'Social enterprise in Europe: Recent trends and developments', *Social Enterprise Journal*, **4** (3), 202–228.

Dey, P. and C. Mason (2018), 'Overcoming constraints of collective imagination: An inquiry into activist entrepreneuring, disruptive truth-telling and the creation of "possible worlds"', *Journal of Business Venturing*, **33** (1), 84–99.

Doherty, B., H. Haugh and F. Lyon (2014), 'Social enterprises as hybrid organizations: A review and research agenda', *International Journal of Management Reviews*, **16** (4), 417–436.

Dufays, F. and B. Huybrechts (2014), 'Connecting the dots for social value: A review on social networks and social entrepreneurship', *Journal of Social Entrepreneurship*, **5** (2), 214–237.

Gartner, W. B. (1988), '"Who is an entrepreneur?" is the wrong question', *American Journal of Small Business*, **12** (4), 11–32.

Haugh, H. (2007), 'Community-led social venture creation', *Entrepreneurship Theory and Practice*, **31** (2), 161–182.

Haugh, H. (2012), 'The importance of theory in social entrepreneurship research', *Social Enterprise Journal*, **8** (1), 7–15.

Huybrechts, B. and A. Nicholls (2013), 'The role of legitimacy in social enterprise-corporate collaboration', *Social Enterprise Journal*, **9** (2), 130–146.

ICF Consulting Services (2015), 'A map of social enterprises and their eco-systems in Europe: Executive Summary', European Commission: DG Employment, Social Affairs & Inclusion. Accessed 21 February 2019 at https://ec.europa.eu/social/main.jsp?advSearchKey=Map+of+social+enterprises+ and+their+eco-systems+in+Europe&mode=advancedSubmit&catId=22&doc_submit=&policyArea =0&policyAreaSub=0&country=0&year=0.

Johannisson, B. and A. Nilsson (1989), 'Community entrepreneurs: Networking for local development', *Entrepreneurship and Regional Development*, **1** (1), 3–19.

Mason, C., J. Barraket and C. Neesham (2018), 'Guest editorial', *Social Enterprise Journal*, **14** (2), 118–129.

Mauksch, S., P. Dey, M. Rowe and S. Teasdale (2017), 'Ethnographies of social enterprise', *Social Enterprise Journal*, **13** (2), 114–127.

Medina Munro, M. and C. Belanger (2017), 'Analyzing external environment factors affecting social enterprise development', *Social Enterprise Journal*, **13** (1), 38–52.

Michels, R. (1915), *Political Parties: A Sociological Study of the Oligarchical Tendencies of Modern Democracy*, New York: Hearst's International Library Company.

Montgomery, A., P. Dacin and M. Dacin (2012), 'Collective social entrepreneurship: Collaboratively shaping social good', *Journal of Business Ethics*, **111** (3), 375–388.

Moulaert, F., D. MacCallum and J. Hillier (2013). 'Social innovation: Intuition, precept, concept', in F. Moulaert et al. (eds), *The International Handbook on Social Innovation: Collective Action, Social Learning and Transdisciplinary Research*, Cheltenham, UK: Edward Elgar Publishing, pp. 13–24.

Nicholls, A. (2010), 'The legitimacy of social entrepreneurship: Reflexive isomorphism in a pre-paradigmatic field', *Entrepreneurship Theory and Practice*, **34** (4), 611–633.

Nicholls, A. (2018), 'Institutions for inclusive societies: Unfolding the complexity of institutional effects on socioeconomic inequality', Keynote Presentation, 10th International Social Innovation Research Conference (ISIRC), Heidelberg, Germany.

Parkinson, C. and C. Howorth (2008), 'The language of social entrepreneurs', *Entrepreneurship and Regional Development*, **20** (3), 285–309.

Peredo, A.M. and J.J. Chrisman (2006), 'Toward a theory of community-based enterprise', *Academy of Management Review*, **31** (2), 309–328.

Richez-Battesti, N. (2018), 'Changing social economies in changing territories', in X. Itçaina, and N. Richez-Battesti (eds), *Social and Solidarity-based Economy and Territory: From Embeddedness to Co-construction*, Brussels, Belgium: Peter Lang, pp. 13–29.

Sarpong, D. and C. Davies (2014), 'Managerial organizing practices and legitimacy seeking in social enterprises', *Social Enterprise Journal*, **10** (1), 21–37.

Seanor, P. and J. Meaton (2008), 'Learning from failure, ambiguity and trust in social enterprise', *Social Enterprise Journal*, **4** (1), 24–40.

Smith, A., M. Fressoli, D. Abrol, E. Arond and A. Ely (2017), *Grassroots Innovation Movements*, Abingdon, UK and New York, USA: Routledge.

Smith, A., M. Fressoli and H. Thomas (2014), 'Grassroots innovation movements: Challenges and contributions', *Journal of Cleaner Production*, **63**, 114–124.

Spear, R. (2006), 'Social entrepreneurship: A different model?' *International Journal of Social Economics*, **33** (5/6), 399–410.

Spear, R., C. Cornforth and M. Aiken (2007), *For Love and Money: Governance and Social Enterprise*, London, UK: National Council of Voluntary Organisations.

Spear, R. and L. Hulgard (2007), 'Social entrepreneurship and the mobilization of social capital in European social enterprises', in M. Nyssens (ed.), *Social Enterprise*, Abingdon, UK: Routledge, pp. 101–124.

Suchman, M.C. (1995). 'Managing legitimacy: Strategic and institutional approaches', *Academy of Management Review*, **20** (3), 571–610.

Tepsie (2014), 'Social Innovation Theory and Research', a deliverable of the project TEPSIE: 'The theoretical, empirical and policy foundations for building social innovation in Europe'. European Commission 7th Framework Programme, Brussels, Belgium: European Commission, DG Research.

Tracey, P., N. Phillips and H. Haugh (2005), 'Beyond philanthropy: Community enterprise as a basis for corporate citizenship', *Journal of Business Ethics*, **58** (4), 327–344.

Tracey, P. and N. Phillips (2011), 'Bridging institutional entrepreneurship and the creation of new organizational forms: A multilevel model', *Organization Science*, **22** (1), 60–80.

Vestrum, I. (2016), 'Integrating multiple theoretical approaches to explore the resource mobilization process of community ventures', *Journal of Enterprising Communities*, **10** (1), 123–134.

Vurro, C. and T. Dacin (2014), 'An institutional perspective on cross-sector partnership', in M.M. Seitanidi and A. Crane (eds), *Social Partnerships and Responsible Business*, Abingdon, UK: Routledge in association with GSE Research, pp. 306–319.

Weber, C., K. Weidner, A. Kroeger and J. Wallace (2017), 'Social value creation in inter-organizational collaborations in the not-for-profit sector – Give and take from a dyadic perspective', *Journal of Management Studies*, **54** (6), 929–956.

Weick, K.E. (1995), *Sensemaking in Organizations*, Thousand Oaks, USA: Sage.

Young, D.R. (2013), *If Not for Profit, for What?* (1983 Print Edition), Lanham, USA: Lexington Books.

Zasada, M. (2017), 'Entrepreneurial activity in community health promotion organisations: Findings from an ethnographic study', *Social Enterprise Journal*, **13** (2), 144–162.

9 Inclusive value chain development: the role of social enterprise hybrids in smallholder value chains

Bob Doherty and Pichawadee Kittipanya-ngam

Introduction

Despite continued growth in global trade there are concerns regarding the distribution of economic value between stakeholders in regional and international value chains (International Trade Forum, 2017). One of those groups experiencing increasing vulnerability is smallholder farmers who face increasing food insecurity (Bacon et al., 2014). An estimated 2.5 billion people worldwide depend on harvests from about 500 million smallholder farmers (FAO, 2013). Approximately 80 per cent of those facing food insecurity live in rural areas and half are smallholders (Gottlieb and Joshi, 2010). This 'hungry farmer paradox' shows the significant inequalities in the global food system (Bacon et al., 2014). This chapter investigates how hybrid organizations operating in the food system place development goals as central to the design of inclusive value chains, termed 'Inclusive Value Chain Development' (IVCD).

The value retained by smallholders in agrifood supply chains has declined over the past 20 years, whilst economic value accrued further upstream has increased particularly at retail level (Oxfam, 2018). This distribution of value brings into question governance and transparency in supply chains. Reardon et al. (2018) argue that there has been too much focus on smallholder transformation in the on-farm activities in contrast to the supply chain where value is added (off-farm activities).

Orr, Donovan and Stoian (2018) argue that many value chain approaches see performance driven by mainly financial incentives and pay scant attention to social and environmental objectives and the complex system impacts on the value chain. They highlight the risk of high failure rates in developing countries where smallholders are active participants and call for value chain approaches that pay attention to both contextual factors and other performance measures in addition to just price. More recently, the notion of IVCD has emerged which refers to a type of intervention that aims to address poverty through improved linkages between business and poor households within a value chain via targeting marginalized actors such as smallholders (Devaux et al., 2018). IVCD has been defined as a 'positive or desirable change in a value chain to extend or improve productive operations and generate social benefits such as poverty reduction, income and employment generation, economic growth, environmental performance, gender equity and other development goals' (Devaux et al., 2018, p. 102). Emerging in the literature is the potential role that private sector business model innovation in economic or technical advances could play in IVCD. However, it is surprising that other business models such as hybrids, which prioritize social and environmental aspects, do not yet appear in this literature (Kannothra et al., 2018).

Hybrid organizations are defined (Billis, 2010, p. 201) as 'any organization that possesses significant characteristics of more than one economic sector' (public, private or third sector). Social enterprises are seen as an 'ideal type' of hybrid which bridge the public, private and non-profit sectors and are found in a range of industries and locations. They differ from other forms of enterprise as they prioritize the achievement of social and environmental objectives above commercial goals and they differ from other forms of non-profits as they generate income from trading activity (Doherty et al., 2014; Pache and Santos, 2013; Zahra et al., 2009). Hybrids exist in a range of sectors including; health services, social care, retail, clothing, finance and agrifood. There are a growing number of studies investigating how hybrids manage tensions, trade-offs resulting from the dual-mission. However, research concerning how social enterprise hybrids contribute to IVCD is limited. Therefore, our research question is *how do hybrids create and manage value chain development?* We answer this by studying a series of hybrid social enterprise case studies to design a model of hybrid approaches to IVCD. The cases comprise profitable and sustainable social enterprise hybrids based in both the United Kingdom (UK) and Thailand.

Inclusive value chain development

Synthesizing various perspectives on value chain development in agribusiness, supply chain management and development, value chains can be described as the sequence of interlinked agents, activities, networks and markets that transfer inputs and services into products with attributes that consumers are prepared to purchase (Bacon, 2005; Devaux et al., 2018; Donovan et al., 2015; Lambert and Pohlen, 2001). Devaux et al. (2018) argue that standard global value chain analysis has failed to tackle the problems of smallholders in a holistic way. In fact, improving the performance of agricultural value chains stands to benefit large numbers of people (Reardon and Timmer, 2012). The role of smallholders is pertinent in regions such as the Greater Mekong where, for example, in Thailand 64 per cent of farms are smallholdings (Rigg et al., 2018). In fact, this percentage of smallholders has increased in the past 10 years, showing the persistence of the smallholder in countries such as Thailand (Rigg et al., 2018).

The IVCD approach encourages organizations to initiate inclusive innovation and value chain development as this approach can improve the linkages between households and value chains. It provides an approach to linking change processes on both farms and in value chains coupled with integrating a focus on liveli-hoods and policy (Devaux et al., 2018). A number of challenges for incorporating smallholders into value chains have been identified including: power imbalances, meeting quality standards, access to credit, availability of technology inputs and infrastructure and constraints in accessing markets (Donovan et al., 2017). Devaux et al. (2018) highlighted that very few cases of successful IVCD intervention have been documented. These limited cases identify a range of attributes for successful IVCD including; combining agricultural innovation and IVCD, the importance of multi-stakeholder platforms that focus on commercial, technical and institutional innovation (e.g. contract farming), inclusivity of discussions, sharing data, involv-ing research organizations, recognizing power dynamics, application of gender lens, collective marketing and the importance of time to allow results to emerge (Thiele et al., 2011; Swaans et al., 2013). Orr et al. (2018), in their work with smallholders, highlight the importance of business model adaptation but focus on approaches such as contract farming and selling on spot markets plus technical innovations such as refrigeration in transporting crops such as bananas. However, in these studies the evaluation of success has been focused purely on economic or technical measures such as yields, gross margin and no discussion of social and environmental performance.

Current work has focused on private sector firms with two schools of thought, one linking IVCD with a livelihoods focus (Stoian et al., 2012) and the second link-ing agricultural innovation with IVCD (Ayele et al., 2012). Donovan et al. (2015) argue that there is an absence in the literature regarding discussion on the condi-tions necessary for value chain development in achieving sustainability. There is increasing interest in how collaboration and partnership can provide these condi-tions (Donovan et al., 2015). Also, there have been calls for IVCD development to consider positive social and environmental impacts. It is therefore surprising that despite the rise in those organizations that are termed hybrids, which prioritize positive social and environmental impact, limited attention has been paid to the potential role they could play in the IVCD literature (Kannothra et al., 2018).

Hybrid organizations

The prioritization of goals other than revenue growth and profitability distinguishes social enterprise hybrids from organizations in the private sector (Mair and Martí, 2006; Lumpkin et al., 2013). Social goals are broadly construed to include serving the needs of the disadvantaged (Defourny and Nyssens, 2006), unemployed (Pache and Santos, 2013), homeless (Teasdale, 2012) and smallholder farmers (Mason and Doherty, 2016). Environmental objectives include responding to climate change, biodiversity loss and pollution (Austin et al., 2006; Vickers and Lyon, 2013) through initiatives such as leadership development and recycling (Vickers and Lyon, 2013). To achieve sustainable outcomes in all three domains, social enterprises adopt business models that encompass commercial trading as well as creating social and environmental impacts. This is achieved by blending practices from organizations in the private, public and non-profit sectors (Doherty et al., 2014). Although deviation from the institutional conventions anchored in each sector of the economy might appear to be a risk-laden strategy, the outcome has been the development of an increasing global population of social enterprise hybrids that strive to generate social change (Mair and Martí, 2006).

Organizations manifest generic structural features and characteristics that are in some way 'pure' and representative of a distinct and recognizable group of organizations (Billis, 2010; Crittenden and Crittenden, 1997; Haigh and Hoffman, 2012; Somerville and McElwee, 2011). In this view categories are presented as idealized structures from which organizations derive legitimacy from alignment with categorical logics and discourse (Zuckerman, 1999). To elaborate, Billis (2010) presents organizational templates for the categories of private, public and non-profit organizations. Thus private sector organizations are guided by market forces to maximize financial return, owned by shareholders, governed according to size of share ownership, and generate revenue from sales and fees. Organizations in the public sector are characterized as guided by the principles of public benefit and collective choice, owned by citizens and the state, and resourced through taxation. Finally, non-profit sector organizations pursue social and environmental goals, are owned by members, governed by private election of representatives, staffed by a combination of employees and volunteers and generate revenue from membership fees, donations and legacies. Specifically, non-profit distributing organizations are legally prohibited from distributing any residual 'earnings' to those with a managerial or ownership interest (Hansmann, 1980). Organizational forms that do not fit neatly into the institutionalized categories outlined above are labelled hybrids and are found in a range of constellations including private-public, private-non-profit and public-non-profit. Social enterprise hybrids are 'not aligned with the idealized categorical characteristics' of the private, public or non-profit sectors (Doherty et al., 2014, p. 3) and by pursuing the achievement of commercial, social and environmental objectives are thus a classic hybrid organizational form (Battilana and Lee, 2014; Dees and Elias, 1998; Defourny and Nyssens, 2006; Billis, 2010).

Hybrids in agrifood smallholder value chains

Our cases include a range of social enterprise hybrids in both the UK and Thailand operating in agrifood: Akha Ama Coffee (coffee, Thailand), Cafédirect (fair trade coffee, UK), Dairy Home (organic dairy, UK), Divine Chocolate (fair trade chocolate, UK), Doi Tung (community enterprises, coffee and handicrafts, Thailand), Liberation (fair trade nuts, UK), Siam Organic (Jasberry organic rice, Thailand). A number of key characteristics have emerged from how hybrids create and manage value chain development.

Profit and investment

Hybrids employ a number of mechanisms to ensure economic value is shared more equitably amongst stakeholders. Firstly, a number of hybrids purposefully pay more for their raw materials from smallholders through both certification (fair trade) and agreed equitable pricing agreements. This is designed to facilitate livelihood development of smallholder producers; fair trade certification commits hybrids to pay fair prices for agricultural commodities. The calculation of a fair trade price is based on providing a reasonable income to smallholder producers and does not fluctuate in the way that market prices do. Thus, even when the market price for commodities falls below the fair trade price, fair trade certified organizations commit to paying the fair trade price and the fair trade premium. In fact, the fair trade price is agreed in consultation with smallholder farmers. Hybrid owners described how the strategies they devised were explicitly intended to not only generate income for their organization, but also to promote both community economic and supply chain development. Both Dairy Home and Siam Organic (Jasberry rice) have grown their supply of organic milk and organic rice (high in antioxidants) respectively by investing funds in supporting farmer conversion to organic production coupled with investments in farmer training. Siam Organic also requires the farmers to keep at least 25 per cent of their harvests for household consumption (food security), and the company guarantee the purchase of the rest at a pre-agreed premium price. Liberation has invested producer support and development funds to help smallholder producers invest in peanut processing facilities to redistribute economic value.

A number of smallholder farmer groups also own shares in hybrids (Divine, Cafédirect and Liberation) providing a dividend when the hybrid makes a profit. In addition, this shareholding has enabled some of the producer organizations to borrow money at preferential rates against the asset of equity ownership. Hybrids are recognized as delivering social impact and therefore are in a pole position to attract investments from social impact investors, for example Oikocredit and Change Venture (Thailand).

Power and governance

Empowerment of smallholders is a key aim of hybrids; strategies include participatory strategy development (Divine, Doi Tung, Siam Organic), sharing brand property rights, and board-level participation (Cafédirect, Divine, and Liberation). Such policies and practices empower beneficiaries by giving them a voice in organizational strategic direction and governance. One of the founding strategic objectives of Divine was to empower female cocoa farmers in Ghana. This is achieved by requiring 30 per cent female participation at all decision-making levels in the Kuapa Kokoo farmers' cooperative. Cafédirect's surpluses are gifted to a foundation committed to empowering farmers. It is clear that hybrids work to redress power imbalances.

Purpose

Hybrid business models achieve social goals through entrepreneurial means. A key feature of these agrifood hybrids is market access to premium markets. Siam Organic packs and distributes organic rice under its brand Jasberry. Its rice is claimed to have the highest antioxidant level in the world and is able to access premium rice market segments in the USA. At Akha Ama Coffee, instead of selling the cherry and parchment coffee to intermediaries for a low price, the smallholder farmers decided to process and market the coffee themselves and established a chain of high quality coffee bars in Chiang Mai targeting young professionals, expats and tourists, thereby ensuring a better price for their organic coffee and other produce. Development of premium position brand is clearly a strategy to build financial value.

The Akha Ama smallholders also decided to change to an organically sustainable system of mixed multi-cropping for their coffee, reducing the use of chemical fertilizers, herbicides or pesticides. The coffee plants are now grown in-between larger fruit trees and a wide variety of vegetables, providing produce for the smallholders' own consumption and for selling in local markets. This system is beneficial to the soil ecology, produces humus, stabilizes hillsides against erosion and retains moisture during the dry season. Due to constant crop rotation, pests are less liable to negatively affect the plants. Akha Ama has now invested in a school to train the next generation of social entrepreneurs. Hybrids are geared towards reinvestment in the enterprise and supply chain, rather than the capital gain aspect of a standard limited liability company. Divine invests in education and schooling projects, which are designed to improve the attractiveness of cocoa farming to young people because, for adults, this increases the likelihood that their children will stay in the home community and care for them in the future. The smallholder cocoa farmers' cooperative Kuapa Kokoo (based in Ghana), which is a shareholder in Divine, funds – via the fair trade social premium – investments in building schools so that there is better education in rural areas.

Conclusions

It is clear that hybrid business models are able to meet a number of the challenges for incorporating smallholders into value chains. Returning to our research question – *how do hybrids create and manage value chain development?* – social enterprise hybrids, when creating value chains, work to address power imbalances and deliver social benefits due to their social mission. They do this using a number of mechanisms including: designing equitable pricing arrangements in discussion with farmers, for example fair trade certification; providing credit arrangements at preferential rates; and providing access to premium market segments. They are able to build differentiated brands using a combined product quality and social/environmental positioning to create both economic and social value. Social enterprises also purposefully allocate funds to producer support and development to ensure capacity building of farmer organizations, work on gender equality and empowerment (Doherty, 2018), and food security and improvements or adaptations in agronomy, and they therefore take a much longer-term view of IVCD. This focus on farmer livelihoods to address poverty is exactly what is identified as vital in the IVCD literature (Devaux et al., 2018).

Furthermore, new approaches to governance and ownership are employed by hybrids to develop more inclusive value chains that target positive social and environmental change. Equity ownership for producer groups, which increases the economic value received and enables gender empowerment programmes and quotas for female representation at producer organizational level, clearly targets power imbalances within value chains. Moreover, some producer groups are going direct to market via their own social enterprise retail outlets, for example Aka Ahma Coffee, thereby reducing the economic value taken by intermediaries in the value chain.

Social enterprises, due to their multi-stakeholder approach, appear to be well placed to collaborate and develop more inclusive approaches with stakeholders. They work closely with smallholders on business development, creating spaces for negotiation to deal with the complexity of value chain development and any potential conflicting priorities (Battilana et al., 2015). It is clear that social enterprise hybrids provide innovative approaches in terms of profit sharing with smallholders, governance and social entrepreneurship. Thus they demonstrate a wider notion of innovation beyond just technological innovation, which has dominated IVCD literature to date. These identified characteristics provide a useful contribution to the IVCD literature, showing the importance of social entrepreneurship delivering positive social and environmental value.

This chapter has also shown the potential of value chain perspectives for future research into social enterprises. Gary Gereffi (1994) was the first to use the term governance in his influential contribution to *Commodity Chains and Global Capitalism* (Gereffi and Korzeniewicz, 1994). Here, Gereffi (1994, p. 97) defined governance as the 'authority and power relationships that determine how financial, material and human resources are allocated and flow within a chain'. On this basis, Gereffi distinguished between 'producer-driven' and 'buyer-driven' chains and argued that barriers to entry constitute the key determinant of the 'governance structure' of these chains. The dominant questions in most GVC scholarship centre on the generation, control and distribution of economic value. Whilst not dismissing the importance of these questions, we have cast the net wider to consider the role that social enterprise hybrids can play in addressing the imbalances and governance tensions in value chains. These 'hybrid-driven value chains' studied here demonstrate how more inclusive participatory approaches can be more effective in achieving development goals. Future studies on the role of social enterprise hybrids in regional or international supply chains could be enhanced by applying a value chain approach to deepen our understanding of how hybrids create economic, social and environmental value. This analysis could also provide valuable lessons to those more enlightened corporate firms who are aiming to make a positive contribution to achieving sustainable development goal targets by working with smallholders in a more collaborative way.

Acknowledgements

The authors would like to thank our funders, including The British Council, Newton Fund, for the award of a Researcher Link Grant (2015–2016) and Thamassat University, the Rector Fund (2017–2018), for their award to study the management of social enterprises in both Thailand and the UK. In addition, we would like to thank the social enterprise organizations for their support and collaboration.

References

Austin, J., H. Stevenson and J. Wei-Skillern (2006), 'Social and commercial entrepreneurship: same, different or both?', *Entrepreneurship Theory and Practice*, **30** (1), 1–22.

Ayele, S., A. Duncan, A. Larbi and T.T. Khanh (2012), 'Enhancing innovation in livestock value chains through networks: lessons from fodder innovation case studies in developing countries', *Science and Public Policy*, **39** (3), 333–346.

Bacon, C.M. (2005), 'Confronting the coffee crisis: can fair trade, organic, and specialty coffees reduce small-scale farmer vulnerability in northern Nicaragua?' *World Development*, **33** (3), 497–511.

Bacon, C., W.A. Sundstrom, M.E.F. Eugenia, F. Gomez, V.E. Mendez, R. Santos, B. Goldoftas and I. Dougherty (2014), 'Explaining the "hungry farmer paradox": smallholders and fair trade cooperatives navigate seasonality and change in Nicaragua's corn and coffee markets', *Global Environmental Change*, **25**, 133–149.

Battilana, J. and M. Lee (2014), 'Advancing research on hybrid organizing: insights from the study of social enterprises', *The Academy of Management Annals*, **8**, 397–441.

Battilana, J., M. Sengul, A.-C. Pache and J. Model (2015), 'Harnessing productive tensions in hybrid organizations: the case of work integration social enterprises', *Academy of Management Journal*, **58**, 1658–1685.

Billis, D. (2010), *Hybrid Organizations for the Third Sector. Challenges for Practice, Theory, and Policy*, London: Palgrave Macmillan.

Crittenden, W.F. and V.L. Crittenden (1997), 'Strategic planning in third-sector organizations', *Journal of Managerial Issues*, **9** (1), 86–103.

Dees, J.G. and J. Elias (1998), 'The challenges of combining social and commercial enterprise', *Business Ethics Quarterly*, **8** (1), 165–178.

Defourny, J. and M. Nyssens (2006), 'Conceptions of social enterprise in Europe and the United States: convergences and divergences', *Social Enterprise Journal*, **1** (1), 32–53.

Devaux, A., M. Torero, J. Donovan and D. Horton (2018), 'Agricultural innovation and inclusive value-chain development: a review', *Journal of Agribusiness in Developing and Emerging Economies*, **8** (1), 99–123.

Doherty, B. (2018), 'Gender equality and women's empowerment through fair trade social enterprise: case of Divine Chocolate and Kuapa Kokoo in Apostolopoulos', in N. Apostolopoulos, H. Al-Dajani, D. Holt, P. Jones and R. Newbury (eds), *Entrepreneurship and the Sustainable Development Goals*, Bingley: Emerald Publishing, pp. 151–163.

Doherty, B., H. Haugh and F. Lyon (2014), 'Social enterprises as hybrid organizations: a review and research agenda', *International Journal of Management Reviews*, **16** (4), 417–436.

Donovan, J., S. Franzel, M. Cunha, A. Gyau and D. Mithöfer (2015), 'Guides for value chain development: a comparative review', *Journal of Agribusiness in Developing and Emerging Economies*, **5** (1), 2–23.

Donovan, J., D. Stoian and K. Poe (2017), 'Value chain development in Nicaragua: prevailing approaches and tools used for design and implementation', *Enterprise Development and Microfinance*, **28** (1–2), 10–27.

FAO (2013), 'Resilient livelihoods – Disaster Risk Reduction for Food and Nutrition Security Framework Programme', FAO, Rome.

Gereffi, G. (1994), 'The organization of buyer-driven global commodity chains: how US retailers shape overseas production networks', in G. Gereffi and M. Korzeniewicz (eds), *Commodity Chains and Global Capitalism* (No. 149). Santa Barbara, CA: ABC-CLIO, pp. 95–122.

Gereffi, G. and M. Korzeniewicz (eds) (1994), *Commodity Chains and Global Capitalism* (No. 149), Santa Barbara, CA: ABC-CLIO.

Gottlieb, R. and A. Joshi (2010), *Food Justice*, Cambridge, MA: MIT Press.

Haigh, N. and A.J. Hoffman (2012), 'Hybrid organizations', *Organizational Dynamics*, **41** (2), 126–134.

Hansmann, H.B. (1980), 'The role of non-profit enterprise', *Yale Law Journal*, **89**, 835–898.

International Trade Forum (2017), 'Routes to inclusive and sustainable trade', *International Trade Forum*, **4,** International Trade Centre.

Kannothra, C.G., S. Manning and N. Haigh (2018), 'How hybrids manage growth and social–business tensions in global supply chains: the case of impact sourcing', *Journal of Business Ethics*, **148** (2), 271–290.

Lambert, D. and T. Pohlen (2001), 'Supply chain metrics', *International Journal of Logistics Management*, **12** (1), 1–19.

Lumpkin, G.T., T.W. Moss, D.M. Gras, S. Kato and A.S. Amezcua (2013), 'Entrepreneurial processes in social contexts: how are they different, if at all?', *Small Business Economics*, **40** (3), 761–783.

Mair, J. and I. Martí (2006), 'Social entrepreneurship research: a source of explanation, prediction and delight', *Journal of World Business*, **41** (1), 36–44.

Mason, C. and B. Doherty (2016), 'A fair trade-off? Paradoxes in the governance of fair-trade social enterprises', *Journal of Business Ethics*, **136** (3), 451–469.

Orr, A., J. Donovan and D. Stoian (2018), 'Smallholder value chains as complex adaptive systems: a conceptual framework', *Journal of Agribusiness in Developing and Emerging Economies*, **8** (1), 14–33.

Oxfam (2018), 'Ripe for Change: Ending Human Suffering in Supermarket Supply Chains', Oxfam GB for Oxfam International, Oxford.

Pache, A.C. and F. Santos (2013), 'Inside the hybrid organization: selective coupling as a response to competing institutional logics', *Academy of Management Journal*, **56** (40), 972–1001.

Reardon, T., R. Echeverria, J. Berdegue, B. Minten, S. Liverpool-Tasie, D. Tschirley and D. Zilberman (2018), 'Rapid transformation of food systems in developing regions: highlighting the role of agricultural research and innovations', *Agricultural Systems*, In Press, Corrected Proof, available online 26 February 2018. https://doi.org/10.1016/j.agsy.2018.01.022.

Reardon, T. and C.P. Timmer (2012), 'The economics of the food system revolution', *Annual Review of Resource Economics*, **4** (1), 225–264.

Rigg, J., A. Salamanca, M. Phongsir and M. Sripun (2018), 'More farmers less farming? Understanding the truncated agrarian transitions in Thailand', *World Development*, **107**, 327–337.

Somerville, P. and G. McElwee (2011), 'Situating community enterprise: a theoretical explanation', *Entrepreneurship and Regional Development*, **23** (5/6), 317–330.

Stoian, D., J. Donovan, J. Fisk and M. Muldoon (2012), 'Value chain development for rural poverty reduction: a reality check and a warning', *Enterprise Development and Microfinance*, **23** (1), 54–60.

Swaans, K., B. Cullen, A.F. Van Rooyen, A. Adekunle, H. Ngwenya, Z. Lema and S. Nederlof (2013), 'Dealing with critical challenges in African innovation platforms: lessons for facilitation', *Knowledge Management for Development Journal*, **9** (3), 116–135.

Teasdale, S. (2012), 'Negotiating tensions: how do social enterprises in the homelessness field balance social and commercial considerations?', *Housing Studies*, **27** (4), 514–532.

Thiele, G., A. Devaux, I. Reinoso, H. Pico, F. Montesdeoca, M. Pumisacho . . . and D. Horton (2011), 'Multi-stakeholder platforms for linking small farmers to value chains: evidence from the Andes', *International Journal of Agricultural Sustainability*, **9** (3), 423–433.

Vickers, I. and F. Lyon (2013), 'Beyond green niches? Growth strategies of environmentally-motivated social enterprises', *International Small Business Journal*, **32** (4), 449–470.

Zahra, S.A., E. Gedajlovic, D.O. Neubaum and J.M. Shulman (2009), 'A typology of social entrepreneurs: motives, search processes and ethical challenges', *Journal of Business Venturing*, **24** (5), 519–532.

Zuckerman, E. (1999), 'The categorical imperative: securities analysts and the illegitimacy discount', *American Journal of Sociology*, **104** (5), 1398–1438.

10 Social enterprises as rural development actors

Robyn Eversole and Mary Duniam

Introduction

In the quest for sustainable development, rural development is a persisting policy concern. Around the globe, rural areas provide the key resources – such as food, fibre, energy, and ecosystem services – necessary to sustain urban settlements. They are home to diverse communities of rural people and a range of rural industries, often including but not limited to agriculture. At the same time, physical distance from markets and concentration of resources and services in urban areas may disadvantage rural areas and jeopardise community sustainability. This chapter considers social enterprises as rural development actors and explores how they relate to other development actors in rural places.

Rural development refers to planned initiatives that aim to make a positive difference for rural communities (Eversole 2018b). Historically, rural development efforts have often been initiated from outside rural places by national governments, non-governmental organisations (NGOs) or other development actors, who act upon rural communities using a range of policy approaches (Ellis and Biggs 2001). It is only relatively recently that rural communities have been theorised as protagonists rather than passive recipients of development action, and then primarily by practitioner-researchers (Chambers 1983, Annis and Hakim 1987).

While there is a persisting tendency for rural development efforts to be instigated by non-rural people, there is also recognition that the on-the-ground knowledge of rural people themselves is a vital resource. Rural communities are diverse, internally heterogeneous, and capable of instigating their own development action (see e.g. Eversole 2018a). Attention to rural communities as development actors has opened up the opportunity to consider rural communities' own agency and leadership in rural development; including the role that particular kinds of community organisations may play in generating rural development outcomes.

Social enterprises are one kind of organisational actor in rural communities that have the potential to generate important rural development outcomes. While research on the role of social enterprises in rural development is still at a very early stage, it suggests that social enterprises based in rural areas are skilled at mobilising community resources, building social capital, and generating a range of benefits for their local communities (Eversole et al. 2014, Barraket et al. in press). Social enterprises appear to be significant organisational actors generating rural development outcomes from within rural communities.

Rural development actors

Communities in rural places are diverse, but they face some common challenges related to their comparatively small and often scattered populations and disadvantageous positioning in national and global political economies. Rural communities have their own identities and sense of place, but in the broader political economy they tend to be political and economic decision-takers rather than decision-makers. As a result, they often find themselves at the sharp end of unsustainable systems that undermine rural lifestyles and livelihoods (see e.g. Gray and Lawrence 2001, Eversole 2016). Further, small, dispersed rural populations present challenges for cost-effective production and delivery of products and services, and citizen expectations often turn to their local government councils to supply what is lacking (Duniam 2017). Local government is thus a significant development actor in rural communities.

Traditional rural development policies were designed in central policy offices far from rural places (see e.g. Ellis and Biggs 2001). Central governments and, later, large NGOs and international bodies, have long been the dominant rural development actors. Only more recently has attention turned to the roles of on-the-ground rural development actors within rural communities. A number of studies, particularly in the community development field, have drawn attention to rural communities as capable of leading rural development for themselves, from within their particular local contexts (e.g. Chambers et al. 1989, Flora and Flora 2012, Cheshire 2006). The more nuanced recognise that 'rural communities' are themselves comprised of multiple actors, with multiple roles: such as local councils and social enterprises.

Actor-oriented rural development (Long 2001, 2015) and anthropology of development (Olivier de Sardan 2005, Gardiner and Lewis 2015, Eversole 2018a) provide a useful theoretical lens for understanding the diverse actors involved in rural development. They enable us to focus on actors – such as social enterprises – who are involved in rural development processes. 'Actors' may be individuals, groups, and organisations, local and non-local, who interact with each other and influence the nature and direction of change. An anthropological approach to rural development recognises that rural communities that share ties of local residence are neither passive sites of development as imagined by others, nor homogenous groups with a common local agenda.

An anthropological approach can shed light on how different actors with different social positions and roles understand the aims and processes of rural development, and what they do to achieve their desired outcomes. In the context of this chapter, an anthropological approach to rural development allows us to look up close at social enterprises, as one type of development actor within rural communities, to consider the role they play, the logics they employ, the strategies they use, and how they relate to other key rural development actors such as local government councils.

Social enterprises in rural development

An emerging research agenda explores the role that social enterprises play in the social and economic development of local places – especially, though not exclusively, rural places. It has been observed that many social enterprises have a strong place-based focus, and that their work contributes to the social and economic wellbeing of the local communities where they are based; for instance, by growing social capital, providing employment and training opportunities, or filling gaps in available services (see e.g. Steinerowski and Steinerowska-Streb 2012, Eversole 2013, Eversole et al. 2014, Barth et al. 2015).

Further, researchers have started to look beyond the roles that social enterprises play (*what* they do), to explore *how* they work – that is, the strategies they use to generate development outcomes. Using concepts such as bricolage, resourcefulness (Barraket et al. in press) and intermediation (Richter in press), theorists have begun to describe specific strategies that social enterprises are adopting to generate outcomes for local communities in resource-constrained rural areas. A key theme is that social enterprises are skilled at drawing on resources from both within and beyond local communities, and across traditional sectoral and organisational boundaries. As development actors, they may be intentionally positioning themselves to do development differently than mainstream organisations; providing competing institutional logics to econo-centric development institutions (Barth et al. 2015), disrupting prevalent institutional norms (Barraket and Archer 2009), and actively modelling alternative ways-of-working or 'counterwork' (Eversole 2014). These new ways of working may in turn create the basis for systemic change (Dorado and Ventresca 2013).

These studies are beginning to shed light on the potentially important role of social enterprises as rural development actors, and the kinds of strategies and logics that they use to generate development outcomes. At the same time, they raise a number of questions for further work. Little is known about how social enterprises see their role in rural development, or how they articulate the logics that guide their work. Equally, little is known about the relationships between social enterprises and other development actors: for instance, the extent to which they may collaborate or compete; and the extent to which social enterprises are valued or seen as 'legitimate' development actors by others (see e.g. Barth et al. 2015). Yet as the following study shows, these questions are key to understanding, and unlocking, the potential of social enterprises as rural development actors.

Social enterprises in rural Tasmania

Context and methodology

The research described below was undertaken in 2014 in Australia, as part of a PhD project on the relationship between local government and social enterprises. The study used the definition of social enterprises by Barraket et al. (2010): social enterprises are led by an economic, social, cultural, or environmental mission consistent with a public or community benefit, and trade to fulfil their mission (Barraket et al. 2010: 4). Not all social enterprises included in the study identified themselves as social enterprises, but all met this definition.

The research focused on the sparsely populated island state of Tasmania. An earlier study (Eversole and Eastley 2011) had identified the existence of a diverse, emerging social enterprise sector in Tasmania. In the 2014 research, all 29 Tasmanian local government councils were surveyed to determine their knowledge of and interaction with local social enterprises. Based on the results of this survey, four mainly rural councils of different sizes, from different parts of the state, were selected for in-depth study. These councils nominated a total of 32 social enterprises that they had some relationship with, and based on the characteristics of these enterprises and relationships, eight case studies of council–social enterprise relationships were selected for the research project. In-depth interviews were conducted with both council and social enterprise representatives for each case study, exploring social enterprises' roles, strategies, and relationships with local councils. The results were manually analysed to distil key themes and to compare these across organisational and geographic contexts.

Findings and discussion

The Tasmanian research found that local government councils and social enterprises were both playing important rural development roles, but they were working in markedly different ways. Both types of organisations focused on 'community' as central in generating rural development outcomes, and both were deeply embedded in their local rural contexts. Nevertheless, their development logics about rural communities and strategies for working with them were very different. Further, neither local councils, nor social enterprises themselves, had a strong understanding of social enterprise as a concept (Duniam 2017). This meant that it was difficult for actors within these organisations to articulate their logics or why they conflicted.

The eight case-study social enterprises in rural Tasmanian communities had all been established by local community members as a direct response to local community needs. For example, a community rhododendron garden was established to fulfil an unmet need of a group of local volunteers with a common interest and passion for gardening. By establishing the garden, they also created a significant local tourism opportunity:

> [A] volunteer organisation that over the past 33 years has created an asset that's of value that's very difficult to put a value on . . . [The garden] has reached the point now where it's

*becoming of international significance . . . and that's quite an incredible achievement for a
bunch of volunteers . . .*

Another social enterprise was established by volunteers to provide for an unmet
need for people with disabilities within the local community. This enterprise continues to rely heavily on unpaid volunteers for client support positions that in other
contexts would typically be filled by paid staff.

These rural social enterprises emerged organically from communities of place
and operated as change agents within those communities by mobilising resources
(e.g. land, buildings, volunteers), meeting needs, and developing local capabilities.
These social enterprises had been established on-the-ground by local community
members and were self-organising organisations that operated within both mainstream and social economies, involving different kinds of stakeholders in their
membership. Thus, they displayed the characteristics of place-embeddedness,
hybridity, and cross-sector resource mobilisation that have been documented in
other studies. Further, these social enterprises sought to create real change for
participants and local communities. They fostered local social inclusion and community resilience, and empowered community members to draw on and share
their skills and knowledge. While they did not describe themselves explicitly as
rural development actors, they were clearly playing this role: creating opportunity for individual, organisational and community development in rural places
(Duniam 2017).

At the same time, the unique agenda and social mission of each case-study social
enterprise – which ranged from providing cultural opportunities to health services
– was strongly shaped by community needs and deficits. These social enterprises
were responsive to community needs, but they were not particularly strategic
organisationally (Duniam 2017). Their logics for effective work with rural communities emphasised community responsiveness over strategic organisational
development. Further, the case-study social enterprises demonstrated a low level of
knowledge of social enterprise as a concept. All eight simply considered themselves
as not-for-profits, despite their significant trading activities and the reinvestment
of surplus funds back into the enterprise. These organisations met the external
definition of social enterprise provided by the researchers but had not previously
encountered the concept (Duniam 2017). As one respondent reflected:

*. . . I've never looked at it that way . . . but, but I like the sound of it . . . I think it describes it
quite adequately . . .*

Thus, while rural social enterprises were creating important rural development
impacts, they lacked the language to explain their approach and strategy to other
development actors – such as local councils.

Local government councils are another set of development actors in rural communities. Councils represent local people, but they are also highly structured

bureaucratic organisations. Their role, as agents of place, is to strategically shape local places and advocate for their council area and its citizens. While social enterprises emphasise community responsiveness and mobilise local resources to meet needs, councils tend to see their role differently: as strategic leaders who create change *for* communities. This can be conceptualised as a 'philanthropic approach' to rural development: seeking to enact social responsibility by doing something for communities from the top down, rather than empowering communities to build capabilities and resilience from the ground up. Council spokespeople recognised that they had a social responsibility to do some things for community, but generally only in the context of council's strategic community development objectives (Duniam 2017).

The bureaucratic and philanthropic approach adopted by councils regularly gave rise to resourcing concerns. Councils highlighted the difficulties they faced in meeting the expectations from their local communities, particularly expectations that councils would address socio-economic challenges. Elected representatives expressed concern about the balancing act of prioritising community need against the limited resources of councils in rural areas. Typically, councils employed standardised top-down philanthropic mechanisms, such as annual Community Funding Grants, and struggled to understand how to weigh up social value against a dollar cost (Duniam 2017).

While the four case-study councils all had some relationships with social enterprises, they had little understanding of social enterprises' role, or how it might differ from that of other community organisations. For councils, social enterprises were just part of the broad landscape of community organisations, as described by one council spokesperson:

> ... all the activities that are actually happening and all the different community organisations ... it'll never go away whatever happens in the future ... you're still gonna have these small organisations because that's how people get on with one another, that's how people meet other people through all these variety of organisations.

This impression was further reinforced by the fact that some social enterprises sought funding support from councils. Councils characterised this as the usual philanthropic community resourcing – not social investment – and expressed it as a reason to avoid close collaborative relationships with social enterprises (Duniam 2017). Situating council–social enterprise relationships within the established institutional roles and logics of council-as-philanthropic-grant-maker and social-enterprise-as-not-for-profit-grant-recipient obscured opportunities for institutional innovation. It was difficult for councils to see how social enterprises were different than any other 'community' actor, let alone how social enterprises' logics and strategies might suggest new ways of responding to rural resource constraints.

Overall, there was a marked contrast between the rural development logics of social enterprises and local councils, even though both focused on rural communities and their development. In the four council areas studied, social enterprises were operating as 'bottom-up' change agents leveraging local skills and resources to respond to local needs; in many ways they were shaping people to shape place. Local councils, in turn, sought to shape place strategically from the top down by providing civic leadership and local services to local communities, but their activities did not generate economic value or community capacity development. Nor did councils acknowledge the value created by social enterprises – despite evidence that social enterprises were generating both social and economic value. Further, because both councils and social enterprises had little understanding of the social enterprise concept, it was difficult for either type of organisation to articulate how and why they worked differently, or how they might collaborate to achieve rural development outcomes (Duniam 2017).

Conclusions

As rural communities and policy makers grapple with rapid change and sustainability challenges, it is important to move beyond simplistic caricatures of rural communities to consider how diverse actors within those communities understand and contribute to rural development outcomes. Emerging research on rural social enterprises suggests that social enterprises, as one type of organisational actor, are playing significant – if largely invisible – roles in rural development. The Tasmanian research described above contributes to an emerging literature on the potential of rural social enterprises as rural development actors. Taking an anthropological approach has illuminated strategies and logics employed by social enterprises in rural development, and how these differ markedly from the strategies and logics of local councils. These differences impede their ability to work together in the present, but suggest promising terrain for the future.

The social enterprises in this study demonstrated a clear intent to stimulate economic and social change in rural areas, working with diverse stakeholders in rural communities. They articulated this mission in terms of a grounded responsiveness to local community needs. Local councils, by comparison, also saw themselves as change agents and shapers of local places and the communities living there. Yet councils took a strategic approach that conceptually separated themselves, as leaders and benefactors, from communities as the recipients of development action. Councils' approach to community development was thus largely directive or 'top down', while social enterprises took a more 'bottom-up' approach.

More importantly, these embedded logics influenced how the organisations saw themselves, and how they saw each other. The innovative potential of social enterprises to work in resource-constrained rural areas to leverage and grow resources was evident in all four council areas, yet largely overlooked. In the absence of a strong conceptual understanding of the role of social enterprise, case-study social enterprises positioned themselves as traditional community-based not-for-profits, and councils treated them as such.

This chapter has highlighted the need for further research to deepen our understanding of social enterprises as contributors to sustainable rural development. In rural areas, where human and financial resources are often thin on the ground, how are social enterprises mobilising resources for change, and to what extent is this work understood and leveraged – or misunderstood and ignored – by traditional development actors such as local councils and extra-local development organisations (state and national governments, NGOs, etc.)? Further, how do enterprising grassroots community groups themselves explain their work in contexts where 'social enterprise' as a concept is unknown or poorly understood? Finally, given that the logics and strategies of social enterprises may differ markedly from those of other development actors, how could improving mutual understanding and coordination contribute to more impactful rural development action in the future?

References

Annis, S. and P. Hakim (1987), *Direct to the Poor: Grassroots Development in Latin America*, Boulder, CO: L. Rienner.

Barraket, J. and V. Archer (2009), 'Changing the rules in use: an examination of the role of social enterprise in local governance', paper presented at the International Social Innovation Research Conference 2009: Social Innovation: Reconfiguring Markets, Blurring Sector Boundaries and Challenging Institutional Arrangements, Oxford University, 14–16 September 2009.

Barraket J., N. Collyer, M. O'Connor and H. Anderson (2010), *Finding Australia's Social Enterprise Sector: A Final Report*, Australian Centre for Philanthropy and Non-profit Studies, QUT, Queensland.

Barraket, J., R. Eversole, B. Luke and S. Barth (in press), 'Resourcefulness of locally-oriented social enterprises: implications for rural community development', *Journal of Rural Studies*. https://doi.org/10.1016/j.jrurstud.2017.12.031.

Barth, S., J. Barraket, B. Luke and J. McLaughlin (2015), 'Acquaintance or partner? Social economy organizations, institutional logics and regional development in Australia', *Entrepreneurship & Regional Development*, **27** (3–4), 219–254.

Chambers, R. (1983), *Rural Development: Putting the Last First*, Harlow: Pearson Education.

Chambers, R., A. Pacey and L. Thrupp (1989), *Farmer First: Farmer Innovation and Agricultural Research*, London: Intermediate Technology Publications.

Cheshire, L. (2006), *Governing Rural Development: Discourses and Practices of Self-Help in Australian Rural Policy*, Aldershot: Ashgate.

Dorado, S. and M.J. Ventresca (2013), 'Crescive entrepreneurship in complex social problems: institutional conditions for entrepreneurial engagement', *Journal of Business Venturing*, **28** (1), 69–82.

Duniam, M. (2017), 'Local government and social enterprises in Tasmania: exploring relationships that build community value', PhD thesis, University of Tasmania.

Ellis, F. and S. Biggs (2001), 'Evolving themes in rural development 1950s to 2000s', *Development Policy Review*, **19** (4), 437–448.

Eversole, R. (2013), 'Social enterprises as local development actors: insights from Tasmania', *Local Economy*, **28** (6), 567–579.

Eversole, R. (2014), 'Social enterprise as counterwork: building a new development paradigm', in H. Douglas and S. Grant (eds), *Social Entrepreneurship and Enterprise: Concepts in context*, Melbourne: Tilde University Press.

Eversole, R. (2016), *Regional Development in Australia: Being Regional*, London and New York: Routledge.

Eversole, R. (2018a), *Anthropology for Development: From Theory to Practice*, New York and London: Routledge.

Eversole, R. (2018b), 'Rural development' in H. Callan (ed.), *The International Encyclopedia of Anthropology*, Oxford: Wiley.

Eversole, R., J. Barraket and B. Luke (2014), 'Social enterprises in rural community development', *Community Development Journal*, **49** (2), 245–261.

Eversole, R. and K. Eastley (2011), *Tasmanian Social Enterprise Study: Baseline Study Report*, Burnie: Institute for Regional Development.

Flora, C.B. and J.L. Flora (2012), *Rural Communities: Legacy and Change*, fourth edition, Boulder, CO: Westview Press.

Gardiner, K. and D. Lewis (2015), *Anthropology and Development: Challenges for the Twenty-First Century*, London: Pluto Press.

Gray, I. and G. Lawrence (2001), *A Future for Regional Australia: Escaping Global Misfortune*, Cambridge: Cambridge University Press.

Long, N. (2001), *Development Sociology: Actor Perspectives*, London and New York: Routledge.

Long, N. (2015), 'Activities, actants and actors: theoretical perspectives on development practice and practitioners', in P. Milone, F. Ventura and J. Ye (eds), *Constructing a New Framework for Rural Development*, Research in Rural Sociology and Development, Volume 22, Bingley: Emerald Group.

Olivier de Sardan, J.P. (2005), *Anthropology and Development: Understanding Contemporary Social Change*, London: Zed Books.

Richter, R. (in press), 'Rural social enterprises as embedded intermediaries: the innovative power of connecting rural communities with supra-regional networks', *Journal of Rural Studies*.

Steinerowski, A.A. and I. Steinerowska-Streb (2012), 'Can social enterprise contribute to creating sustainable rural communities? Using the lens of structuration theory to analyse the emergence of rural social enterprise', *Local Economy*, **27** (2), 167–182.

11 Social and ecological entrepreneurship in a circular economy: the need for understanding transitional agency

Malin Henriksson, Martin Hultman, Nils Johansson, Anna Kaijser and Björn Wallsten[1]

Introduction

Recently, ideas of circling the economy and in particular on the resource and energy flows that sustain it have been brought, at least rhetorically, into the core of state policies (European Commission, 2015) and business (Geissdoerfer et al., 2017). Simultaneously, the research on the topic has seen a remarkable proliferation and a recent literature review found over a hundred definitions of the term circular economy (Kirchherr et al., 2017). There are plenty of reasons to be reflexive when emerging concepts become so dominant in the environmental and social debate that all actors must relate to them, perhaps especially whenever such terms seem inherently fuzzy and elusive, like in this case. In the research we envision on social entrepreneurship (SE), we ask whether the concept of the circular economy is consistent enough to trigger environmental challenges to be taken seriously and create agency for a transition towards a less resource-intensive and more sustainable economy or whether it implies 'greenwashing' of existing, unsustainable patterns of production and consumption.

Previous studies have demonstrated that the adoption of circular economy practices often becomes a side activity without generating any significant agentic energy towards more sustainable practices (Corvellec and Stål, 2017). For example, one of the world's largest clothing retailers has built a take-back system which they state is based on circular economy principles, in which a returned bag of used clothes entails a voucher of 5 euros to buy new ones. However, and quite contradictory to the stated environmental ambitions, such voucher-based strategies encourage more consumption and thus fit perfectly in line with the unchanged core activity of these businesses: to sell large quantities of cheap clothes (Corvellec and Stål, 2017). Adopting a critical stance towards the concept of circular economy and how it has so far been used in different contexts, we argue that a focus on grassroots social entrepreneurs may implicate certain changes in circular economy-related research as well as entrepreneurship writ large. Combinations of these two research fields might furthermore provide fruitful trajectories going forward.

Background

A significant tendency within previous research on circular economy has been its bias towards large technical systems, such as waste management and industrial actors (European Commission, 2015; Geissdoerfer et al., 2017). If all the grandiose visions of circular economy were ever to be realized, waste management systems and industrial actors would for sure have a role to play in that transition. This is not to say, however, that many of the interesting initiatives that challenge linear thinking should be allowed to go under the radar. On the contrary, we see great reasons to engage in research on agents addressing a circular economy transition from below, a movement that is driven by social entrepreneurs and loosely organized citizens. Research on grassroots initiatives is still in the early stages, as indicated, for example, by the open questions and qualitative methods which have dominated this research to date (Galkina and Hultman, 2016). The field is thus in need of new perspectives, questions and methods. Recognition of and research on such ideas and initiatives can furthermore inspire more sustainable consumption patterns and circular business models on a greater scale, and thereby contribute to reaching several of the UN sustainable development goals as well as national environmental objectives. Research could highlight what can broadly be termed green entrepreneurship, and more specifically study ecopreneurs and social entrepreneurs as central actors (Isaak, 2002; Hockerts, 2006; Schaper, 2010; Hultman et. al., 2016).

In this chapter, we argue that transdisciplinary critical scrutiny of circular economy initiatives has the potential to inform and expand the transformative potential of the growing field of SE. We argue that ecopreneurship and SE are interesting lenses by which to explore disruptive forms of organizational models aimed towards facilitating a circular economy that is truly circular, and that different initiatives (non-profit and commercial) and different forms of entrepreneurship should also be included in the spectrum of scrutiny. We propose that an intersectional perspective enriches the ways in which the relationship between these initiatives and their outside worlds can be exposed. For example, we suggest investigations into whether these initiatives address and reach out to certain users but not others, and how and where such demarcation lines are drawn. We see distinct merits in scrutinizing the power dynamics of ecopreneur/social entrepreneur initiatives and how institutions such as legislation, policy and cultural norms affect and frame these dynamics. This is important to explore in order to further understand these actors' spaces of operation and further encourage their transformative work. Thus, we are obliged to ask whether these kinds of initiatives and activities serve to sustain the unsustainable, or whether they can actually contribute to tilting the economy into a more sustainable trajectory.

Circular economy, social entrepreneurs and ecopreneurs

Today, growing movements of concerned citizens and innovative entrepreneurs question how as well as what we consume, and instead strive to enable new, innovative forms of consumption based on circular economy models of bio-based and renewable resource use. In different ways, these actors use creative strategies to limit the leakage of resources and emissions, thereby keeping resources 'within the economy whenever possible' (European Commission, 2015). Social entrepreneurs include, for example, entrepreneurs who want to 'make a difference', philanthropists who invest in companies with such ambitions, and non-profit organizations that use strategies from the business community to reach out to larger audiences with their initiatives (Mair et al., 2006). When connected to environmental issues Hultman and others have argued that the concept of ecopreneurship has evolved towards its 'second phase', in which society and businesses are open to more radical initiatives in terms of ambitions to change and modes of operation (Hultman et.al., 2016). The underlying motives for such a new phase are the mounting problems and the proven inability of the linear economy to come to grips with significant issues including climate change, pollution and resource depletion. Schaper describes some characteristics of actors that he labels ecopreneurs: 'they have the ability to identify a feasible business opportunity, their activities have an overall positive effect on the environment, and they see the move towards a more sustainable future as valuable' (Schaper, 2010: 8). In a sense, they act on Elisabeth Shove's (2012: 72) argument that many modern societal 'needs', which are seen as non-negotiable, have relatively short lifespans and do change rapidly.

The two conceptual categories of ecopreneurs and social entrepreneurs cover a wide range of stakeholders; to some extent they overlap with each other. A shared problem for ecopreneurs and social entrepreneurs is that their businesses rarely have explicit market advantages or advantages for the user in terms of lower prices and higher performance (Karakaya et al., 2014). These entrepreneurs most often suffer from a lack of profitability and low returns, but their activities bring environmental and social benefits by, for example, keeping mineral resources in the ground through reuse and recycling practices. This lack of profitability is of course not a consequence of their business model per se, but a combination of this model and how the societies subsidize, for example, fossil fuels and extractive industries (Hultman et al., 2016). For example, the fossil fuel sector as well as the mining sector receives higher subsidies and political support than the renewable fuel sector (IEA, 2011) and metal recycling sector (Johansson et al., 2014), respectively. Hence, fossil practices are institutionally rewarded, while regenerative practices are intuitively punished. Another example is seen in how mobility innovations such as bike and car pools face difficulties to become established solutions, due to how urban infrastructure planning is performed, the inaptitude of political decision making and the norms and values embedded in fossil-driven motorization (Hanson, 2010; Wangel et.al., 2013).

Changing existing consumption patterns and creating innovative business models have been recognized as vital steps towards circular economy (Soper, 2008; Bradley and Hedrén, 2014; EPA, 2015). This suggests that research on circular economy should focus its efforts, not on downstream waste management solutions, but rather upstream on product life cycles, and the consumption and production phase of products (Johansson and Corvellec, 2018). A possible approach to investigate the transition towards circular economy is to critically analyze entrepreneurial activity in different sectors in need of change. Here, we will use the Swedish context in order to illuminate how to choose areas of interest for analysis. Sweden is interesting due to its high ambition regarding sustainable development, for example related to transport (Hysing and Isaksson, 2015), food (Swedish Government, 2017) and waste management (Johansson and Corvellec, 2018).

The Swedish EPA repeats the well-known fact that production of animal products, including dairy, is more resource intensive than plant-based alternatives (EPA, 2015). Consumption of animal products carries a significant part of every country's total contribution to climate change (Peters et al., 2010), and replacing these products with plant-based alternatives can lower the emission of greenhouse gases (GHGs) significantly. For example, replacing dairy milk products with oat-based alternatives means a reduction of one third of the GHG emissions (Dahllöv and Gustavsson, 2008). Similarly, the reuse and redistribution of food through food banks can potentially reduce the ever-increasing food wastage, which affects the climate in an order of magnitude that is comparable to the total GHG emissions of countries such as USA or China (FAO, 2013). In terms of climate impact, transportation is the most emission-intensive sector in a country like Sweden (Minx et al., 2008). This sector's emissions come almost exclusively from the burning of fossil fuels, and a transition towards other less fossil intensive modes of transportation would thus contribute to significant emission savings.

The Swedish Environmental Protection Agency asserts that consumption patterns are difficult to change, since a high level of consumption is a strong societal norm and associated with desires and identity formation (EPA, 2015). While we acknowledge such structural difficulties, we would also like to emphasize the inspirational potential of alternative consumption initiatives from ecopreneurs and social entrepreneurs with high levels of transitional agency (cf. Soper, 2008). The extent to which such agents contribute to sustainability is poorly understood. They offer products and services that require less resources and/or are free or more affordable than conventional products or services, and they play an important role in disseminating visions of sustainable futures to their users and consumers. Still, it is important to reflect upon who is targeted by their activities, the possibilities of ecopreneur initiatives to reach significantly larger audiences, and the role of policy in enabling or hampering the spreading and deep scaling of initiatives and practices that may contribute to the circular economy.

Definitions of nature, environmental problems, human and non-human subjects, and ideals for sustainable human–nature interaction, do not simply reflect a reality of material conditions, but are also embedded in social relations (e.g. Feindt and Oels, 2005; Robbins, 2012). What is regarded as environmentally sustainable behavior is highly contextual and closely tied to social relations based on, for instance, income level, gender, age, and ethnicity, and also contingent on which environmental issue you focus on – problems like toxic leakages, GHG emissions, and waste issues, for example, require different kinds of actions. This means that there might be conflicts of interest among different environmental issues. As certain types of behavior are broadly recognized as environmentally sustainable with reference to certain environmental issues, they also become entangled with the formation of subjectivities that might be in conflict with other matters of environmental and social sustainability.

Advancing SE within circulating economies

What is to be considered a legitimate environmentalist subject is a matter of negotiation and varies over time and space (see Agrawal, 2005; Bradley, 2009). Recent studies in Sweden (see e.g. Bradley, 2009) suggest that the ability to be regarded as an environmentally friendly subject requires sustainable literacy in the form of certain environmental knowledge along with certain gender, class and ethnic features. Unfortunately, social structures such as these are often black boxed in research on the circular economy. We therefore argue for the engagement of intersectionality as a useful theoretical perspective that can help identify and analyze how social dynamics play out and affect and influence consumers as well as the activities of ecopreneurs and social entrepreneurs.

Intersectionality has evolved within feminist theory, as a sensitive tool for understanding power dynamics. It serves to shed light on how various structures of power based on categories like gender, race, class and age cannot be separated from each other, but always interact in all relations and encounters (de los Reyes and Mulinari, 2005; Kaijser and Kronsell, 2014). Relevant research questions when addressing transitional agency of social and ecological entrepreneurship can beneficially be divided in two sets.

The first of these deals with their possible contribution to the circular economy. For example: What are the expected environmental impacts of these initiatives? What capacity do they have to influence the level of consumption and the transition towards circular flows in the economy? Also, it is possible to go beyond the activities as such and look at the institutional configuration of their operations: Which existing public policies and instruments hinder or help these initiatives? What kind of policies and instruments can be envisioned to help these initiatives arise and grow?

The second set of questions relates more to the visions and outreach of these initiatives: How do ecopreneurs/social entrepreneurs translate ideas of circular and bio-based economy into practice? How do they envision their contribution to a more sustainable economy? Also, which audiences are the respective initiatives targeting, or omitting? How may their strategies be developed in order to reach a wider range of users and consumers?

To further advance the assessments of these initiatives and strengthen their potential to contribute towards sustainable consumption in a Swedish context, we suggest that interdisciplinary approaches that combine life cycle analysis (LCA) with ethnographic studies including in-depth interviews, on-site observations, workshops and document analysis provide a useful trajectory going forward (Bribián et al., 2011). However, the environmental impacts of SE are complex. For example, repair activities of a bike kitchen may not primary lead to avoided car traffic, but rather to prolonged lifespan of bicycles, and thus to fewer bikes being produced. How the activities of social entrepreneurs and ecopreneurs may change consumption patterns in practice thus needs to be mapped through in-depth interviews with both entrepreneurs and users, and through on-site observations.

Some final words

We argue that studying examples of how social entrepreneurs and ecopreneurs can contribute to social change and more sustainable production and consumption patterns by generating knowledge and expertise on the conditions in which these actors operate, and what kinds of public efforts can support and empower them. Support through policy instruments needs emphasis since such instruments are a key tool to achieve government-defined targets such as the UN sustainability goals as well as national environmental quality objectives. Existing research indicates that researchers' cooperation and dialogue with private and public actors is important to contribute to a process of change (Gawell et al., 2009). The results generated through research of this kind should therefore also aim to help to raise awareness of and knowledge about the various initiatives and highlight their role as encouraging transformative agency. By involving initiatives from key sectors, the results from these types of studies might serve as inspiration to other social entrepreneurs and ecopreneurs, but also form the basis for policy instruments and target public entities such as municipalities, county councils and other authorities.

NOTE
1 All authors contributed equally to this work.

References

Agrawal, A. (2005), *Environmentality: Technologies of Government and the Making of Subjects*, Durham, NC: Duke University Press.

Bradley, K. (2009), 'Planning for eco-friendly living in diverse societies', *Local Environment*, **14** (4), 347–363.

Bradley, K. and J. Hedrén (2014), "Utopian thought in the making of green futures", in K. Bradley and J. Hedrén (eds), *Green Utopianism. Perspectives, Politics and Micro-practices*, London: Routledge, pp. 1–20.

Bribián, I. Z., A. V. Capilla and A. A. Usón (2011), 'Life cycle assessment of building materials: comparative analysis of energy and environmental impacts and evaluation of the eco-efficiency improvement potential', *Building and Environment*, **46** (5), 1133–1140.

Corvellec, H. and H. I. Stål (2017), 'Evidencing the waste effect of Product-Service Systems (PSSs)', *Journal of Cleaner Production*, **145**, 14–24.

Dahllöv, O. and M. Gustafsson (2008), 'Livscykelanalys av Oatly havredryck', Master's thesis, Lund University.

de los Reyes, P. and D. Mulinari (2005), Intersektionalitet, Malmö: Liber.

EPA, Environmental Protection Agency (Naturvårdsverket) (2015), 'Hållbara konsumtionsmönster. Analyser av maten, flyget och den totala konsumtionens klimatpåverkan idag och 2050', Report 6653.

European Commission (2015), Closing the loop – an EU action plan for the circular economy, Brussels, accessed 10 October 2018 at http://eur-lex.europa.eu/legal-content/EN/TXT/?uri=CELEX:52015 DC0614.

FAO (2013), Food wastage footprint online, accessed February 16 2017 at http://www.fao.org/docrep/018/i3347e/i3347e.pdf.

Feindt, P. and A. Oels (2005), 'Does discourse matter? Discourse analysis in environmental policy making', Journal of Environmental Policy and Planning, 7 (3), 161–173.

Galkina, T. and M. Hultman (2016), 'Ecopreneurship – assessing the field and outlining the research potential', Small Enterprise Research, 23 (1), 58–72.

Gawell, Malin, Bengt Johannisson and Mats Lundqvist (2009), Samhällets entreprenörer: en forskarantalogi om samhällsentreprenörskap, Stockholm: KK-stiftelsen.

Geissdoerfer, M., P. Savaget, N. M. Bocken and E. J. Hultink (2017), 'The Circular Economy – a new sustainability paradigm?', Journal of Cleaner Production, 143 (1), 757–768.

Hanson, S. (2010), 'Gender and mobility: new approaches for informing sustainability', Gender, Place and Culture, 17 (1), 5–23.

Hockerts, K. (2006), 'Introduction to Part IV – ecopreneurship: unique research field or just "more of the same"?', in J. Mair, J. Robinson and K. Hockerts (eds), Social Entrepreneurship, Basingstoke: Palgrave Macmillan, pp. 209–213.

Hultman, M., K. J. Bonnedahl and K. J. O'Neill (2016), 'Unsustainable societies – sustainable businesses? Introduction to special issue of small enterprise research on transitional ecopreneurs', Small Enterprise Research, 23 (1), 1–9.

Hysing, E. and K. Isaksson (2015), 'Building acceptance for congestion charges – the Swedish experiences compared', Journal of Transport Geography, 49, 52–60.

IEA (2011), 'World energy outlook', International Energy Agency, Paris, France.

Isaak, R. (2002), 'The making of the ecopreneur', Greener Management International, 38, 81–91.

Johansson, N., J. Krook and M. Eklund (2014), 'Institutional conditions for Swedish metal production: a comparison of subsidies to metal mining and metal recycling', Resources Policy, 41, 72–82.

Johansson, N. and H. Corvellec (2018), 'Waste policies gone soft: an analysis of European and Swedish waste prevention plans', Waste Management, 77, 322–332.

Kaijser, A. and A. Kronsell (2014), 'Climate change through the lens of intersectionality', Environmental politics, 23 (3), 417–433.

Karakaya, E., A. Hidalgo and C. Nuur (2014), 'Diffusion of eco-innovations: a review', Renewable and Sustainable Energy Reviews, 33, 392–399.

Kirchherr, J., D. Reike and M. Hekkert (2017), 'Conceptualizing the circular economy: an analysis of 114 definitions. Resources, conversation and recycling', 127, 221–232.

Mair, J., J. Robinson, and K. Hockerts (eds) (2006), Social Entrepreneurship, New York: Palgrave Macmillan.

Minx, J. C., K. Scott and G. Peters (2008), 'An analysis of Sweden's carbon footprint. WWF Sweden', accessed 24 August 2018 at http://www.wwf.se/source.php/1242860/4553_Swedenscarbonfootprint_SIDA.pdf.

Peters, G. M., H. V. Rowley, S. Wiedemann, R. Tucker, M. D. Short and M. Schulz (2010), 'Red meat production in Australia: life cycle assessment and comparison with overseas studies', Environmental Science and Technology, 44(4), 1327–1332.

Schaper, M. T. (2010), 'Understanding the green entrepreneur', in M. T. Schaper (ed.), Making Ecopreneurs: Developing Sustainable Entrepreneurship', Farnham: Gower Publishing, pp. 7–20.

Shove, E. (2012), 'Energy transitions in practice: the case of global indoor climate change', in G. Verbong, and D. Loorbach (eds), *Governing the Energy Transition: Reality, Illusion or Necessity?*, London: Routledge, pp. 51–74.

Soper, K. (2008), 'Alternative hedonism, cultural theory and the role of aesthetic revisioning', *Cultural Studies*, **22** (5), 567–587.

Swedish Government (2015), *Smart industry – en nyindustrialiseringsstrategi för Sverige*, N2015, 38.

Swedish Government (2017), *A food strategy for Sweden – more jobs and sustainable growth throughout the country.* Government proposition 2016/17:104.

Wangel, J., S. Gustafsson, and Ö. Svane (2013), 'Goal-based socio-technical scenarios: greening the mobility practices in the Stockholm City District of Bromma, Sweden', *Futures*, **47**, 79–92.

12 Gender and social entrepreneurship research: contemporary themes

Kate V. Lewis and Colette Henry

Introduction

Contemporary scholarship recognizes the growing importance of entrepreneurship globally, and increasingly acknowledges that entrepreneurship is a gendered phenomenon (Jennings and Brush, 2013). As a consequence, research in the area of gender and entrepreneurship has attracted considerable attention from researchers, practitioners and policy makers in recent years, and its theoretical reach has extended beyond the traditional commercial/for-profit sector into social and non-profit ventures (Clark Muntean and Ozkazanc-Pan, 2016). Indeed, there is a small body of work that covers the point at which considerations of gender intersect with the domain of social entrepreneurship (SE) scholarship. While it is undoubtedly both a niche and emergent area of focus, the research that characterizes it is relatively robust in that it tends to take gender as its central focus (rather than merely as a by-product of a larger or supposedly more important dimension of interest). However, as is typical of any embryonic lens to understanding a pre-existing phenomenon, there is currently more that is *unknown* than *known*. This has theoretical and methodological implications in terms of what informs the area currently, as well as what research may extend its boundaries as scholars seek to move understanding forward.

At present, research is more often quantitative, using moderate- to large-scale samples, or grounded in secondary data analysis (i.e. a type of 'map via review' approach) – as opposed to intensive, smaller-scale, qualitative studies oriented to paradigms that seek to capture voice rather than attribute activity. There is some irony that a 'gender as variable' approach has a catalytic role in the research origins of this as a distinct topic, given that as the knowledge base moves from emergent to established it is argued that research must instead be characterized by a 'gender as lens' approach. In light of this, the chapter offers an overview of how gender is conceptualized in SE by articulating key contemporary themes in the gender and SE literature. In so doing, the chapter highlights both the known and the unknown in relation to the socially entrepreneurial endeavours of women, and points to the value of ongoing investigations in this field.

Gender and SE scholarship

Three primary explanatory divisions in respect of the existing research literature on gender and SE can be identified. The first consists of work that seeks to establish the presence of women in terms of socially entrepreneurial behaviour and articulates *what we know*; the second focuses on the knowledge gap: that is, *what we do not know* about women in SE; while the third theme constitutes research that draws upon *learning from other disciplines*. These three themes are discussed below.

What we know

Research within this thematic division can broadly be characterized as counting exercises that seek to capture a sense of what is already occurring in terms of female SE activity (some drawing on empirical data and others on the secondary analysis of large pre-existing data sets). The focus is on 'doing' rather than 'being' with an emphasis on writing up 'success stories' – though some of these do take a genuinely analytic approach and are published in robust academic journals (e.g. Datta and Gailey, 2012).

So, from such research what is known about women relative to SE activity? We know that women participate, but (to date) to a lesser extent than men. However, evidence suggests that the extent of the gap in participation is not as prominent as in commercial (or for-profit) entrepreneurship (Bernardino et al., 2018). Indeed, Teasdale et al. (2011) argue that increasingly equal levels of female participation by women as social entrepreneurs is a deliberate rejection of the hierarchical organizational structures of business that were constructed to both serve and perpetuate the interests of men. They assert that it may also be a means of rebelling against modern male-dominant conceptualizations of heroic capitalistic forms of entrepreneurship, as well as against the ongoing positioning of the male social entrepreneur as a type of 'Robin Hood' who creatively destructs (as per Schumpeter) societal inequalities while continuing to occupy a protector and provider status (Marlow, 2014).

Large-scale quantitative data sets centred around cross-country analysis of entrepreneurial behaviour reinforce many of these conclusions. For example, data from the Global Entrepreneurship Monitor (GEM) indicated that social enterprises were more likely to be started by men than women (Terjesen et al., 2011). However, taking a more fine-grained approach and using a different phase of the same longitudinal data collection methodology (i.e. GEM data from 2009 specific to the United Kingdom), Levie and Hart (2011) found some hitherto anomalous patterns of engagement. Their analysis showed that social entrepreneurs in the United Kingdom were more likely to be female, and women were more likely to engage in socially entrepreneurial behaviour if they resided in an economically deprived area. They were also more likely to participate in their social venture on a full-time basis than their male counterparts.

Also using a large-scale quantitative data set from the United Kingdom (secondary analysis of the Citizenship Survey and Labour Force Survey), Teasdale et al. (2011) found that third sector organizations employed around twice as many men as women, which was a similar ratio to the public sector (but, the opposite of the private sector). There was a higher proportion of women managers and professionals in smaller rather than larger third sector organizations, and only a tenth of women working in the sector reached the highest levels compared to a fifth of men (whereas the same proportion of women and men reached lower managerial positions). Unusually, women were only slightly less likely to initiate and lead third sector social ventures than men (this considered to be a proxy for acting as a social entrepreneur).

In being socially entrepreneurial, women tend to work at a local (cf. global) scale and in a 'grass roots' mode rather than at the social innovation end of the activity spectrum. Some argue that this is a direct corollary of the role of women as conduit between community, business and society (Clark Muntean and Ozkazanc-Pan, 2016; Dimitriadis et al., 2017), and because volunteering is often the antecedent to their engagement. This is not unrelated to the argument that the female contribution to the domain of SE is merely an extension (or projection) of existing roles (often tied to gendered norms or traits, and those related to class) (Levie and Hart, 2011).

What we do not know

The second theme that characterizes current research on women and SE takes the opposite stance to the above and is oriented to narrating what is not known: that is, a form of gap analysis that in turn sets out an agenda for future research. This work coalesces around the primary conclusion that what is not known about female social entrepreneurs is understanding 'why' they do what they do (Levie and Hart, 2011), and 'how' they do it (either in terms of tangible manifestations of behaviour and process or, in a more nuanced sense, how sense of such activity is made relative to the whole of their life).

Other imperatives reported as being essential to moving the research agenda forward feature more abstract concerns related to the primacy of gender within the knowledge schema: for example, moving beyond the one-dimensional interpretation of the rationale for female engagement as being inherently related to a gendered 'caring and sharing' rationale (Teasdale et al., 2011). The promulgation of this type of reductive, gendered, pseudo explanation of socially entrepreneurial activity by women is said to be, in part, due to the relative immaturity of the domain of inquiry itself. However, many such assumptions that are given a degree of explanatory power are rooted in ascriptions derived from culture, embeddedness related to community, family or other units of belonging (and the constraints that ensue as a cost or consequence of membership), and a trait-driven approach to behaviour (Nicolás and Rubio, 2016). For example, altruism and 'social-mindedness' are suggested as being more characteristic of women than men (Huysentruyt, 2014). More useful is when such claims are used as theoretical springboards from which more complex extrapolations can be postulated. For example, Themudo (2009) argues that the proclivity of women to be pro-social means that it is probable that as the relative share of resources and participation in the economy by women increases, the supply of private resources (fiscal or otherwise) being directed to the non-profit sector as a result should also, in turn, increase.

Notwithstanding the above, gendered ascriptions have the potential to amplify and reinforce one another at a micro level, while at a macro level, broader structural influences may also be deterministic (particularly in differing regional and country level geographic contexts). Indeed, issues of 'place' have the potential to acutely affect both the experience and execution of socially entrepreneurial behaviour by women (Dimitriadis et al., 2017): for example, the contrast between developed and developing country contexts, where SE may be enacted as a micro-enterprise shaped by a micro-finance intervention in the latter environment, as opposed to social innovation in the context of a business model social enterprise in the former. The geo-context is especially pertinent to consider where women may be both the target of an initiative and the primary actors, especially given that it may result in a dual emphasis (i.e. on the socially entrepreneurial activity as well as its broader relationship to the potential for social inclusion, empowerment and economic sustainability and/or poverty reduction for women) (Datta and Gailey, 2012; Fotheringham and Saunders, 2014).

Following on from this power of gendered ascription is the categorization of related roles (the most obvious being care-giving in the maternal sense) and whether these, and their correlated behavioural patterns, further or limit our understanding of how women enact SE. For example, women are more likely to be involved in a social enterprise as a volunteer or employee (cf. leader, founder or social innovator) (Jennings and Brush, 2013) and female socially entrepreneurial activity is more likely to be of a small scale, at a local level and be needs driven (cf. large-scale, globally ambitious endeavours driven by a social innovation) (Themudo, 2009). Dimitriadis et al. (2017) point out that there is also a risk of the reproduction of existing models of behaviour and argue that as the social sector is predominantly female and often operates under a charity model schema, it socially validates the appropriateness of charitable activity for women (cf. a commercialization model of social enterprise). This, on top of the trait-driven, role-based conditioning that occurs early on in the female life-cycle, may mean that women choose roles in the SE context (as in others) that validate those inclinations. This essentially then represents a forced, or at least coercive rather than voluntary, relationship with third sector engagement for many women (Teasdale et al., 2011).

This same diminished set of expectations around behaviour by women was faced early on in the pursuit of understanding generic (cf. social) entrepreneurship but has, over time and with evidence, been replaced by a far subtler and fine-grained understanding. It is likely that the same transition, and cycle of knowledge development, can occur in respect of understanding gendered SE engagement. However, we can hope that it occurs with greater haste given the foundations and awareness that already exist in the broader domain of investigation, and is facilitated by the adoption of a cumulative (rather than merely incremental) approach to knowledge generation given the overlaps in both real-world experience and theory-building.

Learning from other disciplines

The third, and final, theme is research that draws upon frameworks derived from other disciplines, or the individual domains of SE and female entrepreneurship (rather than the nexus of the two). It further articulates (in a more theoretically complex fashion) the voids in understanding and reasons those out (either in terms of lack or need) via the application of such theory. For example, while existing literature suggests that patterns of participation and progression by female social entrepreneurs mimic barriers faced by women in other public spheres of life, these patterns remain underscored by the tendency of the private to impede or enable action. However, we do not understand how, or if, the power and influence of structure, and the possible diminishment of the agentic power of women, occur in the same shape and form as 'for-profit' entrepreneurship.

Scholars advocate the need for gender-specific, empirically driven research in the domain of SE, and associated gendered theoretical conceptualizations, with some very specific and well-grounded caveats. For example, not only does the work need to be theoretically driven, gendered in its foundations, deep in intent, and broad in scope, but it must also (and essentially) draw upon feminist critiques. It also needs to move beyond what Marlow (2014) describes as a preoccupation with exploring whether there is something essential that conceptually bridges the link between the feminine and the social. Methodologically, this then signals a need for research design that privileges voice, subjectivity, narrative, story and richness, and gives greatest primacy to methods that are sensitive to the spectrum of feminist inquiry. These methods must also seek to support the problematization of the gender-neutral and gender-blind assumptions related to theorizing in the field of SE (Clark Muntean and Ozkazanc-Pan, 2016). Echoing such calls, Calas et al. (2009) argue that liberal, psychoanalytic and radical feminism perspectives would reframe entrepreneurship as a social change activity that may benefit women (cf. an economic-only imperative).

While every new perspective on a phenomenon needs to nurture and feed its impetus, it must do so mindfully and in a way that leverages accumulated understanding from its origin platforms. In this sense, the fact that gender is further along its theoretical trajectory in terms of both temporality and nuance is both useful and inspiring when approaching the topic from a primarily SE starting point. A reflection of this is that much of the existing research is by gender scholars (rather than SE researchers). This work is theoretically driven and takes as its starting point women (logically). Conversely, SE researchers tend to take the activity, output or organizational form as a starting point and probe gender as a departure point in terms of demography only. Gender scholars in particular put forward scholarship in the area as an integral part of moving the knowledge frontier forward, and argue eloquently and assertively for the creation of a gender-aware framework via which to explore female experiences of SE (Clark Muntean and Ozkazanc-Pan, 2016). The underpinning belief is that women are active in distinct ways and that the why and how of that is mostly opaque (other than the acceptance that what is known is, in no limited way, driven by stereotype, norm and culturally ascribed role-oriented assumptions) (Haugh, 2005). Jennings and Brush (2013) are especially emphatic in 'daring' scholars of women's entrepreneurship to boldly pursue SE as a topic of importance.

Conclusion

In a relatively under-developed area of focus such as gender and SE it is somewhat unusual to already have a corpus of work that looks backwards as well as forwards. However, this reflects two primary characteristics of the area itself: its modernity and its hybridity. The study of SE is neither mature nor well anchored from a disciplinary perspective. However, it does epitomize the real-time curiosity and relevance in terms of the phenomenon itself, and the way it has captured the imagination of researchers, policy makers and practitioners alike. In tandem with this 'newness' is the relative youthfulness of gendered understandings of female for-profit entrepreneurial behaviour and the hybridity that exists when this is coupled with a drive to understand what socially entrepreneurial behaviour from a gendered perspective may contribute to the 'field' as a whole. The swift pace of, and enthusiasm for, ongoing investigation in this area is set to result in an ever-expanding evidence base.

References

Bernardino, S., Freitas Santos. J. and Cadima Ribeiro, J. (2018), 'Social entrepreneur and gender: What's personality got to do with it?, *International Journal of Gender and Entrepreneurship*, **10** (1), 61–82.

Calas, M. B., Smircich, L. and Bourne, K. A. (2009), 'Extending the boundaries: Reframing "entrepreneurship as social change" through feminist perspectives', *Academy of Management Review*, **34** (3), 552–569.

Clark Muntean, S. and Ozkazanc-Pan, B. (2016), 'Feminist perspectives on social entrepreneurship: Critique and new directions', *International Journal of Gender and Entrepreneurship*, **8** (3), 221–241.

Datta, P. B. and Gailey, R. (2012), 'Empowering women through social entrepreneurship: Case study of a women's cooperative in India', *Entrepreneurship Theory and Practice*, **36** (3), 569–587.

Dimitriadis, S., Lee, M., Ramarajan, L. and Battilana, J. (2017), 'Blurring the boundaries: The interplay of gender and local communities in the commercialization of social ventures', *Organization Science*, **28** (5), 819–839.

Fotheringham, S. and Saunders, C. (2014), 'Social enterprise as poverty reducing strategy for women', *Social Enterprise Journal*, **10** (3), 176–199.

Haugh, H. (2005), 'A research agenda for social entrepreneurship', *Social Enterprise Journal*, **1** (1), 1–12.

Huysentruyt, M. (2014), 'Women's social entrepreneurship and innovation', *OECD Local Economic and Employment Development (LEED), Working Papers*, 2014/01, Paris: OECD.

Jennings, J. E. and Brush, C. G. (2013), 'Research on women entrepreneurs: Challenges to (and from) the broader entrepreneurship literature?', *Academy of Management Annals*, **7** (1), 663–715.

Levie, J. and Hart, M. (2011), 'Business and social entrepreneurs in the UK: Gender, context and commitment', *International Journal of Gender and Entrepreneurship*, **3** (3), 200–217.

Marlow, S. (2014), 'Exploring future research agendas in the field of gender and entrepreneurship', *International Journal of Gender and Entrepreneurship*, **6** (2), 102–120.

Nicolás, C. and Rubio, A. (2016), 'Social enterprise: Gender gap and economic development', *European Journal of Management and Business Economics*, **25** (2), 56–62.

Teasdale, S., McKay, S., Phillimore, J. and Teasdale, N. (2011), 'Exploring gender and social entrepreneurship: Women's leadership, employment and participation in the third sector and social enterprises', *Voluntary Sector Review*, **2** (1), 57–76.

Terjesen, S., Lepoutre, J., Justo, R. and Bosma, N. (2011), *Global Entrepreneurship Monitor: Report on Social Entrepreneurship*, London: London Business School.

Themudo, N. S. (2009), 'Gender and the nonprofit sector', *Nonprofit and Voluntary Sector Quarterly*, **38** (4), 663–683.

13 Māori Indigenous research: impacting social enterprise and entrepreneurship

Ella Henry and Léo-Paul Dana

Introduction

This chapter draws together the social entrepreneurship, social capital and cultural capital literature to inform the analysis of a research project in New Zealand that has incorporated Māori Indigenous researchers, a Māori social enterprise and its local community that are facing extreme challenges and seeking solutions. It contributes to the small but growing field that highlights Indigenous perspectives on social entrepreneurship and the context within which these endeavours occur. We argue that social enterprise delivers more than business activity, whether through for-profit or non-profit businesses. Indigenous social enterprise and social entrepreneurs also bring together Indigenous communities to work collaboratively for cultural revitalization and social change. Further, we explore the role of Indigenous researchers and Indigenous research methodologies in contributing to cultural revitalization and social change.

Connecting with the social entrepreneurship literature

The social entrepreneurship literature brings together a range of disciplines, including entrepreneurial studies, social innovation and non-profit management, which suggests a focus on identity, networks and institutions will enrich theorizing in the field (Dacin et al. 2011). Grimes et al. (2013) also highlight the debate around what makes social entrepreneurship distinct from other forms of organizing and point to the importance of the founder's motivation and compassion as key ingredients in social enterprise formation. They argue 'that, in order to fully understand embedded agency, social entrepreneurship scholars must start by examining the environmental and market conditions that give rise to particular social entrepreneurial opportunities' (Grimes et al. 2013, p. 461). For Chell et al. (2010, p. 486) social entrepreneurship involves the same levels of opportunity identification and exploitation as commercial entrepreneurship, but these are to 'enhance social wealth. The central driver for social entrepreneurship is the social problem being addressed in an innovative and entrepreneurial way.' They urge further cross-country studies to better understand this phenomenon.

Building on these debates about identifying, defining and developing theory for social entrepreneurship, social entrepreneurs and social enterprise, Dacin et al. (2010) developed an entrepreneurship typology, distinguishing between conventional, institutional, cultural and social entrepreneurs, with the latter two focusing on non-profit organizations delivering cultural enlightenment and social change and wellbeing. They proffer the notion that:

> *Relational resources, such as social capital and "social skills," are the elements of an actor's social network or interpersonal context . . . Cultural resources, defined in terms of the norms, values, roles, language, attitudes, beliefs and aesthetic expressions of a community . . . we believe that the ability to collect, understand and leverage cultural knowledge constitutes a key resource from which social entrepreneurs can and must draw.* (Dacin et al. 2010, p. 49)

This literature leads into more specific domains of social entrepreneurship or emerging fields that draw on similar views about entrepreneurship and enterprise. For example, ethnic (Dana 2007; Volery 2007), immigrant (Chand and Ghorbani 2011), Indigenous (Dana 2015; Dana and Anderson 2007; Foley and O'Connor 2011; Tapsell and Woods 2010) subsistence (Viswanathan et al. 2014) and, alongside that, Māori entrepreneurship (Frederick and Henry 2004; Henry 2012) are evolving similar research interests. These also focus on identity, founder motivations, environmental and historical impacts, as well as the commitments of these diverse populations of entrepreneurs to enhance social wealth and to embrace cultural enlightenment, social change and wellbeing for their communities of interest. A growing number of researchers also acknowledge the relevance of social and cultural capital and their potential to enhance or impede social innovation and enterprise (Casson and Giusta 2007; Chell et al. 2016; Kerlin 2006). Bosma et al. (2016, p. 55) link social entrepreneurship to social capital in local neighbourhoods and argue that 'both high and low levels of social capital in a local environment may create higher degrees of social entrepreneurial activity'. Thus, a discussion of social and cultural capital is relevant to this analysis.

Social and cultural capital

According to Woolcock (1998 p. 155), 'To physical and human capital, sociologists and political scientists . . . have thus begun to speak of *social* capital, a broad term encompassing the norms and networks facilitating collective action for mutual benefit'. Bosma et al. (2016) distinguish between social capital at the macro (institutions, norms and cultural attitudes), meso (local or regional collectives) and micro level (personal social networks and resources). Alongside social capital, cultural capital focuses on shared values and beliefs (Lamont and Lareau 1988). Bourdieu (1977) coined the term cultural capital when analysing the impacts of culture on the class system. Adler and Kwon (2002) suggest that cultural capital can be acquired by means of social capital, thereby suggesting the link between the two. Based on her work with impoverished communities of colour Yosso (2005, p. 82) writes:

Communities of Color are places with multiple strengths. In contrast, deficit scholars bemoan a lack of cultural capital . . . CRT (critical race theory) shifts the research lens away from a deficit view of Communities of Color as places full of cultural poverty or disadvantages and instead focuses on and learns from these communities' cultural assets and wealth.

These perspectives inform the analysis of an Indigenous and Māori social enterprise and their access to and application of social and cultural capital.

Indigenous and Māori entrepreneurship

Early writers on Indigenous entrepreneurship have worked to develop relevant, multi-disciplinary approaches, but all have focused on the key goals of Indigenous enterprise to empower and rebuild communities, to address poverty and the impacts of colonization and to enhance self-determination (Dana and Anderson 2007; Foley 2004; Henry 2007, 2012; Peredo et al. 2004). Hindle and Moroz (2010, p. 363) define Indigenous entrepreneurship as 'the creation, management and development of new ventures by Indigenous people for the benefit of Indigenous people'. For Cahn (2008) Indigenous business brings together cultural and social factors in unique ways and for Frederick and Henry (2004) Indigenous entrepreneurs use standard business practice to benefit their communities rather than the individual. These same attributes can be applied to Māori entrepreneurship.

Māori are the Indigenous people of New Zealand, which became a British Colony on 6 February 1840 with the signing of the Treaty of Waitangi. Prior to colonization Māori enjoyed extensive interactions with the outside world from the arrival of Captain Cook in 1769. These frequently involved trade with the growing number of visitors to the South Pacific including whalers, missionaries and ships to or from the New South Wales Penal Colony. Māori were actively engaged in manufacture and trade with over £34 000 of goods being produced for the Sydney market in 1831 at a time when fewer than 200 non-Māori lived in the country (Petrie 2006). However, after signing the Treaty Māori suffered the consequences of encroaching state power, through military might and repressive legislation, resulting in the Land Wars (Belich 1988) and consequent expropriation of land and economic power (Walker 1990). By the close of the nineteenth century Māori faced destitution and extinction, about which Newman (1881, p. 477) stated, 'Taking all things into consideration, the disappearance of the race is scarcely subject for much regret. They are dying out in a quick, easy way and are being supplanted by a superior race'. By the twentieth century, particularly post-WWII, as significant numbers of Māori relocated to the cities, there was a rekindling of Māori language and culture, which Walker (1990) termed the Māori Renaissance. As of the 1970s a rise in activism and protest occurred, demanding that the Treaty be honoured and increasing the aspirations for self-determination and sovereignty.

Māori entrepreneurs have contributed to this renaissance through cultural, linguistic and economic revitalization (Henry 2012; Henry et al. 2017). One could argue that the history of commercial enterprise became embedded in Māori culture from the eighteenth century because it resonated for a people who had drawn on risk-taking and opportunity exploitation over the centuries of the Austronesian diaspora across the South Pacific (Chambers and Edinur 2015). However, these shared values of exploration, innovation, discovery and risk-taking, the cultural wealth and assets of Māori people, may also be enhanced by social capital, which in turn is a characteristic of kinship society predicated on tribal networks and relationships. Taken together, these assets, cultural and social, have been negatively impacted by a recent history of colonial expropriation and economic disadvantage. These negative factors have been ameliorated by cultural revitalization and the growing body of knowledge being generated by Māori scholars who are part of this renaissance. The following is one such example of Māori researchers and Māori social enterprise working collaboratively to find strategies and solutions for their communities of interest.

The research project

In 2014 the government allocated significant funding over 10 years for 11 National Science Challenges. These were designed to take a more strategic approach to science investment, with specifically targeted goals to achieve major and enduring benefits across a wide range of areas. Each is underpinned by specific principles to be mission-led, have high levels of science quality, ensure purposeful collaboration, and maximize stakeholder engagement and public participation. They must have strong Māori involvement and give effect to Vision *Mātauranga*, which is the policy created by the Ministry of Research, Science and Technology 'to provide strategic direction for research of relevance to Māori' (MRST 2007, p. 2).

The impetus for Māori-centric research has been integral in the discourse amongst Māori scholars for decades, particular in the emerging field of Kaupapa Māori, a term to describe critical theory for and by Māori (Smith 1987). For Nepe (1991), Kaupapa Māori is derived from distinctive cultural, epistemological and metaphysical foundations, which were marginalized as Eurocentric knowledge systems were integrated as part of the colonial experience (Henry and Pene 2001; Smith 1996). Vision Mātauranga policy and goals are closely linked to the notion of partnership between Māori and the Crown.

Within one of these, the Building Better Homes, Towns and Cities Challenge, Vision Mātauranga is exemplified in the metaphorical image of a traditional meeting house (whare) which illustrates the partnership between Māori and non-Māori researchers who share a common vision for improving the built environment and its communities. Alongside this ontological foundation for the research are a range of research projects that draw on Kaupapa Māori methodology. For Cooper (2012, p. 64) 'Kaupapa Māori . . . must stand aloof from the concerns of science and centre Māori epistemologies as a starting point for research'. The methodological principles that inform these research methods were articulated as:

- research that is for, with and by Māori where possible;
- research that validates *te reo me ngā tikanga* Māori (Māori language and culture);
- research that empowers and results in positive outcomes for Māori; and
- research that benefits both researchers and end users.

These principles were applied in the research project outlined below.

Neighbourhood regeneration: an Indigenous perspective

The Tamaki Regeneration Project covers three Auckland suburbs, which were developed in the 1930s as a large state (social) housing area. They are relatively close to Central Auckland, with in-demand coastline properties bordering the harbour, bus and rail access. The project encompasses diverse business and industry interests, as well as schools, Marae (Māori community centres), Kōhanga (Māori-language early child-care), under-utilized open space and an aging housing stock on large properties. Amongst the longer-term residents are one of the highest proportions of Māori and Pacific peoples in Auckland. The Tamaki Redevelopment Company is a joint venture between national and local governments which aims to deliver 7500 new homes and community facilities over 10–15 years. As part of the process government transferred ownership and management of 2800 Housing New Zealand properties in the area. Between 2013 and 2018 a number of developments occurred, removing the old and replacing it with new in a mixed portfolio of market-value, affordable and social housing. To facilitate this development social housing tenants were moved until the new housing was available for their return. Many of those tenants had lived in the area for decades, some being forcibly removed in the public eye (Miller 2017). Whilst for many the transformation is impressive and those who own property in the area have seen massive increases in their capital gains, for the most vulnerable, the social housing tenants, the impact has been devastating.

One local non-governmental organization, Mad Ave Community Trust, has been working in the community development sector since 2010. Directors of the Trust are both well-known Māori social entrepreneurs in the area who work in media, health and community enterprise. Mad Ave Community Trust specializes in building and implementing a wide range of creative and innovative programmes that foster community cohesion and wellbeing.[1] The Trust bases its organizational structure and strategy on what it describes as 'Indigenous wisdom and innovative technologies that culminates into generative outcomes' (Patuwai 2018). In 2018 the Trust hosted an event entitled Home Fires where they opened the doors of two houses owned by Trust directors in a street where every other home had been demolished and whilst the rebuild of new, high-density dwellings was occurring. These homes would be difficult for many of the local residents to purchase at market prices. The Trust wanted to share stories from those who had been negatively affected by the regeneration project. Their objective was to give voice to the voiceless.

The research team gave support in the form of sponsorship, made presentations during the event and worked with young locals and community researchers afterwards to compile, analyse and disseminate their images and stories as research outputs and outcomes. Participants shared these stories of loss and the consequent social and health issues as whole streets were demolished and families and long-standing communities were separated. The event attracted many still living in the area and others who had moved out. They were joined by artists, musicians and representatives from local government and other community organizations. Youths in the area had created art, painting murals to express their sense of loss. People came and shared food and stories throughout the week. It was clear to those who participated that this was a meaningful and warmly received event. The Home Fires gathering provided an opportunity to share and reflect, to co-create strategies and build resilience. Further, as a consequence of the event and relationship with the researchers the Trust has developed a programme to facilitate saving for and buying affordable homes and the young artists are looking to build their activities into a cooperative enterprise. Both researchers and the researched were part of the development of this new knowledge and concomitant community connections and resources, enhancing social capital. This event and other initiatives growing out of it give weight to the notion that researchers have the potential to not only create new knowledge but also to strengthen the communities they study, particularly when the researchers and the researched share common values and cultural connections.

Conclusion

This case illustrates how social entrepreneurs and researchers who share cultural capital (in this case, the shared values and world view of an Indigenous people) might work collaboratively to enhance the social capital of the enterprise at the macro, meso and micro-levels. It also contributes to the literature that focuses on the ways that Māori Indigenous research and researchers can contribute to building the capacity of social enterprise that represents the interests of impoverished or disadvantaged communities who seek to find local solutions to their broader challenges and concerns. It calls for more research for, with and by Indigenous peoples to address Indigenous issues and concerns whilst contributing to Indigenous theory development. Finally, it asks non-Indigenous scholars, institutions, journals, publishers, reviewers and other holders of institutional knowledge and power to walk alongside Indigenous peoples in this endeavour.

NOTE

1 http://www.madave.co.nz/about-us. Accessed 25 February 2019.

References

Adler, P.S. and S-W. Kwon (2002), 'Social capital: Prospects for a new concept', *Academy of Management Review*, **27** (1), 17–40.

Belich, J. (1988), *The New Zealand Wars and the Victorian Interpretation of Racial Conflict*, Auckland, NZ: Auckland University Press.

Bosma, N., V. Schutjens and B. Volker (2016), 'Local social entrepreneurship and social capital', in H. Westlund and J. Larrson (eds), *Handbook of Social Capital and Regional Development*, Cheltenham, UK and Northampton, USA: Edward Elgar Publishing, pp. 55–81.

Bourdieu, P. (1977), *Outline of a Theory of Practice*, Cambridge, UK: Cambridge University Press.

Cahn, M. (2008), 'Indigenous entrepreneurship, culture and micro-enterprise in the Pacific Islands: Case studies from Samoa', *Entrepreneurship and Regional Development: An International Journal*, **20** (1), 1–18.

Casson, M. and M.D. Giusta (2007), 'Entrepreneurship and social capital: Analysing the impact of social networks on entrepreneurial activity from a rational action perspective', *International Small Business Journal*, **25** (3), 220–244.

Chambers, G.K. and H.A. Edinur (2015), 'The Austronesian diaspora: A synthetic total evidence model', *Global Journal of Anthropology Research*, **2** (2), 53–65.

Chand, M. and M. Ghorbani (2011), 'National culture, networks and ethnic entrepreneurship: A comparison of the Indian and Chinese immigrants in the US', *International Business Review*, **20** (6), 593–606.

Chell, E., K. Nicolopoulou and M. Karataş-Özkan (2010), 'Social entrepreneurship and enterprise: International and innovation perspectives', *Entrepreneurship and Regional Development*, **22** (6), 485–493.

Chell, E., L.J. Spence, F. Perrini and J.D. Harris (2016), 'Social entrepreneurship and business ethics: Does social equal ethical?', *Journal of Business Ethics*, **133** (4), 619–625.

Cooper, G. (2012), 'Kaupapa Māori research: Epistemic wilderness as freedom?', *New Zealand Journal of Educational Studies*, **47** (2), 64–73.

Dacin, P.A., M.T. Dacin and M. Matear (2010), 'Social entrepreneurship: Why we don't need a new theory and how we move forward from here', *Academy of Management Perspectives*, **24** (3), 37–57.

Dacin, M.T., P.A. Dacin and P. Tracey (2011), 'Social entrepreneurship: A critique and future directions', *Organization Science*, **22** (5), 1203–1213.

Dana, L-P. (ed.) (2007), *Handbook of Research on Ethnic Minority Entrepreneurship: A Co-evolutionary View on Resource Management*, Cheltenham, UK and Northampton, USA: Edward Elgar Publishing.

Dana, L-P. (2015), 'Indigenous entrepreneurship: An emerging field of research', *International Journal of Business and Globalisation*, **14** (2), 158–169.

Dana, L-P. and R.B. Anderson (eds) (2007), *International Handbook of Research on Indigenous Entrepreneurship*, Cheltenham, UK and Northampton, USA: Edward Elgar Publishing.

Eketone, A. (2008), 'Theoretical underpinnings of Kaupapa Māori directed practice', *Mai Review*, **1**, 1–11.

Foley, D. (2004), *Understanding Indigenous Entrepreneurship: A Case Study Analysis*, unpublished doctoral thesis, University of Queensland, Australia.

Foley, D. and A.J. O'Connor (2011), 'Social capital and the networking practices of Indigenous entrepreneurs', *Journal of Small Business Management*, **51** (2), 276–296.

Frederick, H. and E. Henry (2004), 'Innovation and entrepreneurship amongst Pākehā and Māori in Aotearoa/New Zealand', in C. Stiles and G. Galbraith (eds), *Ethnic Entrepreneurship: Structure and Process, International Research in the Business Disciplines*, vol. IV, Oxford, UK: Elsevier Press, pp. 115–140.

Grimes, M.G., J.S. McMullen, T.J. Vogus and T.L. Miller (2013), 'Studying the origins of social entrepreneurship: Compassion and the role of embedded agency', *Academy of Management Review*, **38** (3), 460–463.

Henry, E. (2007), 'Kaupapa Māori entrepreneurship', in Dana, L-P. and R. Anderson (eds), *International Handbook of Research on Indigenous Entrepreneurship*, Cheltenham, UK and Northampton, USA: Edward Elgar Publishing, pp. 536–548.

Henry, E. (2012), *Te Wairua Auaha: Emancipatory Māori Entrepreneurship in Screen Production*, unpublished doctoral thesis, Auckland University of Technology, NZ.

Henry, E., L-P. Dana and P. Murphy (2017), 'Telling their own stories: Māori entrepreneurship in the mainstream screen industry', *Entrepreneurship and Regional Development*, **30** (1–2), 118–145.

Henry, E. and H. Pene (2001), 'Kaupapa Māori: Locating Indigenous ontology, epistemology and methodology in the academy', *Organization*, **8** (2), 234–242.

Hindle, K. and P. Moroz (2010), 'Indigenous entrepreneurship as a research field: Developing a definitional framework from the emerging canon', *International Entrepreneurship and Management Journal*, **6** (4), 357–385.

Kerlin, J.A. (2006), 'Social enterprise in the United States and Europe: Understanding and learning from the differences', *Voluntas: International Journal of Voluntary and Nonprofit Organizations*, **17** (3), 247–263.

Lamont, M. and A. Lareau (1988), 'Cultural capital: Allusions, gaps and glissandos in recent theoretical developments', *Sociological Theory*, **6** (2), 153–168.

Mad Ave Community Trust (2018), *Mad Ave Community Trust*, accessed 24 October 2018 at www.gleninnesvillage.co.nz/product.php?id=192.

Miller, C. (2017), 'Glen Innes resident Niki Rauti moves into new house', *NZ Herald* online, accessed 24 October 2018 at www.nzherald.co.nz/nz/news/article.cfm?c_id=1andobjectid=11938474.

MRST (2007), *Vision Mātauranga: Unlocking the Innovation Potential of Māori Knowledge, Resources and People*, Wellington, NZ: Ministry of Research Science and Technology, accessed 24 October 2018 at royalsociety.org.nz/assets/Uploads/Vision-Matauranga-document-2007.pdf.

Nepe, T.M. (1991), *Te toi huarewa tipuna: Kaupapa Māori, an Educational Intervention System*, unpublished Masters thesis, University of Auckland, NZ.

Newman, A.K. (1881), 'A study of the causes leading to the extinction of the Māori', *Transactions and Proceedings of the Royal Society of New Zealand*, vol. 14, pp. 459–477.

Patuwai, T. (2018), Interview with Mad Ave Community Trust Director, Tamati Patuwai, at their premises in Glen Innes, 22 January.

Peredo, A.M., R.B Anderson, C.S. Galbraith and B. Honig (2004), 'Towards a theory of Indigenous entrepreneurship', *International Journal of Entrepreneurship and Small Business*, **1** (1–2), 1–20.

Petrie, H. (2006), 'Maori enterprise: Ships and flour mills', in I. Hunter and D. Morrow (eds), *City of Enterprise: Perspectives on Auckland Business History*, Auckland, NZ: Auckland University Press, pp. 27–49.

Smith, G.H. (1987), *Aonga Māori: Preferred Māori Teaching and Learning Methodologies*, unpublished paper, Auckland, NZ: Auckland University.

Smith, L.T. (1996), *Ngā Aho o Te Kākahu Mātauranga: The Multiple Layers of Struggle by Māori in Education*, unpublished doctoral thesis, University of Auckland, NZ.

Tapsell, P. and C. Woods (2010), 'Social entrepreneurship and innovation: Self-organization in an Indigenous context', *Entrepreneurship and Regional Development*, **22** (6), 535–556.

Viswanathan, M., R. Echambadi, S. Venugopal and S. Sridharan (2014), 'Subsistence entrepreneurship, value creation, and community exchange systems: A social capital explanation', *Journal of Macromarketing*, **34** (2), 213–226.

Volery, T. (2007), 'Ethnic entrepreneurship: A theoretical framework', in L-P. Dana (ed.), *Handbook of Research on Ethnic Minority Entrepreneurship: A Co-evolutionary View on Resource Management*, Cheltenham, UK and Northampton, USA: Edward Elgar Publishing, pp. 30–41.

Walker, R. (1990), *Ka Whawhai Tonu Mātau: Struggle Without End*, Auckland, NZ: Penguin Books.

Woolcock, M. (1998), 'Social capital and economic development: Toward a theoretical synthesis and policy framework', *Theory and Society*, **27** (2), 151–208.

Yosso, T.J. (2005), 'Whose culture has capital? A critical race theory discussion of community cultural wealth', *Race Ethnicity and Education*, **8** (1), 69–91.

14 Social entrepreneurship in the Middle East and North Africa

Ghadah Alarifi, Paul Robson and Endrit Kromidha

Introduction

The social entrepreneurship (SE) literature acknowledges that there is a link between the national context and SE activity in a country. Living within shared geographical territories often gives rise to relative bonds in terms of a shared identity, expectations, and interests. Consequently, there exists a symbiotic relationship between SE organisations and the national territories within which they exist (Seelos et al. 2011). Tapsell and Woods (2010) stressed the view that context matters in SE research, especially where governments and regulations are involved. Consequently, social enterprise varies according to political, economic, cultural and historical factors (Teasdale 2012). It is thus critical when examining social enterprises within a regional context to explore the political, cultural and religious background of the region.

Focus on social enterprise has increased globally in recent years. The Middle East and North Africa (MENA) region is no exception (Halabi, Kheir and Cochrane 2017). According to Zanganehpour (2015), the emergence of interest in SE in the MENA region dates to the events that occurred after the Arab Spring. In the spring of 2011 a series of pro-democracy uprisings began that eventually enveloped Tunisia, Morocco, Syria, Libya, Egypt and Bahrain. Post-revolution, social activists in MENA countries began to realise the significance of human potential for curbing the challenges facing the region (Jamali and Lanteri 2016). Scanning the global landscape for ideas, innovative and conscientious individuals have turned to SE for potential solutions to some of the regional challenges. Doumit (2017) conducted a thorough literature review and carried out field visits to contextualise the concept of social enterprise in the MENA region and found that, as in the rest of the world, the region's social enterprise sector seems to be growing and that individuals as well as groups in both the non-profit and for-profit sectors are disrupting different for-profit and non-profit models, to make a positive social impact.

The social enterprise sector in the MENA region has observed some growth in the past decade. Rampant unemployment, enduring poverty, drastic environmental changes, as well as food and water scarcity, are some of the major problems that have bewildered even the most efficient public servants (Zanganehpour 2015). The challenging state of affairs has propelled social entrepreneurs to break into various sectors and ensure service delivery at the grass-roots level (Jamali and Lanteri 2016). Additional challenges and opportunities are unique to the MENA region. This chapter reviews literature on social enterprise in the MENA region, gives an overview of the region's social enterprise landscape and explores the existing prospects and challenges that regional social enterprises face.

Social entrepreneurship research in the MENA region

The existence of SE in MENA is evident from the number of globally recognised support bodies that operate in the region such as Acumen, Ashoka and the Schwab Foundation. However, the region remains largely unexplored in the SE academic literature. Studies examining social entrepreneurs and social enterprises in the region are scarce.

The region is affected by the cultural and religious antecedents of these countries, which would appear conducive to the development of SE. For instance, Muin, Abdullah and Bahari (2014) conducted a study to define SE according to an Islamic perspective. The authors identified a lack of an Islamic SE model, focusing exclusively on the Qur'an (Muslims' holy book) and Al-Hadith (the words and actions of Prophet Muhammad). The study analysed secondary data on Islamic SE and conducted a comparative analysis of existing models of SE, concluding that none of the studied models catered to the Islamic perspective on SE. The authors stressed that, in Islamic countries, the Qur'an and Al-Hadith mandated SE work through 'Al-Falah', that is, using one's finance and property for humanitarian purposes. Moreover, the authors argued that SE in an Islamic society should entail concepts of welfare, justice and the ideology of Zakat and Waqf.

Islam teaching advances the concepts of helping those in need, Ehsan (giving care) and compassion for others. One of the five pillars of Islam, Zakat (almsgiving) is a religious obligation that individuals have to give to the poor and people in need, and this is rewarded in the afterlife (Lambarraa and Riener 2015). Waqf (endowment) is an act of worshipping God and it is rewarded as long as the Waqf is used in this life and afterlife of the donor. Furthermore, it is a mechanism for development and social welfare. Corporate organisations have a religious obligation and social responsibility which they fulfil by paying the Zakat. The payment of Zakat depends on the wealth of the payer. In the case of business enterprises Zakat is 2.5% of the enterprise's net profits. In Saudi Arabia, Zakat is mandatory on business enterprises and is collected by the Zakat and Income Tax Department (Al-Sakran 2001).

Characteristics of social entrepreneurs in MENA

Abdou et al. (2014) found that social entrepreneurs in the Middle East share the following six common characteristics: (a) the individuals involved tend to be highly educated and have acquired graduate and post-graduate degrees; (b) as children and young adults, these individuals generally actively participated in volunteer work; (c) most of these entrepreneurs have lived abroad and explain that their experiences abroad influenced their professional aspirations; (d) they usually have first-hand experience with the problems they are striving to solve; (e) they envision systematic change and often collaborate with governments to make far-reaching impacts; and (f) they have identified gaps in service or product delivery in different sectors.

Challenges faced by social enterprises in the MENA region

Social enterprises in MENA must overcome many challenges, some of which occur globally, whereas some are uniquely local. Like other enterprises, social enterprises must face red tape and monopolies, often influenced by their countries' respective governments. The challenges social enterprises face in the Middle East can be grouped into three distinct categories: legal-related challenges, the need for better financial support and a lack of social and cultural awareness (Abdou et al. 2014; Doumit 2017).

Legal challenges

A challenge that social enterprises in the MENA region face is lack of a legal framework defining them in the market. Usually, these enterprises work as informal entities, and even when they register themselves, they must adopt legal forms specific to other organisational types (e.g., cooperatives, nongovernmental organisations, non-profit organisations or commercial licences). In the Kingdom of Saudi Arabia, a relatively developed economy, social enterprises have no special legal licence, and SE is not well established in the country in comparison with its regional counterparts (Alarifi 2018). The legal challenge is exacerbated in Saudi Arabia since Saudi law does not support the establishment of nongovernmental organisations (NGOs) (Montagu 2010). Finding an umbrella organisation to help overcome this challenge is an option for some social enterprises. The only alternative route is for social enterprises to gain a commercial licence to operate. Similar challenges exist in other MENA countries, and social entrepreneurs employ creative solutions to address this challenge. For example, a social enterprise providing online education in Egypt adopted the legal status of a corporation to avoid government prosecution, meanwhile functioning as a non-profit to acquire international funding for catering to less privileged areas (Doumit 2017).

Awareness challenges

Although SE has received global recognition, the concept is underutilised in the MENA region. Doumit (2017) noted the very low awareness regarding the concept of 'social enterprise' in the MENA region. Since many MENA countries depend on foreign aid and have weak government structures, citizens have mostly encountered the concept through international initiatives. Nonetheless, such initiatives might resemble SE, but use different terminologies which can engender confusion among stakeholders in the region. Thus, the public generally regards SE as part of voluntary and charity-based programmes.

This confusion indicates a lack of clarity as to what social enterprise actually is in the MENA region. For example, a perception in Egyptian society is that social ventures are all about charity and the non-profit sector (Elsayed 2018). This hampers public recognition of the country's social enterprise sector (Jamali and Lanteri 2016). Similarly, Lebanese people deem SE synonymous with not-for-profit enterprise (Abdou et al. 2014). As in other MENA regions, Saudi society confuses SE with social work and volunteerism (Alzalabani et al. 2013). To determine the way forward for the SE sector in Saudi Arabia, Bitzenis and Vlachos (2013) utilised secondary data to generate theoretical propositions. Analysing future SE prospects in Saudi Arabia, the authors held that the Saudi government needs to understand and perpetuate the determinants of SE to resolve this issue. A solution to this confusion in regards to the SE concept would be that governments would establish a guideline or an interpretation to what is considered a social enterprise.

Funding challenges

Social entrepreneurs in MENA countries often face funding challenges. One reason for this challenge is the absence of a legal framework for social enterprises in the region. Halabi et al. (2017) found that social enterprises in Jordan, Morocco and Palestine face strict government policies and lack of funds. Those governments hold strict policies in charitable giving, donations and receiving money from overseas entities as part of anti-terrorism laws. Abdou et al. (2014) further supported the argument that countries in the MENA regions lag behind in funding social enterprises. The SE sector in Egypt remains largely untapped (Abdou and Ebrashi 2015) mainly because of the prevalence of red tape and the Egyptian government's tight legislative and funding framework. It is recommended that governments should clearly define SE in the MENA region, nurture youth-led social enterprises by providing incubation and funding, and benchmark social and economic standards to observe the potential of social enterprises.

Social entrepreneurship: a way forward for MENA problems

Rapid population growth in the MENA region is putting pressure on diminishing resources. Statistics shows that the MENA region's population quadrupled from the 1950s to the year 2000 (Tabutin et al. 2005). The population of Saudi Arabia alone grew from 4,086,539 in 1960 to 32,552,336 in 2017, with 49% of the Saudi population under 25 years old.[1] Saudi Arabia witnessed an average population growth of 3.67% from 1998 to 2002, whereas the average growth in Gross Domestic Product (GDP) for the same period was 1.8% (Mahoney and Alboaouh 2017). Another major problem the nation has to deal with is a high rate of unemployment. According to the Saudi General Authority for Statistics the unemployment rate of 2017 was 12.6% (83.9% for women). Unemployment rates for women in the MENA region are the highest in the world (International Labour Organization 2017). Youth unemployment is also high across the region (International Labour Organization 2013; Zanganehpour 2015). To address this problem it has been suggested that 83–90 million new jobs need to be created (Mirkin 2010), while Sulphey and Alkahtani (2017) suggest that Arab countries would need about 51 million new jobs by the year 2020. Traditionally the public sector has acted as a buffer to unemployment, providing up to 40% of jobs (Zanganehpour 2015). However, political and financial pressures mean it is unlikely this will continue. Governments also play a major role in the region's economic development through job creation, human capital development and the provision of social services, but severe stress on natural resources linked to population growth has nullified their impact, also creating strains on health care, fully funded education and similar government-provided services for citizens (Abdou, Fahmy, Greenwald and Nelson 2010).

Even though it is difficult to solve large unemployment issues, social entrepreneurs can focus on bringing minorities and neglected groups closer to the labour market particularly through training, education programmes and development of community centres. The end result could be the equitable development that has hitherto eluded the region, as well as enhanced availability of basic services (Sulphey and Alkahtani 2017). Abdou et al. (2014) provided a framework for leveraging an SE model, and this could enable marginalised communities to capitalise on their human potential for society's greater benefit.

SE also has the potential to bring positive changes to the otherwise 'catastrophic' health and education sectors of Jordan, Morocco and Palestine (Halabi et al. 2017), through the simultaneous provision of employment and training programmes, and delivery of health and educational services at the grassroots level. While unlikely to make a substantive difference to the overall rate of unemployment, social enterprises have been shown (in other countries) to be an effective mechanism for employing marginalised groups, or delivering niche health and educational services. However, Kreitmeyr (2018) analysed the SE landscape in Jordan and Morocco and argued that instead of driving progressive changes, the concept cements neo-liberalism and strengthens authoritarian regimes in these countries. Kreitmeyr's (2018) findings are unique as a critique of SE in the MENA region.

Cultural antecedents also play a pivotal role in defining the concept of social enterprise in the MENA region. For instance, in some conservative areas in Iran, women are not allowed to socialise in public places; however, they are able to do so in women-only gyms. In such areas, women not only visit gyms for the purpose of exercising, but also regard gyms as social places where they can meet friends and network with one another. For such women, a gym that enables them to 'socialise' is a social enterprise (Doumit 2017). This is not unique to Iranian culture; in other MENA countries where obesity levels are high, gym owners who focus on solving this problem are considered as social entrepreneurs. The creation of gyms and leisure centres can help support niche groups or minorities in their communities by providing a cradle of hope and enrichment. This perhaps illustrates that MENA regions face some unique culturally embedded challenges, and that SE can offer solutions that may not be seen as socially valuable in other countries or regions of the world. To understand cultural differences, Hofstede (1980) explained that national cultures have different dimensions, uncertainty avoidance being one of them: when uncertainty avoidance is high, people feel uncomfortable and display uncertainty regarding their future. Hofstede (1980) mentioned that they (Arab countries) tend to have high power distance, high uncertainty avoidance, collectivism and masculinity. Those cultural differences contributed to the region's unique differences and challenges. For example, the high uncertainty avoidance contributed to people's preference for government employment, while high masculinity contributed to women's high unemployment rates.

Education also plays its part in shaping the social entrepreneurial context of the MENA region. Formal education in many of the MENA countries, through schools and universities, is not designed to shape social entrepreneurial tendencies of students. For example: in Saudi Arabia there are 24 governmental universities (1,400,272 students) and 10 private universities (88,716 students). Only one university covered SE in the curriculum, as an elective course for business students (Alarifi 2018). Iqbal, Melhem and Kokash (2012) suggested that Saudi universities should focus more on introducing entrepreneurship subjects and training. Danish and Smith (2012) in their research on Saudi female entrepreneurs, encourage Saudi policy makers to focus on entrepreneurship education and training programmes that will equip them with skills needed to succeed. Furthermore, most of the MENA countries' education systems are dominated by passive learning, and memorisation. Students are not encouraged to question the accuracy of the information given, which is often framed as being irrelevant to their future lives and careers. The Saudi education system is no exception for those traits (Hamdan 2014), and does not support independence, critical thinking and creativity (Elyas and Picard 2013). A study by Kirby and Ibrahim (2011) on Egyptian university students showed that there is confusion among them about the meaning of SE. In general, culture in the MENA area still plays a very important role in shaping the cognation and norms of individuals, and is not conducive to SE. If governments in the region focus on formal and informal education supporting social entrepreneurship this may lead to a positive shift in the awareness and prevalence of SE in the region.

The above analysis of the literature on social entrepreneurship in the MENA region shows that the region faces many challenges and SE can help marginalised groups in delivering niche social, health and educational services. Nonetheless, social entrepreneurs face many challenges unique to their sector. In prominent MENA countries, such as Lebanon, Saudi Arabia, Egypt, Jordan and Morocco, these challenges relate to lack of public awareness, funding and distinct legislative status and insufficient government support.

Research agenda

The current review has found substantial gaps in the literature on SE in the Middle East. Scholars need to work on better conceptualising SE with reference to the Islamic context, identify common characteristics and specify what sets SE apart from other forms of social organisation, social work and volunteerism. Scholarship on SE in the MENA region is still in its infancy and more quantitative as well as qualitative research is needed. An important problem is the lack of studies analysing the motivation of social entrepreneurs in individual MENA countries. Although some studies have observed the proclivities of social entrepreneurs in the region, studies analysing the differences in motivation and personal antecedents of social entrepreneurs across different countries are lacking. Research focused on understanding why SE exists in MENA would benefit from analysis of the forms it takes, and comparison with other regions to develop greater understanding of how SE is contextually embedded. Furthermore, research on SE in the MENA region should focus on both the 'giving end' and 'receiving end'; few or no studies describe the first-hand experiences of social enterprises in such a way as to determine the success rate of SE in addressing problems and improving service delivery. Finally, although Kreitmeyr (2018) has criticised SE in Jordan and Morocco as reinforcing neoliberal and authoritarian politics, most of the available literature on SE in Egypt, Lebanon and Saudi Arabia, it could reasonably be argued, (over-)emphasises the advantages of SE. Little to no critique of the concept has been conducted, and there is little consideration of any negative consequences of SE in these important MENA countries. Finally, it is critical to highlight the importance of investigating the institutional voids that give opportunities for social enterprises, and how social entrepreneurs are able to overcome the absence of supportive policy frameworks. Any measures to introduce such frameworks should focus on the establishment of both national legal systems, and grass roots support to facilitate SE.

NOTE
1 General Authority for Statistics, Kingdom of Saudi Arabia, accessed 10 November 2018 at www.stats.gov.sa/en.

References

Abdou, E. and R. El Ebrashi (2015), 'The social enterprise sector in Egypt: current status and way forward', in D. Jamali and A. Lanteri (eds), *Social Entrepreneurship in the Middle East*, London: Palgrave Macmillan, pp. 37–62.

Abdou, E., A. Fahmy, D. Greenwald and J. Nelson (2010), 'Social entrepreneurship in the Middle East. Toward Sustainable development for the next generation', Wolfensohn Center for Development, The Middle East Youth Initiative Working Paper, 10.

Abdou, E., A. Fahmy, D. Greenwald and J. Nelson (2014), 'Social entrepreneurship in the Middle East [eBook]', Wolfensohn Center for Development at Brookings, Dubai School of Government, Silatech.

Alarifi, G. (2018), *The Institutional Environment, Entrepreneurial Orientation and Performance of Saudi Social Enterprises*, Doctoral Thesis, Royal Holloway University of London, 10 August.

Al-Sakran, S. A. (2001), 'Leverage determinants in the absence of corporate tax system: the case of non-financial publicly traded corporations in Saudi Arabia', *Managerial Finance*, 27 (10/11), 58–86.

Alzalabani, A., R. S. Modi and M. N. Haque (2013), 'Theoretical perspective of social entrepreneurship: A study of determinants of social entrepreneurship in the context of Saudi Arabia', *Journal of Modern Accounting and Auditing*, **9** (4), 571.

Bitzenis, A. and V. Vlachos (2013), 'International Conference on International Business 2013 Proceedings', accessed 26 September 2018 at https://www.researchgate.net/publication/289531290_International_Conference_on_International_Business_2013_Proceedings.

Danish, A. and H. Smith (2012), 'Female entrepreneurship in Saudi Arabia: opportunities and challenges', *International Journal of Gender and Entrepreneurship*, **4** (3), 216–235.

Doumit, G. (2017), 'Social entrepreneurship in the Middle East: Old practice, new concept', *Stanford Social Innovation Review*, accessed 26 September 2018 at https://ssir.org/articles/entry/social_entrepreneurship_in_the_middle_east_old_practice_new_concept#.

Elsayed, Y. (2018), 'At the intersection of social entrepreneurship and social movements: The case of Egypt and the Arab Spring', *VOLUNTAS: International Journal of Voluntary and Nonprofit Organizations*, **29** (4), 819–831.

Elyas, T. and M. Picard (2013), 'Critiquing of higher education policy in Saudi Arabia: towards a new neoliberalism', *Education, Business and Society: Contemporary Middle Eastern Issues*, **6** (1), 31–41.

Halabi, S., S. Kheir and P. Cochrane (2017), *Social Enterprise Development in the Middle East and North Africa: A Qualitative Analysis of Lebanon, Jordan, Egypt and Occupied Palestine, Cairo, Egypt and Beirut, Lebanon*, Lebanon: Wamda, accessed 26 September 2018 at https://wamda-prod.s3.amazonaws.com/resource-url/e2981f10ea87448.pdf.

Hamdan, A. K. (2014), 'The reciprocal and correlative relationship between learning culture and online education: a case from Saudi Arabia', *International Review of Research in Open and Distance Learning*, **15** (1), 309–336.

Hofstede, G. (1980), 'Culture and organizations', *International Studies of Management & Organization*, **10** (4), 15–41.

International Labour Organization (2013), *Global Employment Trends for Youth 2013*, Geneva, Switzerland: ILO.

Iqbal, A., Y. Melhem and H. Kokash (2012), 'Readiness of the university students towards entrepreneurship in Saudi Private University: an exploratory study', *European Scientific Journal, ESJ*, **8** (15), 109–131.

Jamali, D. and A. Lanteri (2015). 'Introduction', in D. Jamali and A. Lanteri (eds), *Social Entrepreneurship in the Middle East*, London: Palgrave Macmillan, pp. 1–14.

Kirby, D. A. and N. Ibrahim (2011), 'The case for (social) entrepreneurship education in Egyptian universities', *Education & Training*, **53** (5), 403–415.

Kreitmeyr, N. (2018), 'Neoliberal co-optation and authoritarian renewal: social entrepreneurship network in Jordan and Morocco', *Globalizations*, accessed 26 September 2018 at DOI: 10.1080/14747731.2018.1502492.

Lambarraa, F. and G. Riener (2015), 'On the norms of charitable giving in Islam: two field experiments in Morocco', *Journal of Economic Behavior & Organization*, **118** (C), 69–84.

Mahoney, J. and K. Alboaouh (2017), 'Religious and political authority in the Kingdom of Saudi Arabia', *Manas Journal of Social Science*, **6** (2), 241–257.

Mirkin, B. (2010), *Population Levels, Trends and Policies in the Arab Region: Challenges and Opportunities*, New York: United Nations Development Programme, Regional Bureau for Arab States.

Montagu, C. (2010), 'Civil society and the voluntary sector in Saudi Arabia', *The Middle East Journal*, **64** (1), 67–83.

Muin, M. A. A., S. Abdullah and A. Bahari (2014), 'Model on social entrepreneurship: identify the research gap based on Islamic perspective', paper presented at International Conference on Social Entrepreneurship (ICSE2014), Awana Hotel, Genting Highlands, Malaysia, 7–9th November.

Seelos, C., J. Mair, J. Battilana and T. M. Dacin (2011), 'The embeddedness of social entrepreneurship: understanding variation across local communities', in C. Marquis, M. Lounsbury and R. Greenwood (eds), *Communities and Organizations* (Research in the Sociology of Organizations, Volume 33), London: Emerald Group Publishing, pp. 333–363.

Sulphey, M. M. and N. S. Alkahtani (2017), 'Economic security and sustainability through social entrepreneurship: the current Saudi Scenario', *Journal of Security and Sustainability Issues*, **6** (3), 479–490.

Tabutin, D., B. Schoumaker, G. Rogers, J. Mandelbaum and C. Dutreuilh (2005), 'The demography of the Arab world and the Middle East from the 1950s to the 2000s', *Population*, **60** (5), 505–615.

Tapsell, P. and C. Woods (2010), 'Social entrepreneurship and innovation: self-organization in an indigenous context', *Entrepreneurship and Regional Development*, **22** (6), 535–556.

Teasdale, S. (2012), 'What's in a name? Making sense of social enterprise discourses', *Public Policy and Administration*, **27** (2), 99–119.

Zanganehpour, S. (2015), 'The rise of social entrepreneurship in the Middle East: a pathway for inclusive growth or an alluring mirage?' in D. Jamali and A. Lanteri (eds), *Social Entrepreneurship in the Middle East*, London, UK: Palgrave Macmillan, pp. 67–83.

15 Hybrid social entrepreneurship in emerging economies – a research agenda

Diane Holt and Bev Meldrum

Introduction

Addressing the complex deprivations facing those in vulnerable communities in emerging economies is a pressing global challenge. Across the world various types of hybrid social enterprises (Haigh et al., 2015; Holt and Littlewood, 2015; Lyon and Al Faruq, 2018) deliver goods, services, programmes, innovations and/or initiatives that are related in some way to addressing these deprivations. Successful hybrid social enterprises combine social/environmental goals with financial security (Dacin et al., 2011; Doherty et al., 2014). Their importance for socioeconomic development and poverty alleviation has now been recognised by national governments. In South Africa the Decent Work Country Programme (2010) and the New Growth Path Framework (2011) suggest that growth in co-operatives, non-governmental organisations, social businesses and informal savings schemes will offer increasing opportunities for the creation of new jobs. In the developing world these hybrid enterprises often focus on bridging institutional voids left by the state (Mair et al., 2012) associated with intractable societal problems. Such problems include multi-dimensional poverty, lack of access to education, lack of empowerment, poor health, and inadequate nutrition (Alkire and Santos, 2010; Sen, 1999).

Such enterprises can range across a continuum from non-profit to for-profit and may operate under varied designations (including fairtrade, social enterprise, community-based organisation, non-profits etc.) but they all have some element of income generation within their strategic activities and/or facilitate income generation amongst their beneficiaries. The specific definitional boundary conditions of a social enterprise often remain contested (e.g. Rivera-Santos et al., 2015). In part, this is due to variability in the business models emerging in diverse local contexts to address particular development needs (see Littlewood and Holt, 2018; Battilana and Lee, 2014; Doherty et al., 2014). Therefore notions of hybrid social enterprises incorporate a more inclusive framing than the social enterprise definitions typically emerging in some developed countries, and bring in these various alternative organisational forms. In this chapter we therefore adopt this inclusive focus for suggesting a research agenda that covers all types of enterprises that sit within these emerging spaces, recognising this by referring to them as hybrid social enterprises. Whilst on the surface they are very varied they all share three common characteristics. They all:

- have some trading elements and/or enterprise-based activity in their income generation model;
- place the achievement of their social and/or environmental mission at the heart of their business model and strategies; and
- do not profit maximise but reinvest some, if not all, of their surpluses in achieving their core social and/or environmental mission.

Differences in the Global South

Our broad and inclusive framing reflects the heterogeneity of hybrid social enterprise organisational forms and business models present in contexts such as sub-Saharan Africa (see Rivera-Santos et al., 2015; Littlewood and Holt, 2018) and other emerging economies in the Global South. In such settings, applying hard definitional boundaries about what is and what is not a social enterprise – for example having a full asset lock, a particular legal status or specific governance structure – does not reflect the specific institutional variabilities emerging in the Global South.

Research is emerging that suggests that such hybrid social enterprises are 'different' in Africa and other developing world contexts to those found in Europe, the United States and other developed countries (see Rivera-Santos et al., 2015; Littlewood and Holt, 2018). In part these differences are related to the variety of institutional voids they experience (Mair et al., 2012), structural holes (after Burt, 1992), the intersection of multiple 'wicked' sustainable development challenges (Rittel and Webber, 1973) as evidenced by the sustainable development goals (United Nations, 2018), and the lack of various capabilities and functionings of beneficiary communities (after Sen, 1999). The social innovations (Mair et al., 2012; van der Have and Rubalcaba, 2016) and business models (Seelos and Mair, 2015) that arise to fill these voids and address these capabilities thus also differ. The constraints they experience also have important contextual considerations. An income generation scheme that facilitates women selling cosmetics (Scott et al., 2012) or sanitary pads in local villages is only feasible if culturally women can travel outside their home village safely. This then speaks to the institutions that these women experience from a normative perspective (Oliver, 1991; Scott, 2008, 2013) rather than focusing only on an absence of institutions. It is the nuanced consideration of these intersecting institutional influences (regulatory, normative and cultural-cognitive) as well as their absences that are explored by Amine and Staub (2009) in their consideration of women entrepreneurs in sub-Saharan Africa (SSA).

One institution that is much more dominant in emerging economies than in Europe is that of the informal economy. In many parts of SSA this is a legitimate, socially resilient, market space; for instance 87% of Kenyan firms and individuals reported buying from the informal economy (Kapila, 2006). Some countries have developed a dual economy, such as Brazil and South Africa, with formal and informal spaces and legal structures (May and Meth, 2007), and a robust informal economy presence. Hybrid social enterprises are often embedded in economically and socially challenging environments, and especially in the developing world such enterprises may emerge in, interact with or draw from, a large and legitimate informal economy (Webb et al., 2009).

The informal/formal economy

In 1972 the International Labour Organization first used the term the 'informal economy' to describe the institutional space in which millions of households across the developing world earn an income and trade on a daily basis. Typically the informal economy in the Global South is a 'subsistence marketplace' (see Viswanathan and Sridharan, 2009) and located economically in the base-of-the-pyramid (BoP) (see Kolk et al., 2014). Some estimates suggest that more than 70% of the global population is earning a living in such marketplaces (Kiss et al., 2012; Kshreti, 2011), where individuals are excluded from secure employment and the formal market. Encouraging private sector development as part of an economic growth strategy is increasingly recognised by national governments, international bodies, bilateral development agencies and civil society organisations in sub-Saharan Africa (Kaijage and Wheeler, 2013; UNIDO, 2008). Entrepreneurship education is seen as a way to promote private sector development but entrepreneurship research is considered underdeveloped (Von Graevenitz et al., 2010). Such entrepreneurship training and initiatives facilitating micro small business creation in these developing world contexts are often delivered by hybrid social enterprises or may focus on promoting the development of social entrepreneurs and their enterprises in both the formal and informal economy contexts. The importance, and interaction, of these formal/informal institutional spaces cannot be underestimated in any discussion of social entrepreneurship (SE) in emerging economies.

Overview of social entrepreneurship research in emerging economies

Two decades into the research agenda of SE researchers have access to a growing body of research. In 2005 the *Social Enterprise Journal* was launched, the first of its kind. Since that time it has published 218 articles. Of these 11.5%, or 25 articles, have related directly to emerging economies, with more than half relating to countries in Asia, one third in Africa, and the remainder in South America. The first articles relating to social enterprise in emerging economies were published in the journal in 2007, and both focused on social enterprises in Pakistan. Despite the relatively small number of articles, 15 different countries are represented, and topics include contextual understanding of social enterprise, leadership and motivational drivers, governance, clusters of social enterprise activities, social enterprise as a solidarity economy and fairtrade, as co-operatives and as micro-franchises. Other published papers have looked at process and governance, social capital and scaling. The number of articles on emerging economies, in this journal, has been increasing each year – with 2017 seeing five articles published.

When we explore the studies from across a range of journals we can see that the majority of studies have focused, at least in part, on the debates surrounding defini-tions. Much more work is yet to be done on de-constructing the multi-dimensional and complex nature of SE (Hossain et al., 2016). Sengupta et al. (2018) refer to SE as 'strongly community embedded'. This embeddedness refers to the contextual differences that can be found in SE in different national, regional and even local communities. Despite the importance of context in SE, few studies on SE really focus in on the influence of historical, cultural and indigenous factors at a macro level specific to emerging markets (Doherty et al., 2014; Rivera-Santos et al., 2015).

A combined search of EBSCO Business Source Premier and the University of Cape Town's Primo database for the terms 'social enterpr*' (to ensure 'social enter-prise', 'social entrepreneurship' and 'social entrepreneur' were included), 'research agenda' and 'emerging econom*' (to include 'economy' and 'economies'), followed by a filtering process identified 34 articles of note. The search was restricted to 'Peer Reviewed Articles', that were available online, and published since 2008.

This review of the research field highlighted an increased interest in SE as an approach for international development and addressing wicked problems (Katzenstein and Chrispin, 2011; Sodhi and Tang, 2014). The role of traditional institutions, such as the state, changes, social enterprise is seen as being able to fill institutional gaps – both existing gaps and those newly created by changes (Nega and Schneider, 2014a, 2014b).

Just as the importance of context in mainstream management literature has been increasing (e.g. Julian and Ofori-Dankwa, 2013), the same is true of SE literature. This is particularly noticeable in emerging market contexts as there are often stark differences between them and developed markets, as well as between the different sub-contexts, such as at country-level (Rivera-Santos et al., 2015; Dafuleya, 2014).

As a nascent area of research a considerable number of studies have been descrip-tive in nature, using a case study methodological approach (Larson, 2012; Elmes et al., 2012; Gupta et al., 2015). Some have focused on a particular sector (Warnecke and Houndonougbo, 2016), others have looked at a particular context within an emerging market (Kabbaj et al., 2016; Warnecke, 2018), and some have looked at both (Dafuleya, 2014; Hoque and Nahid, 2015; Agrawal and Sahasranamam, 2016; Munro et al., 2016).

Areas of research have focused on social and environment issues including renew-able energy (Warnecke and Houndonougbo, 2016; Munro et al., 2016; Sengupta and Sahay, 2017), the water sector (Hoque and Nahid, 2015), burial services

(Dafuleya, 2014), agricultural services (Diochon and Ghore, 2016), entrepreneur support (Larson, 2012; Galvin and Iannotti, 2015) and poverty alleviation (Elmes et al., 2012; Groch et al., 2012). This is unsurprising as these are key issues within poverty contexts.

Apart from notable exceptions (Meyskens and Carsrud, 2011; Rivera-Santos et al., 2015) there is a lack of inter-country comparison across the studies. Between these two studies more than 600 social enterprises were compared in 21 different emerging economies. However, in the main descriptive studies on social enterprise in particular contexts take a single company/country/ sector/issue focus. One key area for the future is to bring together examples to build up comparisons across different emerging markets.

A broad framing of social enterprise is used across the studies identified in our review, as is expected, as the contexts are so varied. Hybrid organisations are referred to in relation to social enterprises in both Africa and India (Meyskens and Carsrud, 2011; Rivera-Santos et al., 2015; Holt and Littlewood, 2015 etc.). Agrawal and Sahasranamam (2016) also discuss corporate SE, a form not mentioned in other contexts.

The majority of published studies focused on the social enterprise itself as the unit of analysis. Two studies used the social entrepreneur as their focus – in these cases the objective of the study was to analyse the individuals' capabilities and motivations for establishing the social enterprise (Gupta et al., 2015; Ghalwash et al., 2017). Yet, even though there is increased interest in the measurement of impact of business in mainstream management literature, only two studies referred to the evaluation of the impact of social enterprises in emerging markets (Galvin and Iannotti, 2015; Urban, 2015).

Towards a research agenda

In developing a research agenda for hybrid social enterprises in emerging economies we identify: (i) broad, overarching considerations and (ii) some more detailed research questions. Firstly we consider overarching themes that might impact the types of studies that future researchers should consider.

In the developing world the problems such organisations seek to address through enterprise-based business models are complex and multifaceted, and intersect with a vast range of actors at all levels of society. Yet if such organisations are to deliver on their transformative potential for systematic, equitable and sustainable development across Africa and elsewhere in the developing world a longitudinal, not just cross-sectional, understanding is needed, to move beyond the descriptive to a multi-layered, contextualised exploration. This is vital in identifying the factors behind their success or failure, how their business models evolve and grow over time, the impact they have on beneficiaries and key stakeholders, how they interact with multiple actors and intersectionalities such as gender, ethnicity, age (Crenshaw, 1989) and the influence of their external environment (Littlewood and Holt, 2018; Sengupta et al., 2018) in complex shifting economic landscapes that include both formal and informal components.

It is in these overlapping market places at the intersection between the formal and informal, and amongst those experiencing poverty, that development initiatives are increasingly focused, in particular on social enterprise entrepreneurial-based initiatives. Yet 'research in business in institutional settings where poverty is dominant remain[s] very limited' (Bruton, 2010: 6), lacking empirical research, conceptually undeveloped and fragmented, with little systematic analysis focused on the intersection of poverty, entrepreneurial processes and developing world contexts especially in places such as Africa (Rivera-Santos et al., 2015).

The strategic and operational development of these kinds of organisations also often remains opaque because they are situated within hard-to-reach, 'adverse' environments where publicly available data is limited. It is also difficult to identify a sample of 'failed' organisations, or when the services or goods they deliver for beneficiary groups in poverty contexts are not utilised, are unsuccessful or even have negative impacts. The complex external environments in which these hybrid social enterprises are embedded require research that considers various units of analysis set in a variety of fieldwork contexts, in various settings in emerging economies across the world.

Thus we suggest that more studies are needed that:

- extend our research from the descriptive to the comparative;
- adopt a longitudinal perspective to see shifts over time;
- incorporate the consideration of differing contexts, especially from an institutional point of view;
- address the influence of the informal economy and also the nexus where the formal and informal interact; and
- actively research in communities that are often hidden or hard to access.

Secondly, there are many research questions that need to be explored in emerging economy contexts. Our chapter has introduced some of these but we might also consider research questions such as the following.

- What factors determine the success or failure of hybrid social enterprises in emerging economies? What do we consider success to be and for whom?
- What are the strategies, business models, resource profiles and operational aspects of hybrid social enterprises in such contexts? How do they change over time?
- How do hybrid social enterprises grow, how can they scale out and scale up their impact?
- Is 'growth' necessary? Is it different in such contexts?

- What role do both the sources and types of finance play in the success or otherwise of hybrid social enterprises?
- Are there unintended consequences to different growth trajectories?
- What role do cross-sector partnerships and alliances play in achieving inclusive growth objectives for their beneficiary communities?
- How do these enterprises navigate their institutional environments? Are they influenced by national and sub-national institutional differences?
- How do the institutional contexts influence such organisations and their beneficiary groups?
- What social innovations are leveraged by various hybrid social enterprises and what are the issues that need to be considered for emerging economy contexts?
- How do individual, household and community characteristics/contingencies influence the delivery of the hybrid social enterprises mission?
- How do intersectionalities (e.g. race and gender) of beneficiaries interact to hamper the delivery of hybrid social enterprises' objectives?

Hybrid social enterprises are important actors in enhancing wellbeing and resilience at individual, household or community levels, and they offer opportunities for inclusive growth in marginalised, low income communities, often set in informal economy contexts in emerging economies around the world. Yet as enterprises we still know little about them but we do know that they (and their actors, beneficiary groups and institutional environments) are likely to be very different to commercial and/or social enterprises studied in mainstream markets in the Global North. We believe that this chapter may offer interesting avenues for future scholars to consider and explore.

References

Agrawal, A. and S. Sahasranamam (2016), 'Corporate social entrepreneurship in India', *South Asian Journal of Global Business Research*, **5** (2), 214–233.

Alkire, S. and M.E. Santos (2010), *Acute multidimensional poverty*, Oxford: Oxford Poverty and Human Development Initiative.

Amine, L.S. and K.M. Staub (2009), 'Women entrepreneurs in sub-Saharan Africa: An institutional theory analysis from a social marketing point of view', *Entrepreneurship and Regional Development*, **21** (2), 183–211.

Battilana, J. and M. Lee (2014), 'Advancing research on hybrid organizing – Insights from the study of social enterprises', *Academy of Management Annals*, **8** (1), 397–441.

Bruton, G.D. (2010), 'Business and the world's poorest billion', *Academy of Management Perspectives*, **24** (3), 6–10.

Burt, R. (1992), *Structural Holes*, Cambridge, MA: Harvard University Press.

Crenshaw, K. (1989), 'Demarginalizing the intersection of race and sex: A black feminist critique of anti-discrimination doctrine, feminist theory and antiracist politics', *University of Chicago Legal Forum*, **8**, 139–167.

Dacin M.T., Dacin P.A. and P. Tracey (2011), 'Social entrepreneurship: A critique and future directions', *Organization Science*, **22** (5), 1203–1213.

Dafuleya, G. (2014), 'Enterprising in the face of death: Social entrepreneurship in African burial societies', *Journal of Enterprising Culture*, **20** (3), 357–378.

Diochon, M. and Y. Ghore (2016), 'Contextualizing a social enterprise opportunity process in an emerging market', *Social Enterprise Journal*, **12** (2), 107–130.

Doherty, B., Haugh, H. and F. Lyon (2014), 'Social enterprises as hybrid organizations: A review and research agenda', *International Journal of Management Reviews*, **16** (4), 417–436.

Elmes, M., Jiusto, S., Whiteman, G., Hersh, R. and G. Guthey (2012), 'Teaching social entrepreneurship and innovation from the perspective of place and place making', *Academy of Management Learning and Education*, **11** (4), 533–554.

Galvin, M. and L. Iannotti (2015), 'Social enterprise and development: The KickStart model', *VOLUNTAS: International Journal of Voluntary and Nonprofit Organizations*, **26** (2), 421–441.

Ghalwash, S., Tolba, A. and A. Ismail (2017), 'What motivates social entrepreneurs to start social ventures?' *Social Enterprise Journal*, **13** (3), 268–298.

Groch, K., Gerdes, K., Segal, E. and M. Groch (2012), 'The grassroots Londolozi model of African development: Social empathy in action', *Journal of Community Practice*, **20** (1–2), 154–177.

Gupta, S., Beninger, S. and J. Ganesh (2015), 'A hybrid approach to innovation by social enterprises: Lessons from Africa', *Social Enterprise Journal*, **11** (1), 89–112.

Haigh, N., Walker, J., Bacq, S. and J. Kickul (2015), 'Hybrid organizations: Origins, strategies, impacts, and implications', *California Management Review*, **57** (3), 5–12.

Hoque, M. and K. Nahid (2015), 'Business format in social entrepreneurships for Bangladesh's water sector', *Journal of Global Entrepreneurship Research*, **5** (1), 1–17.

Holt, D. and D. Littlewood (2015), 'Identifying, mapping and monitoring the impact of hybrid firms', *California Management Review*, **57** (3), 107–125.

Hossain, S., Saleh, M.A. and J. Drennan (2016), 'A critical appraisal of the social entrepreneurship paradigm in an international setting: A proposed conceptual framework', *The International Entrepreneurship and Management Journal*, **13** (2), 347–368.

Julian, S.D. and J.C. Ofori-Dankwa (2013), 'The institutional difference hypothesis', *Strategic Management Journal*, **34** (11), 1314–1330.

Kabbaj, M., K. El Ouazzani Ech Hadi, J. Elamrani and M. Lemtaoui (2016), 'A study of the social entrepreneurship ecosystem: The case of Morocco', *Journal of Developmental Entrepreneurship*, **21** (4), 1650021.

Kaijage, E. and D. Wheeler (2013), *Supporting Entrepreneurship Education in East Africa*, London: Department for International Development.

Kapila, S. (2006), *Unleashing the entrepreneurial potential of micro and small enterprises in Kenya: Some experiences and directions*, paper prepared for the Commission on Legal Empowerment of the Poor, presented at UNHAITAT, Nairobi, 26 November.

Katzenstein, J. and B. Chrispin (2011), 'Social entrepreneurship and a new model for international development in the 21st century', *Journal of Developmental Entrepreneurship*, **16** (1), 87–102.

Kiss, A.N., Wade, M.D. and S.T. Cavusgil (2012), 'International entrepreneurship research in emerging economies: A critical review and research agenda', *Journal of Business Venturing*, **27**, 266–290.

Kolk, A., M. Rivera-Santos and C. Rufín, C. (2014), 'Reviewing a decade of research on the "base/bottom of the pyramid" (BOP) concept', *Business and Society*, **53** (3), 338–377.

Kshetri, N. (2011), 'Institutional and economic foundation of entrepreneurship in Africa', *Journal Development Entrepreneurship*, **16**, 9–35.

Larson, G. (2012), 'A needle in a haystack: How a new tool is unlocking entrepreneurship in Africa', *Kennedy School Review*, **12**, 76–80.

Littlewood, D. and D. Holt (2018), 'Social entrepreneurship in South Africa: Exploring the influence of environment', *Business and Society*, **57** (3), 525–561.

Lyon, F. and A. Al Faruq (2018), 'Hybrid organisations and models of social enterprise in Ghana and Bangladesh'. In L.J. Spence, J.G. Frynas, J. Muthuri and J. Navare (Eds.), *Research Handbook on Small*

Business Social Responsibility: Global Perspectives, Cheltenham, UK and Northampton, MA: Edward Elgar Publishing, pp. 320–340.

Mair, J., I. Marti and M. Ventresca (2012), 'Building inclusive markets in rural Bangladesh: How intermediaries work institutional voids', *Academy of Management Journal*, **55** (4), 819–850.

May, J. and C. Meth (2007), 'Dualism or underdevelopment in South Africa: What does a quantitative assessment of poverty, inequality and employment reveal?', *Development Southern Africa*, **24**, 271–287.

Meyskens, M. and A. Carsrud (2011), 'The role of partnerships on the legal structure and local choice of nascent social ventures', *Journal of Enterprising Culture*, **19** (1), 61–77.

Munro, P., G. van Der Horst, S. Willans, P. Kemeny, A. Christiansen and N. Schiavone (2016), 'Social enterprise development and renewable energy dissemination in Africa: The experience of the community charging station model in Sierra Leone', *Progress in Development Studies*, **16** (1), 24–38.

Nega, B. and G. Schneider (2014a), 'NGOs, the state, and development in Africa', *Review of Social Economy*, **72** (4), 485–503.

Nega, B. and G. Schneider (2014b), 'Social entrepreneurship, microfinance, and economic development in Africa', *Journal of Economic Issues*, **48** (2), 367–376.

Oliver, C. (1991), 'Strategic responses to institutional processes', *Academy of Management Review*, **16** (1), 145–179.

Rittel, H.W. and M.M. Webber (1973), 'Dilemmas in a general theory of planning', *Policy Sciences*, **4** (2), 155–169.

Rivera-Santos, M., D. Holt, D. Littlewood and A. Kolk (2015), 'Social entrepreneurship in sub-Saharan Africa', *Academy of Management Perspectives*, **29** (1), 72–91.

Scott, L., C. Dolan, M. Johnstone-Louis, K. Sugden and M. Wu (2012), 'Enterprise and inequality: A study of Avon in South Africa', *Entrepreneurship, Theory and Practice*, **36** (3), 543–568.

Scott, W.R. (2008), *Institutions and Organizations*, Los Angeles, CA: Sage Publications.

Scott, W.R. (2013), *Institutions and Organizations: Ideas, Interests, and Identities*. Los Angeles, CA: Sage Publications.

Seelos, C. and J. Mair, J. (2005), 'Social entrepreneurship: Creating new business models to serve the poor', *Business Horizons*, **48** (3), 241–246.

Sen, A. (1999), *Development as Freedom*, New York, NY: Knopf.

Sengupta, S. and A. Sahay (2017), 'Comparing mission statements of social enterprises and corporate enterprises in the new and renewable energy sector of India: A computer aided content analysis study', *Journal of Global Entrepreneurship Research*, **7** (1), 1–16.

Sengupta, S., A. Sahay and F. Croce (2018), 'Conceptualizing social entrepreneurship in the context of emerging economies: An integrative review of past research from BRIICS', *International Entrepreneurship and Management Journal*, **14**, 771–803.

Sodhi, M. and C. Tang (2014), 'Buttressing supply chains against floods in Asia for humanitarian relief and economic recovery', *Production and Operations Management*, **23** (6), 938–950.

UNIDO (2008), *Creating an enabling environment for private sector development in sub-Saharan Africa*, Vienna: United Nations Industrial Development Organisation.

Urban, B. (2015), 'Evaluation of social enterprise outcomes and self-efficacy', *International Journal of Social Economics*, **42** (2), 163–178.

van der Have, R.P. and L. Rubalcaba (2016), 'Social innovation research: An emerging area of innovation studies?', *Research Policy*, **45** (9), 1923–1935.

Viswanathan, M. and S. Sridharan (2009), 'From subsistence marketplaces to sustainable marketplaces: A bottom-up perspective on the role of business in poverty alleviation', *Ivey Business Journal*, **73** (2), 1–15.

Von Graevenitz, G., Harhoff, D. and R. Weber (2010), 'The effects of entrepreneurship education', *Journal of Economic Behavior and Organization*, **76** (1), 90–112.

Warnecke, T. (2018), 'Social entrepreneurship in China: Driving institutional change', *Journal of Economic Issues*, **52** (2), 368–377.

Warnecke, T. and A. Houndonougbo (2016), 'Let there be light: Social enterprise, solar power, and sustainable development', *Journal of Economic Issues*, **50** (2), 362–372.

Webb, J.W., L. Tihanyi, R.D. Ireland and D.G. Sirman (2009), 'You say illegal, I say legitimate: Entrepreneurship in the informal economy', *Academy of Management Review*, **34** (3), 492–510.

16 Social entrepreneurship through the lens of the 'everyday': inquiring the rhythms of female micro-credit recipients

Pascal Dey and Laurent Marti

Introduction

Recent years have witnessed an increasing interest among academics as to whether, and to what extent, social entrepreneurship (SE) offers the requisite means for establishing an alternative form of capitalism (e.g. Baglioni, 2017; Dey, 2014; Driver, 2012; Horn, 2013; Nicholls & Teasdale, 2017; Shaw & de Bruin, 2013). While SE has become an integral part of a broader conversation about the need for radically transforming the purpose and function of business in society, differing perspectives on the subject matter do exist. On one end of the spectrum we find those purporting that SE puts a unique opportunity in front of us to realize a more compassionate, fair or 'humane' market economy (Driver, 2012). Commentators in this tradition have conceived of SE as an antidote against common 'sins' of capitalism (Baglioni, 2017), such as overly self-interested and profit-maximizing forms of doing business (Yunus, 2009). The general thinking is that by combining social and market logics SE precipitates not just a higher form of profit, but a higher form of economy (Driver, 2012). On the other end of the spectrum we find critical evaluations delineating SE as a Trojan horse of capitalist expansion. These critics have pointed out that social enterprises, by addressing essentially political goals with business techniques, represent an inappropriate invasion of the community sector by capitalist ideals (Paton, 2003). A related concern is that governments' use of social enterprise policies effectively transforms civil society into a 'governable terrain' (Carmel & Harlock, 2008) by normalizing capitalist 'virtues' such as enterprise, competitiveness, and innovation (Dey & Steyaert, 2012). Since social enterprises are said to be (overly) wedded to the logics of the market (Dart, 2004), SE is charged with causing a democratic deficit, a decline in political participation or decision-making (Eikenberry & Kluver, 2004; Horn, 2013). Thus, SE is perhaps less the alternative to market capitalism that many see in it.

Even if we applaud research addressing the alter-capitalist potential of SE (Shaw & de Bruin, 2013), our basic contention is that the relationship between social enterprises and capitalism remains poorly understood. This chapter addresses this shortcoming by sketching out a conceptual framework that allows us to relax the binary opposition between 'alternative' versus 'conventional' around which the academic debate currently revolves. Theoretically, we draw on French philosopher Henri Lefebvre's (2004; Lefebvre & Régulier, 1985) work on rhythms, everyday life and capitalism. We thereby use micro-finance as an illustrative vignette to focus on how debt – the paradoxical agent of both poverty alleviation and the financializa-tion of poverty (Federici, 2014; Graeber, 2011) – works to engage female borrowers in repetitive production rhythms and repayment schedules underpinning the 'accumulation process' (Lefebvre, 2002).

Capitalism, everyday life and rhythms

Lefebvre's work on rhythms, from which this chapter draws, marks a continuation of his previous investigations of capitalist survival and expansion (Lefebvre, 1976), and in particular his tri-part critique of everyday life (Lefebvre, 1991, 2002, 2005). Lefebvre's work aspires to understand how capitalism shapes, and is shaped by, every-day life; that is, the aggregate of people's routines, skills, experiences and trajectories. The basic premise thus is that capitalism, to survive, pervades "previously untapped areas of quotidian experience" (Edensor, 2010, p. 13) by ordering, channelling and negotiating people's rituals, movements and ways of thinking according to the desid-eratum of commercial life and modes of production (Edensor & Holloway, 2008). Understanding capitalism according to Lefebvre requires addressing the everyday, locally and empirically, as 'in the making'. Everyday life is more than just a sub-system within a larger system, but rather represents the very 'base' from which capitalism "endeavours to constitute itself as a system, by programming this base" (Lefebvre, 2005, p. 41). This 'programming' involves multifaceted and diverse attempts to make everyday life – including the activities directly related to work and consumption as well as the seemingly most intimate moments of leisure and privacy – coterminous with the accumulation of capital. An apt example of how people's non-work-related time is transformed into the time of markets can be seen in how advertising compa-nies use outdoor billboards to pitch products and services to commuters who spend a significant amount of their commuting time waiting or queuing (Cronin, 2006).

Lefebvre's (2004) treatise on rhythms, which only appeared posthumously, expands some of his earlier work on the controversial and shifting relationship between the everyday and the circuits of capitalist accumulation. In vernacular as well as academic diction, rhythms index repetition, ordering and regularity. They manifest themselves in different phenomena such as the heartbeat (physiological rhythm), the tides (natural rhythm), after-work drinks or pedestrian movements (social rhythm) or workers' movements in the assembly line (rhythms of production). While different interpretations of rhythm do exist, many of which focus exclusively on its temporal dimension (Simpson, 2012) – different speeds, slow-downs, arrested developments, (ir)regular beats, etc. – rhythms are understood here as spatio-tem-poral constellations or unities (Schatzki, 2009, 2010). In Lefebvre's (1996) words: "Every rhythm implies the relation of a time with a space, a localized time, or if one wishes, a temporalised place" (p. 230). While each rhythm has its time (its regular intervals, its stops and beginnings, accelerations and slow-downs, its duration) and its space (the specific location in which it takes place, or the way in which it defines space in particular ways), rhythms differ in terms of the specific forms of spatial and temporal existence they prompt (Smith & Hetherington, 2013), and the kind of finalities (capitalist accumulation, intimacy, friendship, etc.) they precipitate.

A central focus of Lefebvre's critical investigation are linear rhythms,[1] which he conceives of as rhythms originating from human and social activities, especially those of work. Linear rhythms according to Lefebvre are characterized by the type of rational and calculative space-time constellations associated with commerce – as the billboard example (Cronin, 2006) has suggested. Linear rhythms are thereby seen as an 'imposition' (Meyer, 2008), since they set and codify time and shape space to determine how people move (Vedula & Kim, 2018).

The model of the factory offers an emblematic account of how linear rhythms work to rationalize production (to maximize productivity) by strictly determining people's rhythmic movement in time and space: like in a well-oiled machine, factories allo-cate each worker a *position in the labor process* (notably the assembly line); *define the movements* they need to perform; give them a certain amount of *time to complete a task*; define when they are allowed to *take a break*; and offer workers housing close to the factory to reduce their *commuting time*. The factory offers a point in case of how linear rhythms "create quotidian disciplinary conditions" (Reid-Musson, 2017, p. 2) which compose people as a productive force (Edensor, 2010).

However, while the factory is indicative of how people are fully aligned and con-trolled in space-time to cohere to the principle of maximum performance, a recur-rent tension acknowledged by Lefebvre is that linear rhythms pertaining to work are never fully successful in subsuming everyday life to the sphere of production and consumption as there always remains something that escapes the economic imperatives that try to colonize everyday life (Edensor, 2010). It is this excess of everyday life, caused by the complex entanglement and confrontation of dominat-ing rhythms with multifarious vital, natural and cyclical rhythms of nature, the body and the cosmos (Lefebvre, 2003), that capitalism's regular rhythmic unfolding is disrupted and made 'irregular'. Such becoming irregular (Lefebvre, 2004) creates openings in which the person is (temporarily) detached from the regular unfolding of linear space-time (Shields, 1996) upon which the accumulation process is based.

We now use the case of micro-finance to demonstrate the 'use value' of Lefebvre's work for understanding SE.

Empirical vignette: micro-finance

Introduction to micro-finance

Micro-finance was propelled to prominence following the award of the Nobel Peace Prize to Muhammad Yunus and Grameen Bank in 2006. The Grameen Bank addresses poverty by offering small loans to people, mainly women, in Bangladesh who would otherwise be unable to secure financing. Unlike traditional banks which offer loans to people with collaterals, micro-finance institutions like Grameen give loans to poor people without such securities. The credit risk associated with the absence of collaterals is addressed through joint liabilities: rather than giving money to individuals, borrowers are asked to create groups of 5–10 people who act as co-referees (during the application phase) and later as co-guarantors for each other's loans (Ghatak & Guinnane, 1999). Studies suggest that groups of female money lenders ensure a repayment rate of above 95% (Anthony & Horn, 2003; Panjaitan-Drioadisuryo & Cloud, 1999). Women are thus conceived as lower portfolio risks if compared to men as they are associated with fewer write-offs and fewer provisions (D'Espallier, Guérin & Mersland, 2011).[2] Women who receive the loans are expected to make small investments to generate revenue and to eventually lift themselves out of poverty, thus capturing most of the surplus generated by the loan.

Focusing in the ensuing vignette on female micro-entrepreneurs, rather than on micro-finance institutions directly, allows us to take a closer look at the everyday lives of micro-finance's primary beneficiaries to see how becoming micro-entrepreneurs affects women's everyday lives. We thereby use secondary data as our main source of information.

Rhythmanalyzing female micro-entrepreneurs

Becoming part of micro-finance has a direct, immediate effect on women's everyday lives as it affects their repetitions, movements and pauses in time and space (Wozniack, 2017). To take a simple example: many women who receive micro-loans used to be engaged mainly in activities such as child rearing, housekeeping and subsistence farming. Becoming a micro-entrepreneur thus has a potentially disruptive effect on their temporal rhythms as they might spend less *time* at home – with their children, the neighbors and relatives – and spend more time in the fields and in marketplaces. Similarly, becoming a loan recipient changes the spatial movement of women as they might need to travel to faraway places to sell their produce at regular markets. What is crucially at stake in these cursory examples is the prioritization of linear rhythms – the rhythms of production and commerce – over all other types of non-commercial rhythms.

The inclusion of women in the rhythms of financialization is based on a simple principle: debt is used to recode women's everyday life in terms of investments and losses so that women's daily practices and movements are committed to production schemes and repayment schedules. While various scholars have pointed out that micro-finance discursively envisions women as profitable economic agents (Girón, 2015; Radhakrishnan, 2018), it must be stressed that the transformation of women into 'indebted people' is not merely a discursive phenomenon, but an inherently rhythmic one. As Wozniak (2017) aptly points out, debt shapes women's subjectivity and sense of being as they are trained to adapt their existential rhythms of private everyday life to the requirements of commercial life; this adaptation of everyday life is wide-ranging and includes "hours of sleep and waking, meal-times and the hours of private life, the relations [...] with their children, entertainment and hobbies, relations to the place of dwelling" (Lefebvre, 2004, p. 82). So conceived, we can see that linear rhythms that aim in the direction of compliance with the programs of debt service become the norm – they impose themselves on the entirety of women's everyday rhythms.

Particularly noteworthy in regard to debt's linear rhythms are lending schemes which impose a distinct "chrono-normativity" (Freeman, 2005) on women by making their everyday practices and experiences follow timely dictated patters in conformity with repayment deadlines. Repayment schedules convey the essential idea that the best way for any debtor to "avoid 'house breaking' or harassment is to repay loans on time" (Mader, 2013, p. 20). The chrono-normativity of debt creates a situation where women are compelled to adjust their rhythm of life to be able to repay their loans on time. The gravity of debt repayment's chrono-normativity can be sensed in female borrowers' on-going hustle to make ends meet by cutting down on essential goods and services. Research shows that women are at times only able to meet their financial obligations by reducing spending pertaining to, for instance, the nutrition of their families, the education of their children, or the health services of their relatives (Brett, 2006).

Alternatively, Taylor (2011) reports how micro-finance borrowers in parts of India reacted to the rhythmic disciplining and chrono-normativity which came with flows of credit, by accessing extra loans from traditional moneylenders whom micro-finance was supposed to displace, such that "informal moneylending has therein adapted and expanded alongside the rise of microfinance" (Taylor, 2011, p. 499). Female borrowers often seem to have little choice but to take on greater levels of debt to meet basic needs. As a result, they might end up in a vicious cycle of indebtedness and debt repayment.

Evidently enough, the severe rhythmicity and chrono-normativity of repayment schedules designed to ensure predictable cash-flows is at odds with female borrowers' varied income streams, spending habits and private circumstances. Also, the rhythmicity of repayment schedules turns a blind eye to the vagaries and contingencies of people's natural and social rhythms: people fall sick, they get injured or they witness personal tragedies such as the death of a close family member. Unless properly insured, such happenings are antithetical to mechanical rhythms, to linear time-space, since it is very difficult to attune and integrate them to the rhythmic organization of commercial life. Put differently, injuries, death and illnesses operate arrhythmically by causing ruptures in the linear rhythmic flows of micro-finance.

The essential mismatch between financial rhythms and the everyday lives of female micro-entrepreneurs generates various risks. For instance, the inability of a woman to repay a loan on time requires that the other women of her self-help group step in for her. If the group as a whole is not able to repay, then the entire group is not eligible to receive further loans. Research shows that stigma regularly accompanies the experience of not being able to repay the loan and there is a burgeoning literature on (mainly male) micro-entrepreneurs, especially in the field of agriculture, committing suicide to escape the stigma associated with insolvability (Ashta, Khan & Otto, 2015).

As the example of suicide shows, the subjugation of everyday life to the rhythms of micro-finance does not designate a harmonious process. For instance, there is much evidence that micro-finance generates marriage conflicts and cultural tensions, as women are offered new spatial and temporal freedoms through their activity as micro-entrepreneurs. However, while our foregoing elaboration might have suggested that micro-finance reduces women's agency to the "lifetime management of themselves as financial portfolios" (Noys, 2012, p. 12), the point to note is that the linear rhythms of micro-finance are never fully successful in aligning the everyday lives of women with the broader circuits of capitalist accumulation. Consider, as just one example of the excess of everyday life, a study from India which showed that "a significant number of recipients of microcredit used the loans not to support their entrepreneurial ventures, but to begin moneylending activities" (Taylor, 2011, p. 499). Thus under the increasingly seamless matching of micro-finance with the requirements of transnational capital, some female borrowers appropriated the linear rhythms of micro-finance by using microloans to become moneylenders themselves. This indicates that vital rhythms and practices are not necessarily submitted to the accumulation process in that female actors are able to parasitically engage with the linear rhythms of micro-finance so as to pursue their own interests.

Becoming moneylenders themselves suspends the dominant space-time of microcredit as they essentially step outside of the pressures of repayment schedules. This 'stepping out' not only represents a moment of clandestine resistance against the dictate of capital, but an opportunity to produce 'profane time and space' – that is, a type of space-time that has not been programmed, and that hence cannot be fully subsumed to the accumulation process (Halvorsen, 2015). This profanation forms just one example of how the everyday can be disconnected from its regular (i.e. linear or commercial) use and how it can be made available for alternative usages. Interventions into the rhythmic unfolding of micro-finance thus bring into being openings for "creative activity as distinct from [commercial] activity" (Lefebvre, 2004, p. 43) by suspending, at least temporarily, processes of exchange-value production.

Concluding discussion

This necessarily tentative and fragmented attempt to bring the field of research on rhythms, everyday life and capitalism together is important in that it enables us to probe the merit of Lefebvre's work in addressing an important, but still under-explored, question: how is SE related to market capitalism? While the few studies explicitly addressing this question tend to emphasize either the structure of the whole or details of a part, Lefebvre's work brings these opposing perspectives closer together in continuous movements between partially overlapping points of view. Our theoretical reading of extant research on micro-credit, which cannot do justice to the complexity and richness of the subject, has pointed out how female money lenders' everyday practices, routines and movements are at once connected to the reproduction of capitalism, while at the same time including at least the possibility of intermittent moments of rupture and excess.[3]

Rhythms thus offer a conceptual language and analytic sensibility for investigating how multi-layered rhythms – linear (commercial), social, natural, cyclical, physical rhythms – relate to one another in shifting and often contested ways (Borch, Hansen & Lange, 2015). In this way, a rhythm perspective helps us sense the futility of asking whether SE is capitalist or alter-capitalist: SE is neither fully connected to the accumulation process nor completed liberated from it, but a complex overlapping of liberating and reactionary dimensions. Indeed, the truth that is largely going unaddressed in polarized discussions is that SE reactionary and reformist dynamics are not mutually exclusive, but intertwined in complex and shifting ways.

Consequently, although it might be very difficult for social enterprises to be completely 'alternative' – that is, outside or against capitalism – Lefebvre reminds us that there are always intermittent moments of transgression and excess which deserve being studied.

NOTES

1 The idea of linearity might appear inapt in our post-Fordist times where 'non-linear' or flexible forms of labor, such as the gig economy, digital nomadism, or home-working, have become increasingly popular. However, we keep the notion of linearity in this chapter to retain a sensitivity toward how particular work-related rhythms achieve aligning the rhythms of everyday life with a commercial rationale.

2 Perhaps interestingly, research indicates that male loan recipients are more successful in setting up formal businesses (Banerjee, 2013).

3 This duality of micro-credit is also evident in extant research which suggests that the broader effects on women's empowerment are at best mixed (e.g. Stewart et al., 2012; Bali Swain & Wallentin, 2009).

References

Anthony, D. and D. Horn (2003), 'Gender and cooperation: Explaining loan repayment in micro-credit groups', *Social Psychology Quarterly*, **66** (3), 293–302.

Ashta, A., Khan, S. and P. Otto (2015), 'Does microfinance cause or reduce suicides? Policy recommendations for reducing borrower stress', *Strategic Change*, **24** (2), 165–190.

Baglioni, S. (2017), 'A remedy for all sins? Introducing a special issue of social enterprises and welfare regimes in Europe', *Voluntas*, **28**, 2325–2338.

Bali Swain, R. and F. Y. Wallentin (2009), 'Does microfinance empower women? Evidence from self-help groups in India', *International Review of Applied Economics*, **23** (5), 541–556.

Banerjee, A. V. (2013), 'Microcredit under the microscope: What have we learned in the past two decades, and what do we need to know?', *Annual Review of Economics*, **5**, 487–519.

Borch, C., Hansen, K. B. and A.-C. Lange (2015), 'Markets, bodies, and rhythms: A rhythmanalysis of financial markets from open-outcry trading to high frequency trading', *Environment and Planning D: Society and Space*, **33** (6), 1080–1097.

Brett, J. A. (2006), '"We sacrifice and eat less": The structural complexities of microfinance participation', *Human Organization*, **65** (1), 8–19.

Carmel, E. and J. Harlock (2008), 'Instituting the "third sector" as a governable terrain: Partnership, procurement and performance in the UK', *Policy and Politics*, **36** (2), 155–171.

Cronin, A. M. (2006), 'Advertising and the metabolism of the city: Urban spaces, commodity, rhythms', *Environment and Planning D: Society and Space*, **24** (4), 615–632.

Dart, R. (2004), 'Being "business-like" in a nonprofit organization: A grounded and inductive typology', *Nonprofit and Voluntary Sector Quarterly*, **33** (2), 290–310.

D'Espallier, B., Guérin, I. and R. Mersland (2011), 'Women and repayment in microfinance: A global analysis', *World Development*, **39** (5), 758–772.

Dey, P. (2014), 'Governing the social through "social entrepreneurship": A Foucauldian view of the "art of governing" in advanced liberalism', in H. Douglas and S. Grant (eds.), *Social Innovation and Social Entrepreneurship: Context and Theories*, Melbourne: Tilde University Press, pp. 91–107.

Dey, P. and C. Steyaert (2012), 'Social entrepreneurship: Critique and the radical enactment of the social', *Social Enterprise Journal*, **8** (2), 90–107.

Driver, M. (2012), 'An interview with Michael Porter: Social entrepreneurship and the transformation of capitalism', *Academy of Management Learning & Education*, **11** (3), 421–431.

Edensor, T. (2010), 'Introduction: Thinking about rhythm and space', in T. Edensor (ed.), *Geographies of Rhythm: Nature, Places, Mobilities and Bodies*, Aldershot: Ashgate, pp. 1–18.

Edensor, T. and J. Holloway (2008), 'Rhythmanalysing the coach tour: The Ring of Kerry, Ireland', *Transactions of the Institute of British Geographers*, **33** (4), 483–501.

Eikenberry, A. M. and J. D. Kluver (2004), 'The marketization of the nonprofit sector: Civil society at risk?', *Public Administration Review*, **64** (2), 132–140.

Federici, S. (2014), 'From commoning to debt: Financialization, microcredit, and the changing architecture of capital accumulation', *South Atlantic Quarterly*, **113** (2), 231–244.

Freeman, E. (2005), 'Time binds, or, erotohistoriography', *Social Text*, **23** (3–4), 84–85.

Ghatak, M. and T. Guinnane (1999), 'The economics of lending with joint liability: Theory and practice', *Journal of Development Economics*, **60** (1), 195–228.

Girón, A. (2015), 'Women and financialization: Microcredit, institutional investors, and MFIs', *Journal of Economic Issues*, **49** (2), 373–396.

Graeber, D. (2011), *Debt: The First Five Thousand Years*, New York: Melville Publishing House.

Halvorsen, S. (2015), 'Taking space: Moments of rupture and everyday life in Occupy London', *Antipode*, **47** (2), 401–417.

Horn, D. (2013), *Democratic Governance and Social Entrepreneurship: Civic Participation and the Future of Democracy*, London: Routledge.

Lefebvre, H. (1976), *The Survival of Capitalism: Reproduction of the Relations of Production*, London: Macmillan.

Lefebvre, H. (1991), *Critique of Everyday Life, Vol. 1*, London: Verso.

Lefebvre, H. (1996), 'Rhythmanalysis of Mediterranean cities', in E. Kofman and E. Lebas (eds.), *Writings on Cities*, Oxford: Blackwell, pp. 228–240.

Lefebvre, H. (2002). *Critique of Everyday Life, Vol. 2*, London: Verso.

Lefebvre, H. (2003), 'From the social pact to the contract of citizenship', in S. Elden, E. Lebas and E. Kofman (eds.), *Henri Lefebvre: Key Writings*, New York: Continuum, pp. 238–254.

Lefebvre, H. (2004), *Rhythmanalysis: Space, Time and Everyday Life*, New York: Continuum.

Lefebvre, H. (2005), *Critique of Everyday Life, Vol. 3*, London: Verso.

Lefebvre, H. and C. Régulier-Lefebvre (1992), *Éléments de Rythmanalyse: Introduction à la Connaissance des Rythmes*, Paris: Ed. Syllepse.

Mader, P. (2013), 'Explaining and quantifying the extractive success of financial systems: Microfinance and the financialisation of poverty', *Ekonomska istraživanja – Economic Research Special Issue 2013*, 13–28.

Meyer, K. (2008), 'Rhythms, streets, cities', in K. Goonewardena, S. Kipfer, R. Milgrom and C. Schmid (eds.), *Space, Difference, Everyday Life: Reading Henri Lefebvre*, New York: Routledge, pp. 147–160.

Nicholls, A. and S. Teasdale (2017), 'Neoliberalism by stealth? Exploring continuity and change within the UK social enterprise policy paradigm', *Policy & Politics*, **45** (3), 323–341.

Noys, B. (2012), *Persistence of the Negative: A Critique of Contemporary Continental Theory*, Edinburgh: Edinburgh University Press.

Panjaitan-Drioadisuryo, R. D. M. and K. Cloud (1999), 'Gender, self-employment and microcredit programs: An Indonesian case study', *The Quarterly Review of Economics and Finance*, **39** (5), 769–779.

Paton, R. (2003), *Managing and Measuring Social Enterprises*, London: Sage.

Radhakrishnan, S. (2018), 'Of loans and livelihoods: Gendered "social work" in urban India', *Economic Anthropology*, **5** (2), 235–246.

Reid-Musson, E. (2017), 'Intersectional rhythmanalysis: Power, rhythms, and everyday life', *Progress in Human Geography*, **42** (6), 881–897.

Schatzki, T. R. (2009), 'Timespace and the organization of social life', in E. Shove, F. Trentmann and R. Wilk (eds.), *Time, Consumption and Everyday Life: Practice, Materiality and Culture*, Oxford: Berg, pp. 35–48.

Schatzki, T. R. (2010), *The Timespace of Human Activity: On Performance, Society, and History as Indeterminate Teleological Events*, Plymouth, UK: Lexington Books.

Shaw, E. and A. de Bruin (2013), 'Reconsidering capitalism: The promise of social innovation and social entrepreneurship?', *International Small Business Journal*, **31** (7), 737–746.

Shields, R. (1996), *Lefebvre, Love and Struggle: Spatial Dialectics*, New York: Routledge.

Simpson, P. (2012), 'Apprehending everyday rhythms: Rhythmanalysis, time-lapse photography, and the space-times of street performance', *Cultural Geographies*, **19** (4), 423–445.

Smith, R. J. and K. Hetherington (2013), 'Urban rhythms: Mobilities, space and interaction in the contemporary city', *The Sociological Review*, **61** (S1), 4–16.

Stewart, R., C. van Rooyen, M. Korth, A. Chereni, N. R. Da Silva and T. de Wet (2012), 'Do microcredit, micro-savings and micro-leasing serve as effective financial inclusion interventions enabling poor people, and especially women, to engage in meaningful economic opportunities in low- and middle-income countries? A systematic review of the evidence', London: EPPI-Centre, Social Science Research Unit, Institute of Education, University of London.

Taylor, M. (2011), '"Freedom from poverty is not for free": Rural development and the microfinance crisis in Andhra Pradesh, India', *Journal of Agrarian Change*, **11**, 484–504.

Vedula, S. and P. H. Kim (2018), 'Marching to the beat of the drum: The impact of the pace of life in US cities on entrepreneurial work effort', *Small Business Economics*, **50** (3), 569–590.

Wozniak, J. T. (2017), 'Towards a rhythmanalysis of debt dressage: Education as rhythmic resistance in everyday indebted life', *Policy Futures in Education*, **15** (4), 495–508.

Yunus, M. (2009), *Creating a World Without Poverty: Social Business and the Future of Capitalism*, Philadelphia: Public Affairs.

17 The times of social innovation – fictional expectation, precautionary expectation and social imaginary

Rafael Ziegler

This chapter is inspired by a philosophical topic: the relation between time and innovation. More specifically, it explores a distinct future orientation in modern economic theory and capitalist economies, and its implication for social entrepreneurship and social innovation.[1] An obvious starting point for such an investigation is the 'gale of creative destruction', powered by entrepreneurs and their innovations, investors and consumers, and claimed to enable a continuous growth of economic output as well as increase in the standard of living (Schumpeter 1942). As if this were not enough, this growth has to be accelerated (or so the German parliament declared when it passed a *Wachstumsbeschleunigungsgesetz* or Economic Growth Acceleration Law in 2009). Modern history as an upward accelerating spiral of economic progress?

But what is it like to be in such a gale? A subjective entry point is the perspectives of innovators, investors and consumers on an uncertain future. While laws and norms often reduce uncertainty and produce 'institutionalised certainty' (Aspers 2018, 2), a distinct feature of capitalist institutions is to welcome and foster innovations and in this way to institutionalise uncertainty. Enterprises fear that the innovation of a competitor will undermine their business. Continuous innovation leaves consumers with products becoming obsolete just when they got used to them. The institutionalised uncertainty of 'innovation society' is based on a general point: the future of the economy is fundamentally uncertain. Or as John Maynard Keynes put it in 1937:

> *The price of copper, the rate of interest in twenty years, the obsolescence of a new invention, or the position of private wealth owners in the social systems in 1970: About these matters there is no scientific basis on which to form any calculable probability whatever. We simply do not know. Nevertheless, the necessity for action and for decision compels us as practical men to do our best to overlook this awkward fact . . . .* (Keynes 1937, 214)

Economic sociologist Jens Beckert offers a fresh perspective on the uptake of this 'awkward fact' in capitalism (Beckert 2016). Faced with the uncertainty of the future, actors create fictional expectations, stories and images of the future that attract others to support this future pathway, providing it with legitimacy and increasing its achievability. Beckert's central claim: rational calculations and expected utility estimates are not at the heart of the dynamics of capitalist markets, fictional expectations are (and these include, more subtly, calculated predictions as useful fictions, not least to 'save our faces as rational, economic men' (Keynes 1937, 214)). In short, an imaginary future orientation pulsates in the present of capitalist dynamics. Good news for social innovators, the 'unreasonable people', and their creative stories of 'how to change the world' (Elkington and Hartigan 2008, Bornstein 2004)?

Yes, but ... according to the same account, the power of fictional expectations also colonises other forms of agency. Creative and non-economically motivated expressions of agency are fed into capitalism's restlessness (Beckert 2016, 27). The dynamic of capitalism is a complex challenge for social innovation. So what then about the role of fictional expectations and this peculiar future orientation for social innovation? What can we learn from this starting point in the analysis of capitalism about temporal orientation in social innovation?

These are large questions, and this chapter can only suggest what a research agenda in this direction might look like. In order to explore the above-noted ambivalence of fictional expectations for social innovation, it uses a methodological trick. It explores the questions in a societal problem context: sustainability and the (re) production of unsustainability in capitalist dynamics. Social innovation is often presented as a carrier of change towards meeting sustainable development goals (Millard 2018, 42) and for 'smart, sustainable and inclusive growth' (Howaldt et al. 2018, 14). But the sustainability problem context for the present purpose is also methodologically relevant as it reveals *varieties* of temporal orientation, and this in turn sheds light on the 'colonisation' of other forms of creative agency. Put differently, there is something deeply problematic about the tendency to reflect on, and have expectations about, social entrepreneurship and social innovation in terms of capitalist, fictional expectation only, and thus to focus centrally on the expected impact and anticipated return of such initiatives. Accordingly, this chapter will have succeeded, if this seemingly abstract topic and problem, along with alternatives of temporal orientation, become vivid.

The next section will draw on a discourse typology of roughly market, science and civil society centred sustainability discourses (Sachs 1999). Exploring social innovation in relation to these three discourses points to a variety of temporal orientations:

- the fictional expectations of capitalist markets
- the precautionary expectations of Earth systems science
- the social imaginaries of civil society that are just as much about 'present pasts' as they are about 'future presents'.[2]

Anticipating the discussion below, the chapter advances the following claims. Fictional expectation is important for social innovation. However, it is not the only type of temporal orientation. A further important future orientation is precautionary expectation. Moreover, social imaginaries play an important role. They often respond to capitalist expansion dynamics, but they do not do so as a matter of primarily dealing with uncertainty, nor do they necessarily have a future orientation. If these claims and related distinctions are correct, then a further question emerges regarding the relation and ordering of these orientations.

The contest perspective and fictional expectation

In *Planet Dialectics* (1999), Wolfgang Sachs distinguishes three sustainability discourses in his 'political anatomy' of sustainable development. The following sections will introduce these discourses, one per section, starting with the 'contest perspective'. However, it is important to stress right from the start that these discourses, though presented here separately, are in practice blurry and partly interdependent.

According to the contest perspective advanced by economic and political elites, environmental protection is an opportunity for innovation and green growth that the leading nations in the competition should exploit to export their green technologies and gain a competitive edge (Sachs 1999, 78–83). The legitimating narrative of this discourse is that of an economic globalisation that will ultimately raise the standard of living for all, and thus globalise economic progress.

'Green economy' is a gigantic – that is, planetary – opportunity for a new capitalist dynamic. Green-tech pioneers replace the 'brown' capitalist dependency on fossil fuels via the development of renewable energies, improve efficiency via smart grids and so on. This dynamic invites a genre of fictional expectations: 'green' promissory notes.

But first: what are 'fictional expectations'? The term refers to

> the images actors form as they consider future states of the world, the way they visualise causal relations, and the ways they perceive their actions influencing outcomes. The term also refers to the symbolic qualities that actors ascribe to goods and that transcend the goods' material features . . . Actors use imaginaries of future situations and of causal relations as well as the symbolically ascribed qualities of goods as interpretative frames to orient decision-making despite the incalculability of outcomes. (Beckert 2016, 17)

Fictional expectations create as-if futures of a possible world. The adjective 'fiction' does not indicate a contrast to 'truth' or aim to 'debunk' these expectations as lies. Rather, it points to the invitation to belief. Fictional expectations bring actors together 'as believers' in the face of uncertainty, and in this way make a future present more achievable. They are a source of new ideas and innovations, and the focus of interest struggles and politics of expectations. Finally, while they anticipate a future, the formation of such expectations is influenced by the past and present:

the formal and informal institutions and associated distribution of resources, social networks (and one's position in them) as well as culture and its ways of seeing and experiencing the world.

Drawing from the human capability of imagination, fictional expectations are an important source for new cycles of creative destruction. This is evident in the 'green economy' discourse as a promissory note about a more sustainable future. More subtly, in capitalism, market actors are restless due to the threat that others might deviate from established ways of doing things (Beckert 2016, 13ff and 266). This threat is structurally enforced by the profit motive of investors who provide access to resources to which no 'normal claim' exists, as Beckert writes with reference to Schumpeter. Claims are justified by anticipated future success.

Sustainable development as green economy offers a variant of the idea of economic progress, with greater emphasis on the needs of all worldwide and a focus on environmental limitation as a driver of innovation. However, it is still a narrative of expansion and conquest, with sustainability justifying urgency and acceleration towards achieving a 'safe' navigation in the 'Anthropocene' – that is, a planet whose major geological force has become the human species. The human impact has been specifically noteworthy in 'the great acceleration' of the post-World War II years (McNeill and Engelke 2015). It roughly coincides with what Sachs calls the invention of development in post-war US politics. In 1949, President Truman declared an 'era of development' that would make the 'benefits of scientific advances and industrial progress available for the improvement and growth of underdeveloped areas worldwide' (Sachs 1992).

Within this discourse, innovators must offer credible stories. Social innovators have to find ways of promising green products, services and lifestyles. There is also the challenge to find intermediary discourses and images to translate sustainable development goals into more concrete action domains. An example is 'circular economy' and the goals of longer-lasting design, maintenance, repair of products, and the reuse and recycling of waste. This 'circular' image has been so successful that 'the image is taken for reality' (Gregson et al. 2015, 220, drawing on prior work by Alexander and Reno) – an excellent illustration of a fictional expectation that has succeeded in attracting attention and support. Finally, there is the challenge to 'green' existing businesses via corporate social responsibility and social *intra*preneurship (Tracey and Stott 2017).

In this market-contest discourse, finding credible options of future monetary return is a key challenge that actors face. Alternatively, they can seek indirect ways of promising a return for their innovation. An example of the latter are cost-savings ideas that promise a reduction in public expenditure for social problems, and thereby legitimate private and public investment (an idea motivating the interest in social impact bonds). Not surprisingly, impact accounting is an active field of social innovation research, yet facing serious methodological challenges of 'credibly' accounting for (potential) impact.

More subtly, there are questions about the formation of expectations: who is in a position to 'dream' of greener products, who feels entitled to develop green aspirations, and for whom are fictional expectations developed?

The astronaut's perspective and precautionary expectation

According to a perspective advanced by global epistemic communities such as the scientists involved in international climate change research, sustainable development requires the advancement of our knowledge of the planet. Global models of the Earth system fed inter alia by satellite observation specify the right planetary scale of human activities with a view to the global carrying capacity of the Earth. Sachs calls it the astronaut's perspective. Ecological limits rather than economic development take priority (Sachs 1999, 83–86).

This perspective provides the knowledge input for the Anthropocene as a 'meta-narrative of modernity – a narrative in which energy- and resource-intensive industrialisation and capitalism have been accompanied by population booms, increased flows of goods and peoples . . . a category for critique – a way to define excess, limits, thresholds, and boundaries' (Kelly 2017, 11).

The astronaut's perspective puts forward a trump-claim: the consideration of 'hard' environmental limits is to take priority over the 'softer' constraints of society and the 'contest' perspective. The future orientation changes. Earth system scientists offer accounts of boundaries, the transgression of which produces uncertainty (Rockström et al. 2009). The response of the system is uncertain beyond the boundary. Some systems might change in unpredictable ways and cause severe harm. Accordingly, we can refer to this perspective as one of 'precautionary expectation'.

The currently most widely discussed model of such boundaries, the planetary framework model

> is based on critical processes that regulate ES [Earth system] functioning. By combining improved scientific understanding of ES functioning with the precautionary principle, the PB framework identifies levels of anthropogenic perturbations below which the risk of destabilization of the ES is likely to remain low – 'safe operating space' for global societal development. (Steffen et al. 2015, 736)

The narrative is based on a warning of a possibly dangerous exodus from 'safe Holocene' conditions. While fictional expectations seek to attract resources and co-ordinate actors ultimately via positive images of goods, services and associated values, precautionary expectations seek to attract resources and actors for sustainability via a negative image: an uncertain, looming exodus from a 'safe space'.[3] The credibility of this image largely rests on science, and the capability of global, epistemic communities to communicate precautionary expectations.

An implication of pre-cautionary expectations are calls for the 'directionality' of innovation (Leach et al. 2012): 'being clear on the particular goals and principles driving policy and innovation, not leaving them open, undiscussed, or driven by general imperatives of growth or progress, but actively steering them toward the kinds of transformation needed to stay within a safe operating space and meet SDGs.' Normative goals – with sustainable development goals at the most general, global level – are drawn on for a transformation of innovation.

A recent version of putting such 'directionality' into practice is the mission-oriented innovation policy approach (Mazzucato 2016). Accepting both the challenge of societally set goals and the 'extreme uncertainty' (ibid. 150) of direction-changing innovations, there is a call for the entrepreneurial state to take on this uncertainty, with patient, long-term investment in green transitions. Discovery and experimentation are encouraged from basic research to the development and adaption of products and services, and public expenditure is viewed as an investment that should expect fair rewards (Ziegler 2015). In short, the state is called to action to generate markets for policy goals, 'galvanizing green innovation' (Mazzucato 2016).

The power of fictional expectations in capitalist dynamics implies that such stimulation is ambivalent. Not only is 'directing' of innovation difficult, there is also the question whether the markets thereby generated will stay 'sustainably directed' or rather transform into the next wave of the old 'growth goal' (Crépin and Folke 2014, 58). Future orientation in capitalism is 'distorted': short-term expectations are in the way of a relation between present and future that enables green, transformative change (Jackson 2016, 167). Accordingly, sustainability innovation researchers argue that green directionality is insufficient. There must also be a change in the mode of innovation: inclusion of a diversity of approaches, so as to include bottom-up 'grassroots innovation'. Moreover, they call for the consideration of distributional questions of harms and benefits of innovation (Leach et al. 2012). This takes us to a third discourse.

The home perspective and social imaginaries

For the 'home perspective' advanced by international social movements and nature conservation NGOs, sustainable development is a new variant of economic development (Sachs 1999, 86–90). Yet, according to the home perspective, 'development' is based on a linear notion of progress that promises continuous progress over time, ultimately to everyone across the globe. But as material progress for all is only possible at the cost of an increasing crisis of nature, 'sustainable development' is viewed as a contradiction in terms. Therefore, this perspective calls for a replacement of development by justice. There is a call for degrowth, alternative models of wealth and a repayment of ecological debt. There is a call to create space for particular visions of the good, especially of all the indigenous traditions that the 'development discourse' placed as targets to be moved out of 'underdevelopment'. Such particular visions have existed prior to the rise of the capitalist economy, and they have continued to co-exist, even if at the margin. The home perspective calls attention to these traditions and practices, to varieties of experience, not just fictional expectation. It calls attention to the possibility that 'present pasts' might be 'past presents', not as a simple repetition to be sure but as creative, and socially important, adaptions to challenges.

Rather than following the flow of new fictional expectations, the home perspective retrieves social imaginaries of place.[4] While social imaginaries are not static, it is noteworthy that there is no necessary future orientation. There might also be an orientation to the past or perhaps, most interestingly, images of the past might make manifest values that embody the alternative defended and struggled for; or perhaps even directly manifest values of democracy, equality and sustainability (as in the 'real utopias' studied by Wright 2010). If anything, a future-oriented uncertainty is produced by the contest perspective and its expansionist tendencies. But these expansionist tendencies are not just a matter of future uncertainty. For the people affected, they can be certain and present struggles over ways of living and restoring practices in the face of market pressures.

It follows that innovation tends to be seen sceptically in this perspective. There is an emphasis on exnovation – that is, the termination – of unwanted products, services and infrastructures, and on slowing down innovation processes as well as preventing the carrying out of some ideas altogether. Constructively, innovation here calls for the restoration of social imaginaries and associated practices so that they can be passed on from the past to the future – including the creative changes this might necessitate. For example, Slovak social entrepreneur Michal Kravčík and his People and Water call for a 'New Water Paradigm'. The restoration of the small water cycle they aim at retrieves a marginalised tradition of farmers (Kravčík et al. 2012). Roberto Epple and his Big Jump movement call for a reclaiming of rivers by swimmers in the name of nature conservation.[5] River swimming activists like to point out that there were river swimming traditions across Europe up to the early 20th century. Sebastian Schönauer and the Interest-Community for Communal Drinking Water Provision seek to keep decentralised drinking water provision in communal hands against a central provisioning system perceived as dominating hamlets from above.[6] The examples show that innovative action need not emerge out of a context of uncertainty. The perception of civil society organisations and networks of what is dominating them (or nature) provokes creative responses. This is a matter of current struggles and resistance to domination, rather than of future uncertainty. At a very basic level, such creative responses can therefore be consistent with a 'modern' self-understanding that the future is open and that it can be shaped by humans (see endnote 5). However, they are not consistent with a 'modernist' perspective that one model of progress, such as the 'creative destruction' of capitalist markets, is the only and best way to think about innovation and time.

In addition, the 'home perspective' calls for a more fine-grained perspective of innovation. Some social innovations advance fictional expectations within emerging green economy markets, others seek to creatively restore places and practices in response to dominating tendencies of capitalist market provision. For such restoration informal provision and self-provision are important economic modes (Ziegler and von Jacobi 2018). From Thoreau's self-sufficiency experiments at Walden Pond (Thoreau 1854) to the urban garden movement, there have been social innovations critical of market provision and emphasising the opportunities of self- and communal provision.

Such innovations seek to create some security from market competition and space for social relations and community. There is, however, also a positive link to market innovation, as for example in evidence in a strand of Marxist literature: increased productivity gains of capitalist markets could free time for more self-determined ways of working rather than 'toiling' to meet needs.

In communist society, where nobody has one exclusive sphere of activity but each can become accomplished in any branch he wishes, society regulates the general production and thus makes it possible for me to do one thing today and another tomorrow, to hunt in the morning, fish in the afternoon, rear cattle in the evening, criticise after dinner, just as I have a mind, without ever becoming hunter, fisherman, herdsman or critic. (Marx 1846)

This 'utopian expectation' aims at ending work as toil. Yet in practice, it is difficult to transfer the productivity gains of the capitalist dynamic into more free time for those who work. This requires political struggles, and points to the fact that change in self- and communal provision is rarely animated by the lure of future profits (though of course there might be other issues). Therefore, there is also no good or service expansion goal, which might be one reason why social innovation in domestic and communal provision seems understudied in comparison to innovation for market provision. Still, it is important to keep in mind, as Offer discussed in detail (1997), that in spite of the growth of the market economy, self- and communal provision remain a substantial and persistent part of the economy. A key point for the present topic is the absence of a necessary future orientation in self- and informal provision. Moreover, given the evident possibility of creative change in such provisions, what are and can be modes of selection and recognition for such changes?

The renaissance of the entrepreneurial state already encountered above in the astronaut's perspective is via public regulation and provision, enabled by taxation or mandatory labour, a further important part of the modern economy. Arguably there are signs of 'fictional expectations' here too: for example, in the reinvention of cities or states as innovators or entrepreneurial administrators, viewing themselves in competition with other states. A comparative study found that cities such as Barcelona and Shanghai pursue green, urban innovations in order to become more attractive as global cities attracting investment and people (Fan et al. 2017).

Still, the provision of public goods or of goods linked to individual entitlements (for example, public infrastructure for wheelchair accessibility), and of innovations for meeting them, is a matter of political decision-making, ideally even of democratic deliberation. It would be strange to reduce such political process to a marketing of promissory notes to investors and consumers. Here, too, temporal orientation is not necessarily future-oriented.

Summing up, the home perspective points to a variety of modes of provision, alongside capitalist market provision. Yet, these other modes do not exhibit the same future orientation of capitalist market provision. They do not have the central structural selection mechanism of investors anticipating a future return. Rather, social imaginaries and existing ways of doing play an important role, as does political decision-making and deliberation.

Conclusions and contribution to the research agenda

The starting point of this chapter has been the observation that the capitalist economy, and the economic theory studying it, is strongly future-oriented (Beckert 2016). Faced with an uncertain future, and the institutionalised uncertainty of capitalist markets, fictional expectations are a way for 'practical men and women' to co-ordinate action, receive resources, seek legitimacy – and 'overlook the awkward fact'. This provides a rich soil for social innovations and their 'promissory notes' of more progressive, and improved, futures. However, it also exposes them to a powerful selection mode: anticipated return – that is, typically monetary profit expectations and return on investment. Social innovations that aim at market provision can in principle use this selection mode, not least as markets are co-shaped by a moral economy and the values held by innovators, investors and customers. 'Fictional expectations' help explain the great attention paid to 'story-telling' in social innovation practices, and there is a wide research field to better understand the sources of these stories, and their relation to social position (Beckert 2017).

Still, leaving it at that would clearly be unsatisfactory. The institutionalised uncertainty of capitalism is also driver of the unsustainability of the present. Calls for social innovation to transform the capitalist economy towards more sustainable ways of producing and consuming are indicative of this. This takes us to precautionary expectations – that is, the expectations mainly originating from science that a continuation of growth-driven, capitalist dynamics likely lead to a transgression of planetary boundaries (and partly already has). The biosphere might change in unpredictable ways, and the 'safe' place of societies and their economies is at risk. Still, there is no selection mechanism to make precautionary expectations practically effective that is in any way comparable to the dynamic of markets. This suggests that precautionary expectations are relevant for social innovation in at least three ways: there is a challenge of effectively communicating such expectations as knowledge notoriously does not necessitate action. For example, Mathis Wackernagel has invented the ecological footprint as a tool to communicate planetary constraints and with it a different problem perception. Second, precautionary expectations call for new institutions and the change of old ones. Hence there is a need for institutional entrepreneurship to translate precautionary expectations into institutions and to generate markets for green technologies. For example, Walter

Stahel and the Product Life Institutes, founded in 1982, push for policy recognition and industry implementation of 'circular economy'. Third, within such emerging green markets, there is again a place for the fictional expectations. The last point is a source of deep ambivalence: will 'green' fictional expectations as market expectations not inevitably undermine green constraints where profit possibilities arise? It is impossible to tell, but keeping fictional and precautionary expectations apart seems essential.

In addition, this chapter suggests that the future orientation of innovation in capitalism should be complemented by a more balanced account of temporal orientation in social innovation. Social imaginaries are as much about the past, experience and practice as they are about possible futures. The institutionalised uncertainty of capitalism constantly challenges such imaginaries, casting them as present pasts. However, there is creative action in restoring social imaginaries, and with it marginalised ways of doing things, in response to capitalist dynamics. Much indigenous and civil society innovation has such a structure. The negotiation of established practices, in the light of new challenges, is a source of innovation in self-, communal and public provision. But it cannot be captured as fictional expectation. Perhaps, it is often even innovation *par contre coeur*. It is useful to remember that the European use of innovation has emerged with the reformation (Godin 2012): that is, with religious leaders and politics calling for a return to true faith and practice (with Catholics initially cast as the corrupted innovators that have fallen from faith). Future orientation is not a necessary condition for innovation.

Accordingly, there is the question how imaginaries are selected, made credible and assert themselves. For the politics of temporal orientation these distinctions suggest questions for further research. How are temporal orientations and their ordering established? Sustainability science calls for a focus on precautionary expectations, trumping fictional expectations. But how does this happen in practice (or: how could it happen), and what are 'solutions' that social innovations come up with? Likewise, social imaginaries point to further modes of provision, with no specific future orientation, yet still much potential for innovation. How does such co-existence play out in practice? And what further variations of temporal orientation might this question reveal for an account of 'richer presents'?

Methodologically, a focus on temporal orientation in social innovation can contribute to two (interrelated) approaches: hermeneutics and ethics. A focus on temporal orientation points to the importance of hermeneutics in social innovation research. The explanation of innovation processes has to pay attention to practices and the meanings and narratives associated with them (Spinosa et al. 1997). Language is one way in which new spaces are disclosed (Dey and Stayaert 2015, 235). According to the proposal made here, this holds just as much for the narration of fictional expectations as it does for the affirmation of alternative problem perceptions with no specific future orientation (articulating already existing, but potentially marginalised, practices and possibilities) or in alternative modes of future orientation (precautionary expectations). Thus it would be interesting to better understand the role of temporal orientation in the 'texts' of social innovations, including the ideology critique this entails: why are some texts selected rather than others; what is the relation between texts and practices? There is a continuum of belief into the future potential of an idea to the continued belief in an idea as reality in spite of contrary evidence ('the image that is taken for reality'). Second, the varieties of temporal orientation are intrinsically linked to ethics. From the deep link of innovation in markets with a notion of improvement, via the concern with unacceptable harm in precautionary expectations to the emancipatory attempt to creatively respond to dominating tendencies of capitalist economies: ethics is woven into the topic of temporal orientation – and points to the 'eye' of the gale of creative destruction. As an ethical concern, research on 'richer presents' that equally considers varieties of future expectations and past experience is informed by a search for the good and the right that transcends temporal order, and thus distances itself from too much pre-occupation with past and future. 'True happiness is . . . to enjoy the present, without anxious dependence upon the future' (Seneca).

Acknowledgement

I would like to thank Jens Beckert for helpful feedback on the first draft of this chapter, and the participants of the ISIRC 2018 critical social innovation session as well as Philipp Thapa for feedback on the second draft of this text.

NOTES

1 In this chapter, I focus on the strand of social entrepreneurship associated with innovation, and thus the generation and imitation of ideas, their spread, diffusion, scaling etc. In the following, I will for brevity reasons simply refer to social innovators and social innovations. But this is not to claim that all social entrepreneurs have to be innovative. However, as the further discussion in this chapter will make clear, even social enterprises with no ambition of/claim to innovation face the pressure of capitalist dynamics, and for this reason I suggest that the topic is relevant irrespective of earned income school, innovation school or further schools of social entrepreneurship and social enterprise research.

2 'Future present' refers to a possible future that actors in the present (come to) believe in; 'present past' refers to ideas and ways of doing things that actors believe to be 'of the past', even though they co-exist in the present. These complex configurations, and especially the dominating role of (future) expectation over (past) experience, are discussed as a general challenge of modernity by Koselleck (1988).

3 In this chapter I juxtapose 'precautionary' and 'fictional' expectations as different types of future orientations. One focuses on social-ecological systems and the possible dangers related to them; and the other focuses on goods and services and the positive meanings and practices associated with them. However, both share the feature of future orientation and uncertainty, and both share the idea of an open future that can be shaped by humans. At this deeper level, therefore, it is also possible to characterise 'precautionary expectations' as a type of fictional expectation. However, as will be clear from the discussion below, it remains important to distinguish different kinds of fictional expectation, their normative presuppositions and implications.

4 See also Jessop et al. (2013, 124), who use social imaginary in social innovation research as a contrast to a focus on innovation systems as a 'pre-given' reality. The point here is that while capitalist innovation systems constantly change their 'social imaginaries' (due to the process of fictional expectation), 'social imaginaries' are not exhausted by this powerful, yet specific self-understanding.

5 See http://www.bigjump.org/, last accessed 31 May 2018.

6 See http://ikt-bayern.de/wasser/, last accessed 31 May 2018, and for some background in English, Ziegler (2017).

References

Aspers, P., 2018. Forms of uncertainty reduction. Decision, valuation, and contest. *Theory and Society,* **47** (2), 133–149.

Beckert, J., 2016. *Imagined Futures. Fictional Expectations and Capitalist Dynamics.* Cambridge, Mass.: Harvard University Press.

Beckert, J., 2017. *Woher kommen Erwartungen? Die soziale Strukturierung imaginierter Zukünfte.* Köln: Max-Planck-Institut für Gesellschaftsforschung.

Bornstein, D., 2004. *How to Change the World. Social Entrepreneurs and the Power of New Ideas.* Oxford: Oxford University Press.

Crépin, A.-S., and Folke, C., 2015. The economy, the biosphere and planetary boundaries: towards biosphere economics. *International Review of Environmental and Resource Economics,* **8** (1), 57–100.

Dey, P., and Steyaert, C., 2015. Tracing and theorising ethics in entrepreneurship. Toward a critical hermeneutics of imagination. In: A. Pullen and C. Rhodes, eds. *The Routledge Companion to Ethics, Politics and Organizations.* London: Routledge, 231–248.

Elkington, J., and Hartigan, P., 2008. *The Power of Unreasonable People – How Social Entrepreneurs Create Markets That Change the World.* Boston: Harvard Business School Publishing.

Fan, P., et al., 2017. Nature-based solutions for urban landscapes under post-industrialization and globalization. Barcelona versus Shanghai. *Environmental Research,* **156**, 272–283.

Gregson, N., et al., 2015. Interrogating the circular economy: the moral economy of resource recovery in the EU. *Economy and Society,* **44** (2), 218–243.

Godin, B., 2012. Social Innovation: Utopias of Innovation from c.1830 to the Present. *Project on the Intellectual History of Innovation.* CSIIC. Montreal.

Howaldt, J., Kaletka, C., and Schröder, A., 2018. Social innovation on the rise worldwide. What over 1.000 initiatives and projects worldwide reveal about the potential of social innovation to address the great societal challenges. In: J. Howaldt, C. Kaletka, and A. Schröder, eds. *Atlas of Social Innovation.* Sozialforschungsstelle, TU Dortmund University: Dortmund, 12–15.

Jackson, T., 2016. *Prosperity without Growth. Foundations for the Economy of Tomorrow.* London: Routledge.

Jessop, B., Moulaert, F., Hulgard, L., and Hamdouch, A., 2013. Social innovation research: a new state in innovation research? In: S. Moulaert, et al., eds. *The International Handbook on Social Innovation. Collective Action, Social Learning and Transdisciplinary Research.* Cheltenham: Edward Elgar, 110–130.

Kelly, J.M., 2017. Anthropocenes: a fractured picture. In: J.M. Kelly, et al., eds. *Rivers of the Anthropocene.* Berkeley: University of California Press, 1–22.

Keynes, J.M., 1937. The general theory of employment. *The Quarterly Journal of Economics,* **51** (2), 209–223.

Koselleck, R., 1988. *Vergangene Zukunft: Zur Semantik geschichtlicher Zeiten.* Frankfurt: Suhrkamp.

Kravčík, M., J. Kohutiar, M. Gažovič, M. Kovac, M. Hrib, P. Suty, and D. Kravčíková, 2012. *Po nás púšt ́ a potopa? – After us, the desert and the deluge?* Banska Bystrica: D-Press Group.

Leach, M., J. Rockström, P. Raskin, I. Scoones, A.C. Stirling, A. Smith, J. Thompson, E. Millstone, et al., 2012. Transforming innovation for sustainability. *Ecology and Society,* **17** (2), 11.

Marx, K. 1846 (Edited publication 1932). *The German Ideology,* Vol. 1, Part 1. Accessed 31 May 2018 at https://www.marxists.org/archive/marx/works/1845/german-ideology/index.htm.

Mazzucato, M., 2016. From market fixing to market-creating: a new framework for innovation policy. *Industry and Innovation,* **23** (2), 140–156.

McNeill, J.R., and Engelke, P., 2015. *The Great Acceleration: An Environmental History of the Anthropocene since 1945.* Cambridge, Mass.: Harvard University Press.

Millard, J., 2018. How social innovation underpins sustainable development. In: J. Howaldt, C. Kaletka, and A. Schröder, eds. *Atlas of Social Innovation.* Sozialforschungsstelle, TU Dortmund University: Dortmund, 40–42.

Offer, A., 1997. Between the gift and the market: the economy of regard. *The Economic History Review,* **50** (3), 450–476.

Rockström, J., et al., 2009. A safe operating space for humanity. *Nature,* **461** (7263), 472–475.

Sachs, W., ed., 1992. *The Development Dictionary: A Guide to Knowledge as Power.* London: Zed Books.

Sachs, W., 1999. *Planet Dialects: Explorations in Environment and Development.* London: Zed Books.

Schumpeter, J., 1942/1975. *Capitalism, Socialism and Democracy.* New York: Harper Collins Publishers.

Spinosa, C., Flores, F., and Dreyfus, H.L., 1997. *Disclosing New Worlds. Entrepreneurship, Democratic Action and the Cultivation of Solidarity.* Cambridge, Mass.: MIT Press.

Steffen, W., et al., 2015. Sustainability. Planetary boundaries: guiding human development on a changing planet. *Science,* **347** (6223), 736.

Thoreau, H., 1993 [1854]. *Walden and Resistance to Civil Government.* New York: W.W. Norton.

Tracey, P., and Stott, N., 2017. Social innovation. A window on alternative ways of organizing and innovating. *Innovation,* **19** (1), 51–60.

Wright, E. 2010. *Envisioning Real Utopias.* London: Verso.

Ziegler, R., 2015. Justice and innovation – towards principles for creating a fair space for innovation. *Journal of Responsible Innovation,* **2** (2), 184–200.

Ziegler, R., 2017. Citizen innovation as niche restoration – a type of social innovation and its relevance for political participation and sustainability. *Journal of Social Entrepreneurship,* **8** (3), 338–353.

Ziegler, R., and von Jacobi, N., 2018. Fair (economic) space for social innovation? A capabilities perspective. CrESSI Working Papers No. 44. ISBN 978-0-9955852-2-5.

Index